RAF BOMBER COMMAND
AT WAR 1939–45

Dedicated to the men and women of RAF Bomber Command, 1939–1945.

And for My Parents.

RAF BOMBER COMMAND
AT WAR 1939–45

CRAIG ARMSTRONG

Pen & Sword
AVIATION

First published in Great Britain in 2021 by
Pen & Sword Aviation
An imprint of
Pen & Sword Books Limited
Yorkshire - Philadelphia

ISBN 978 1 52670 051 3

The right of Craig Armstrong to be identified
as Author of this work has been asserted by him in
accordance with the Copyright, Designs and Patents Act 1988.

A CIP catalogue record for this book is available from the British Library

Typeset by SJmagic DESIGN SERVICES, India
Printed and bound in the UK by CPI Group (UK) Ltd, Croydon, CR0 4YY

Pen & Sword Books Limited incorporates the imprints of Atlas,
Archaeology, Aviation, Discovery, Family History, Fiction, History, Maritime,
Military, Military Classics, Politics, Select, Transport, True Crime, Air World,
Frontline Publishing, Leo Cooper, Remember When, Seaforth Publishing,
The Praetorian Press, Wharncliffe Local History, Wharncliffe Transport,
Wharncliffe True Crime and White Owl.

For a complete list of Pen & Sword titles please contact
PEN & SWORD BOOKS LIMITED
47 Church Street, Barnsley, South Yorkshire S70 2AS, United Kingdom
E-mail: enquiries@pen-and-sword.co.uk
Website: www.pen-and-sword.co.uk
Or
PEN AND SWORD BOOKS
1950 Lawrence Rd, Havertown, PA 19083, USA
E-mail: Uspen-and-sword@casematepublishers.com
Website: www.penandswordbooks.com

Contents

Introduction

The outbreak of war found RAF Bomber Command in the midst of a period of rebuilding, retraining and expansion. Hopes of the command being able to mount a heavy and sustained attack upon German industrial targets were made impossible by several key factors.

The first was the agreement of the British government to attack only military targets and to avoid civilian casualties. This, in practice, meant that for the early months of the war the command was restricted to the bombing of naval targets and making leaflet raids, codenamed 'Nickels', which dropped propaganda material over German towns and cities. The second restriction was the equipment with which Bomber Command was expected to mount an offensive. The command possessed bombers of varying roles and capabilities ranging from light day bombers to what were described as heavy night bombers. Some of the types in service in 1939 were hopelessly obsolescent and were no match for modern fighter aircraft. Amongst the light day bombers were the Fairey Battle and the Bristol Blenheim.

The Battle was a single engine monoplane design dating back to the mid-1930s. The first Battles had entered service with 63 Squadron in the Spring of 1937. Initial reactions amongst aircrew seem to have been positive, but the truth was that the Battle, with its single Rolls-Royce Merlin engine, was hopelessly underpowered. The Battle could carry a bomb load of 1,000lbs with a crew of three. Although the Merlin was a very fine engine it was not capable of providing adequate power to carry such a combat load and the type had a maximum speed of just 257 mph and a range of 1,000 miles. Furthermore, the Battle was under-armed for its task as a day bomber, carrying only a single defensive Vickers K machine gun and one, largely useless, Browning machine gun mounted in the starboard wing.

The Bristol Blenheim was believed to be a more promising aircraft. Designed as a twin-engine medium bomber, the Blenheim went into service with 114 Squadron at around the same time as the Battle.

With a maximum speed of 285 mph the Blenheim could outpace the biplane fighters of the early 1930s but, once more, was outclassed by the modern monoplane fighters. The Blenheim, too, had a crew of three (pilot, navigator/bomb aimer and wireless operator/air gunner) and better defensive armament than the Battle, boasting a machine gun in the port wing, one or two machine guns in a rear-facing, under-nose blister and a power-operated dorsal turret containing two more Browning machine guns. The Blenheim could carry a bombload of 1,000lbs and had sufficient range to reach Germany. Unfortunately, the Blenheim proved to be a type which was not very robust and was plagued by engine problems.

Amongst what were termed heavy bombers (though they would be medium bombers by later standards) was the Armstrong Whitworth Whitley which had been delivered to 10 Squadron in March 1937. The original Mk I Whitleys were quickly replaced by Mk IIIs and, in 1939, by Mk Vs. Powered by two Merlin engines, the Whitley V could manage a top speed of 230 mph at 16,400 feet, had an operational ceiling of 26,000 feet and a range of 1,500 miles. Defensive armament consisted of a Vickers K machine gun in the nose turret and four Browning machine guns in the tail turret. Offensively, the Whitley could carry a bombload of 7,000lbs. Carrying a crew of five, the Whitley, with its peculiar nose-down flying attitude and broad, square, wing earned the nickname of the 'flying barn-door' but was largely appreciated by those who flew it. The Whitley equipped the squadrons of 4 Group and the crews were the only Bomber Command airmen to be trained in night operations.

Another type classed as a heavy bomber was the Vickers Wellington, a twin-engine monoplane featuring an unusual geodetic fuselage construction which gave it considerable structural strength and a significant durability. The first Wellington was delivered to 99 Squadron in October 1938 and by August 1939 the Wellington equipped eight squadrons in East Anglia. With a top speed of 235 mph, a range of 1,540 miles and a bomb load of 4,500lbs, the Wellington had a crew of five or six and was quickly popular with aircrew. It was nicknamed the 'Wimpy' (after a character in the Popeye cartoons). The Wellington boasted between six and eight Browning machine guns as defensive armament, with two each in nose and tail turrets and optional single guns in two waist or beam positions.

The final heavy bomber was the Handley Page Hampden which was first delivered operationally to 49 Squadron in September 1938. The Air Ministry had been much impressed by the radical design and initial performance of the twin-engine, tapered fuselage bomber and the type featured several positive design features, including a maximum speed of 254 mph, possessed good manoeuvrability and could carry a bombload of 4,000lbs with a range of 1,200 miles. There were, however, several disadvantages to the type. Foremost amongst these failings was the cramped nature of the interior of the bomber, it was quickly nicknamed the 'flying suitcase' or, from its narrow fuselage, the 'flying panhandle', which resulted in poor inter-crew communications and increased levels of fatigue amongst the crew of four. Secondly, the Hampden had inadequate defensive armament consisting of just four hand-operated machine guns.

Despite the shortcomings of some of the types equipping Bomber Command at the outbreak of war the general public were often given reassurances that the aircraft were at the cutting edge of technology. Press reports consistently talked up the abilities of the aircraft (without, of course revealing facts and figures which might be of use to an enemy). For example, the *Illustrated War News* of 22 November 1939 had a feature on the Hampden in which the bomber was described as being 'a formidable night-bomber with a very high speed' as well as good defensive armament.

Bomber Command's initial strategy was for both self-defending formations of bombers operating in daylight, along with more limited numbers of night bombers, mainly drawn from amongst the Whitley-equipped squadrons of 4 Group based in Yorkshire. In the event of a war with Germany, however, the command would immediately be denuded of a large number of light bomber squadrons which would be sent to France as part of the Advanced Air Striking Force (AASF). This planned reduction in operational strength took place two days before the declaration of war when No.1 Group, consisting of ten squadrons of Battles, made its way to bases in France along with two squadrons of Blenheims from another group. These squadrons immediately came under the command of the AASF and did not operate under the auspices of Bomber Command. A further reduction in operational strength took place when the five remaining squadrons equipped with Battles were removed from front-line status and became training and reserve units.

CHAPTER 1

1939 – Feeling the Way

The war opened with the restrictions previously discussed limiting the scope of Bomber Command to wage war. Within an hour of the declaration of war a Bristol Blenheim of 139 Squadron took off from RAF Wyton to make a reconnaissance of German port facilities across the North Sea in an effort to identify German naval units. Upon hearing the report of the Blenheim crew, two flights of Handley Page Hampdens and Vickers Wellingtons took off to seek the naval units, but in the failing light no contact was made and the bombers returned to base.

The restrictions placed upon Bomber Command did, however, allow the force to withdraw nine of its squadrons to create a more suitable reserve. This further reduction, however, meant that Bomber Command entered the war with a front-line force of just 280 aircraft and crews. These aircraft were divided between twenty-three operational squadrons which were further divided between four groups. Bomber Command was run from its HQ which was at Richings Park, Langley, Buckinghamshire. The Commander-in-Chief was Air Chief Marshal Sir Edgar Ludlow-Hewitt. Amongst the early headaches facing Ludlow-Hewitt was the fact that Bomber Command HQ was due to relocate to High Wycombe in March 1940.

Group	Commander	Squadrons	Aircraft Type
2	AVM Maclean	21, 82, 107, 110, 114, 139, 101(Reserve)	Bristol Blenheim
3	AVM Baldwin	9, 37, 38, 99, 115, 149, 214 (R), 215 (R)	Vickers Wellington
4	AVM Coningham	10, 51, 58, 77, 102, 78 (R)	Armstrong-Whitworth Whitley
5	AVM Callaway[1]	44, 49, 50, 61, 83, 144, 185 (R)	Handley Page Hampdens

On the very first night of the war Armstrong Whitworth Whitleys of 51 and 58 Squadrons were dispatched to drop propaganda leaflets over several German towns and cities. Three of the Whitleys from 51 Squadron were tasked with targeting Hamburg while a further seven aircraft from 58 Squadron pressed on for targets including Bremen and the Ruhr area. None of the crews experienced any opposition from the enemy, but three 58 Squadron aircraft experienced engine trouble as they were returning and were forced to make emergency landings in France. The first of the Whitleys to have taken off (K8973) ran out of fuel and the pilot, Squadron Leader J.J.A. Sutton, put his bomber down in an emergency landing at Fécamp while the Whitley of Flight Sergeant Ford (K8990) was put down at St Quentin. Aboard the third Whitley (K8969, GE-G) Flying Officer (F/O) J.A. O'Neill could not locate an airstrip upon which to make an emergency landing and so was forced to put his Whitley down in a cabbage field near Dormans on the eastern bank of the River Marne around 5.54am. Flying Officer O'Neill's aircraft was written off, but the crew were uninjured despite several cabbages entering the aircraft with some force.[2]

Following these initial moves the second day of the war saw another similar Blenheim reconnaissance which identified several German fleet units at Brunsbüttel and Wilhelmshaven. Bomber Command was well aware that the targets, which included the battleship *Admiral Scheer* and the battlecruisers *Scharnhorst* and *Gneisenau*, were likely to be very well defended with both anti-aircraft screens and fighter cover. Despite these fears, the opportunity to destroy or damage such important naval units at the very start of the war was too tempting a target to refuse. Once again, a force of bombers was sent to attack the enemy ships. From RAF Wattisham and Wyton a force of fifteen Blenheims was sent to the latter target while fourteen Wellingtons from RAF Honington and Mildenhall were tasked with attacking the ships at Brunsbüttel and from RAF Scampton twelve Hampdens were also assigned the mission. Weather conditions were very poor and the bomber formations were forced to operate independently of each other.

At the airfields there had been some confusion as the ground crews had to replace armour-piercing bombs with general purpose bombs as the low cloud cover would mean that the far more effective (against naval targets) armour-piercing bombs could not be used effectively. Nos. 107 and 110 Squadrons assigned five crews apiece to the operation and at briefing they were told that the enemy vessels were defended only by machine guns and by their own heavy armaments which, it was hoped, could not be depressed sufficiently to engage low flying targets. Furthermore, and in defiance of the reliance upon tight formation, the crews were ordered to attack from several directions to confuse the defences.

The twelve Hampdens and five Blenheims from 139 Squadron failed to find their targets due to poor weather. The Blenheims, which had been dispatched to attack targets at Wilhelmshaven, fared terribly with no fewer than five being brought down by heavy anti-aircraft fire. Despite several hits being claimed, damage was slight with many of the bombs which did score hits failing to explode. The five aircraft of 110 Squadron were first to attack. The five Blenheims split, with three making attack runs while two others made diversionary attacks from other directions. As the second Blenheim approached to attack a very heavy barrage opened up from the ships and from shore batteries and the third Blenheim was forced to abort its attack and pull up into the safety of the cloud cover. Seconds later one of the diversionary aircraft, Blenheim IV (N6199) was shot down in flames by the flak from the *Admiral Hipper*. The most serious damage of the raid occurred when N6199 crashed on to the cruiser *Emden*, killing nine of her crew along with the four British airmen aboard the Blenheim. Somewhat ironically, the pilot of N6199 was Flying Officer Henry Lovell Emden (a married man from St Leonards-on-Sea, Sussex). Along with Flying Officer Emden were his observer Sergeant Stanley George McKenna Otty, his wireless operator/air gunner Sergeant Raymond Charles Grossey (24), and Aircraftman Ralph Evans (an under-training wireless operator). The bodies of all but Sergeant Grossey, who was on attachment from 42 Squadron, were recovered and buried at Sage War Cemetery, Grossenkneten, Germany.

Around the same time the second flight of Blenheims, from 107 Squadron, arrived on the scene and attempted to attack in the teeth of the now fully-alerted defences. The first aircraft, piloted by Flight Lieutenant William Frank Barton (26), was hit by flak from the *Admiral Hipper* and exploded. The second Blenheim was also hit and crashed with both engines aflame. The third was also hit and crashed near the shore, while the fourth was bracketed by heavy flak and crashed, cartwheeling across the sea. The fifth Blenheim somehow survived the ferocious barrage and managed to straddle the *Admiral Scheer* with its bombs but, once again, the bomb which hit failed to explode. The cost of this failure was paid in the loss of five aircraft and the deaths of fourteen airmen, with a further two becoming the first Bomber Command men to become prisoners of war (PoW). It is unclear which aircraft became the first from Bomber Command to be shot down, but it would appear to have been either N6199 of 110 Squadron or N6184, piloted by Flying Officer John Frederick Ross (23) of 107 Squadron.

For the men of 107 Squadron at RAF Wattisham the return of only one of its aircraft was a bitter blow and surely hammered home that this war was, for the men of Bomber Command, going to be an extremely bloody one. Amongst the losses was Flying Officer Herbert Brian Lightoller (21), the son of Commander Charles Herbert Lightoller, RNR, of Twickenham, Middlesex, and Sergeant Albert Stanley Prince (27) of Chester. Sergeant Prince's aircraft (N6240) crashed in the target area but his observer and wireless operator/air gunner survived to be taken prisoner; they were Sergeant G.F. Booth and Aircraftsman L.J. Slattery.

The Wellingtons of 9 Squadron took off slightly later than the other formations and did locate their targets, but bombing results were poor and the bombers encountered anti-aircraft fire and enemy fighters and a running battle developed during which two of the Wellingtons were lost and all eleven crew killed. These first two Wellingtons to be lost were coded L4268 and L4275 (WS-H). They were piloted respectively by Flight Sergeant Ian Edward Maitland Morley (30) and Flight Sergeant Albion John Turner. Flight Sergeant Morley was a reservist who had, presumably, been called up as hostilities approached and was a married man from Weston-super-Mare. One of the Wellingtons, it is impossible to say which, was claimed as having been shot down by a Messerschmidt Bf 109 and Feldwebel Alfred Held became the first Luftwaffe airman to shoot down an RAF aircraft during the war.

Of the eleven casualties only three bodies were recovered for burial with the remainder being commemorated on the Runnymede Memorial.[3] Four of the Wellington crews reported bombing targets, but little is known of their attacks and navigational errors led to one Wellington dropping bombs on the Danish town of Esbjerg, where two people were killed. Another formation of eight Wellingtons from 149 Squadron had worse fortune with only one claiming to have bombed in the assigned target area while the remainder jettisoned their bombs into the sea after failing to locate any targets. The only damage done by the Wellingtons was to a merchant ship which was hit by bombs jettisoned by an aircraft from 9 Squadron.

In total, seven aircraft had been lost by Bomber Command along with the deaths of twenty-five airmen and two more being held PoW for the rest of the war. Damage to the enemy targets was minimal and it had become clear to many of the airmen who had taken part that the bombs which they were using were poor, with many failing to explode, and that their aircraft were extremely vulnerable in daylight to both flak and fighters. As the shocked survivors made their way homeward, they were painfully aware that their attack had failed largely through the failure of the pre-war bombs with which they had been equipped and that lives and aircraft had been thrown away for little result. At least three bombs had hit the *Admiral Scheer,* but all failed to explode.

In a speech to the House of Commons on 7 September Lord Stanhope paid fulsome tribute to the RAF and particularly to the efforts of Bomber Command which had recently made the news. Lord Stanhope tried to deflect possible criticism of the raid by telling the House that at least two hits had been recorded on a pocket battleship, while the attack had been made in extremely poor weather conditions which had limited effectiveness. Lord Stanhope also explained how many of the airmen involved had joined and been trained since the expansion of the RAF began in the mid-1930s and that a substantial number were volunteers from the Dominions.

Training was continuing apace at this time and the hectic schedule led to further losses. The day after the attack on Brunsbuttel and Wilhelmshaven Bomber Command suffered its first fatal training accident of the war when Pilot Officer Anthony Richard Playfair (26) of 7 Squadron lost control of his Hampden I (L4161) on a training flight. The bomber crashed at Cockwood Farm, Cantley, Yorkshire. Pilot Officer Playfair is listed as being British but his parents lived at Qualicum Beach, British Columbia, Canada. He was reportedly from a theatrical family, his father was an actor and a cousin of Sir Nigel Playfair, the actor and manager of the Lyric Theatre.

Lord Stanhope was also at pains to explain the other ongoing efforts of Bomber Command. He told them how in the last week the command had carried out extensive operations over Germany on three successive nights and that, during the course of these operations, some 10,000,000 leaflets had been dropped over a wide section of German territory, especially the north and west of the country, including the vital Ruhr region. MPs were told that despite the best efforts of the German defences no enemy fighters had intercepted the British bombers and all had returned safely.

In this first week of war the press, following the extremely limited information which they were given, was filled with praise for the efforts of Bomber Command and readers were told of 'a most daring and effective' raid being made on German ports and naval units. The leaflet raids also attracted praise in the national and local press with typical accounts informing readers that 'on numerous occasions flights of the Bomber Command have penetrated far into Germany, dropping leaflets instead of bombs ... These leaflet raids, from which our machines have returned unscathed though not unchallenged, must have a telling effect on people who have repeatedly been assured that their defences are impenetrable.'[4]

These night-time leaflet raids, or 'Nickels', continued when conditions allowed and provided valuable night-flying and navigational experience under wartime conditions for the Whitley crews of 4 Group. Between the second night of the war and Christmas Eve the Whitleys flew a total of 113 sorties on twenty-two nights. They carried leaflets on all of these and, on clearer nights, supplemented this duty with reconnaissance of German territory. These sorties were largely successful with 105 from 113 sorties being completed satisfactorily and losses were low. The first of the four Whitleys which were lost over Germany during this period occurred in the early hours of 9 September when Whitley III (K8950, DY-M) of 102 Squadron failed to return to its base at Driffield. The Whitley had been piloted by Squadron Leader S.S. Murray (who, it appears, was also a qualified interpreter) and he and his four crewmates were taken prisoner by the Germans after the aircraft came down near Kassel.[5] Another aircraft from 102 Squadron was lost on this night when Whitley III (K8985, DY-J) also failed to return. It transpired that a navigational error had caused the Whitley to stray into neutral Belgian airspace and the bomber was forced to land at Nivelles aerodrome where the crew were interned. Flying Officer William Curwin Gavine Cogman and his crew were quickly returned to England, but their aircraft was reported destroyed during the blitzkrieg. A third Whitley was also destroyed on this night when an aircraft of 77 Squadron collided with a French aircraft while taxiing at Buc and was damaged beyond repair.

Aside from the 'Nickel' operations described above, Bomber Command spent most of the remainder of September training and flying some reconnaissance operations. Losses were limited although several aircraft were lost in training or routine accidents. Two 51 Squadron airmen were killed when their Whitley crashed while they were ferrying it to York from

Linton-on-Ouse and the two crew of a Battle were lost when their aircraft crashed into a hillside near Cheltenham during a rainstorm.

From late September until the end of November the Command flew a number of photographic reconnaissance flights over Germany. These operations were largely undertaken by the Blenheim squadrons and a heavy price was paid as the vulnerable Blenheim was no match for the fighters which were often encountered. Over the course of thirty-seven operations on eleven days the Blenheims suffered five aircraft shot down and three other losses.

On 28 September, for example, two Blenheims of 107 Squadron failed to return to their base at Wattisham after being sent on reconnaissance missions. Flying Officer Donald Arthur Strachan and his crew were lost without trace while on a mission to Osnabruck aboard Blenheim IV (N6206).[6] The second aircraft to be lost was (N6212) piloted by the squadron's commanding officer, Wing Commander Ivan McLeod Cameron (31), on a reconnaissance of the Munster area. The Blenheim was shot down near Kiel. Wing Commander Cameron was an Australian, from Bealiba, Victoria, flying with the RAF. He had joined the RAF in 1928 with a short-service commission and had been promoted to the rank of squadron leader in 1937 before being promoted once more and taking over a squadron shortly afterwards. Together with his observer, Sergeant Thomas Cecil Hammond (27) of Dublin, and his wireless operator/air gunner Aircraftsman Thomas Fullerton, Wing Commander Cameron is buried in the Reichswald Forest War Cemetery.

After the debacle of 4 September daylight offensive operations did not take place again for a period of twenty-five days but on 29 September eleven Hampdens were sent to search for and attack German fleet units in the Heligoland area. The Hampdens were dispatched in two formations with the first formation of six making an unsuccessful attack against two enemy destroyers. The second formation was made up of five aircraft from 144 Squadron based at RAF Hemswell and was led by the commanding officer, Wing Commander James Charles Cunningham. None of the five aircraft returned to Hemswell and nothing was known until a German radio broadcast which stated that the Hampdens had run into a hornet's nest of fighters and that all five had been shot down between the islands of Heligoland and Wangerooge.

The radio broadcast was correct and 144 Squadron was forced to come to terms with the loss of twenty of its aircrew, including its commanding officer. The Hampden of Wing Commander Cunningham ((L4134) was shot down in flames having fallen victim to a Bf 109. Wing Commander Cunningham (31), from Louth in Lincolnshire, was killed along with his second pilot/observer, Sergeant Ronald Ernest Herd (25) of Holbeach, Lincolnshire, and one of his wireless operator/air gunners, Sergeant Albert Edward Charles Povey (30) of Lasham in Hampshire. The second air gunner, Aircraftsman H. Liggett was taken as a PoW. The body of Sergeant Herd was buried at Sage War Cemetery while Wing Commander Cunningham and Sergeant Povey are commemorated on the Runnymede Memorial. The other Hampdens lost were piloted by Flying Officer John Tulloch Burrill Sadler (L4121), Flying Officer R.D. Baughan (L4216), Flying Officer Norman Croxen Beck (L4127), and Pilot Officer R.M. Coste (L4132).[7] There were only four survivors from the twenty men who had taken off from Hemswell

In the aftermath of the disastrous raid of 29 September the local media in Lincolnshire highlighted the loss of two men who were well-known locally. The first was Wing Commander Cunningham (with reports mentioning his Grimsby-born wife and his one-year-old daughter) and the second was Flight Sergeant Siriol Williams. The married flight sergeant was a native of Cwmllynfell near Swansea but had married a woman from Cleethorpes three years before the war and was a popular figure in the town. Flight Sergeant Williams had been the second pilot to P/O Coste.

As the winter weather clamped down flying was impossible on many days and operations from 8 October until the beginning of December were limited to speculative sweeps over the North Sea alongside the reconnaissance flights and 'Nickels' referred to above. An extensive programme of training was also undertaken. Losses remained low during the period although there was a constant drain through losses suffered during training.

On 17 November a Blenheim reconnaissance flight identified large numbers of enemy warships in the Heligoland Bight but, concerned over the losses suffered previously in this area, Bomber Command was reluctant to launch an immediate attack over such a heavily defended area. However, the First Lord of the Admiralty, Winston Churchill, urged such an attack before the German fleet could attack British shipping routes. By early December this pressure from the Admiralty was growing irresistible and on 3 December an attack by twenty-four Wellingtons from 28, 115 and 149 Squadrons was authorised. The Wellingtons had been sighted by a patrol ship and the defences were alerted, but the aircraft all ran through the flak (they were ordered not to descend too low) and fighter attacks without suffering any losses. The bombers attacked from 8,000 feet but the ships were all missed. One of the attacking Bf 109s was claimed as having been shot down, but one of the Wellingtons suffered a hang-up of one of its bombs and this dropped accidentally on the island of Heligoland, the first bomb to drop on German soil during the war.

The safe return of the twenty-four Wellingtons served to convince some within Bomber Command that the pre-war beliefs in self-defending bomber formations was vindicated by this raid and the commanders were encouraged to make another effort to hit the enemy shipping. On 14 December the command made another attempt. Twelve Wellingtons from 99 Squadron were ordered to make an attack on enemy shipping in the Jade Estuary following intelligence that the enemy cruisers *Leipzig* and *Nürnberg* were making for the estuary after being torpedoed by a British submarine. The Wellingtons were part of the largest effort made so far by Bomber Command as twenty-three Hampdens and seven Whitleys were also sent off on what was officially described as a North Sea shipping search operation. The Wellingtons, led by their commanding officer, Wing Commander J.F. Griffiths, struggled along in the poor conditions with solid cloud below 1,000 feet. The bombers were forced to descend to 600 feet, despite orders not to attack below 2,000 feet, and came across a convoy in the Schillig Roads, north of Wilhelmshaven. By this time they had been under constant anti-aircraft fire and several had suffered minor damage.

Then a formation of enemy Bf 109 and Bf 110 fighters roared into the attack. The Wellingtons again downed an enemy fighter, but this time the German pilots were not reluctant to press home their attacks and five of the Wellingtons were brought down. Three of the bombers fell to the guns of the enemy while two collided while taking evasive action. There were no survivors from the thirty-six crewmen aboard the Wellingtons. Another Wellington (N2957) was badly shot up and upon return it crashed into a field beside Newmarket racecourse killing three of the crew.

After this severe reverse the upper echelons of Bomber Command seemed to find it unbelievable that the five bombers had all fallen to fighter attack and tried to reassure themselves that flak must have accounted for some. Air Commodore Bottomley wrote a summary of the raid in which he cast doubt upon whether any of the bombers had been shot down by enemy fighters and once more praised the effectiveness of tight bomber formations. Not everyone was convinced. The commander of Bomber Command, Sir Edgar Ludlow-Hewitt, believed that Wing Commander Griffith was in error and should have aborted the sortie when the cloud descended, while the commander of 3 Group (of which 99 Squadron was a part), Air Vice Marshal (AVM) 'Jack' Baldwin, believed that the squadron had been decimated through what was a colossal tactical error.

Four days after the debacle Bomber Command determined to try again and twenty-four Wellingtons from 9, 37 and 149 Squadrons, under the command of Wing Commander Kellet (who had led the raid of 3 December), were detailed to patrol the same locations, although on this occasion the Wellingtons were loaded with armour-piercing bombs and were ordered not to bomb below 10,000 feet. Two of the bombers experienced engine trouble and returned to base; they were the lucky ones. Flying in four flights at 14,000 feet the formation was detected by Freya radar and the Luftwaffe was alerted. Despite this, there was a significant delay in scrambling fighters as the Luftwaffe controllers refused to believe the British would be so foolish as to attack in a cloudless blue sky with no fighter cover.

However, the Bf 109s of 10/JG26 found the Wellingtons as they approached the target area and two Wellingtons were quickly shot down. The fighters broke off as the Wellingtons flew twice over Wilhelmshaven without dropping their bombs before, now reinforced by a formation of Bf 110s of ZG26 and a further number of Bf 109s from JG27, they attacked again as the British formation retreated to the north-west. In a running fight a further seven Wellingtons were shot down by the Bf 110s before a final victim fell to the recently arrived Bf 109s of JG101. Two more Wellingtons were so badly damaged that they had to be ditched on the journey home (one with total loss of life).

In total, twelve of the Wellingtons had been lost from an original formation of twenty-four, although only twenty-two had attacked. Among those shot down were two flight commanders. Squadron Leader Archibald John Guthrie (28) of 9 Squadron was killed along with his crew when Wellington IA (N2872) was shot down off Wilhelmshaven; the Wellington was last seen diving, on fire, into the sea. Squadron Leader Guthrie was from Tamworth, Staffordshire, and he and his crew are commemorated at Runnymede. Squadron Leader Ian Victor Hue-Williams and his crew (aboard N2904, LF-B) were last seen heading out to sea with the starboard wing of their Wellington furiously ablaze. The body of his second pilot,

Flying Officer A.R. Vaughan Williams (23) was washed up and buried at Becklingen, while the others are commemorated at Runnymede.

Some fifty-six of the sixty-five airmen who were in the lost aircraft were killed, while five, all from 37 Squadron, were taken PoW. The aircraft of Sergeant H. Ruse (N936, LF-J) was badly shot up and two of the crew were killed before the Wellington crash-landed on the sand dunes on Borkum Island. Sergeant Ruse, Sergeant T. May and Leading Aircraftman (LAC) H.A. Jones were taken prisoner. Flying Officer P.A. Wimberley was the pilot of N2888 (LF-A) when it was shot down by Leutnant Helmut Lent of ZG26 and he was the only survivor from his crew. Aircraftman 1st class George Warne Geddes was the rear gunner aboard N2889 which was also shot down by Lent. The Wellington broke apart in mid-air and, although Aircraftsman Geddes was alive when picked up by the Germans, he died of his wounds shortly afterwards.[8] For the shattered air and ground crew of the three squadrons the day was appalling. No.9 Squadron at Honington and 37 Squadron at Feltwell had both lost five aircraft while 149 Squadron at Mildenhall had lost two. The belief in the idea of self-defending bomber formations operating in daylight had been shown to be tragically flawed.

Amongst the men to lose their lives was 19-year-old Aircraftman Second Class (AC2) Isaac Davidson Leighton of East Cramlington, Northumberland. Leighton was flying as a Wireless Operator/Air Gunner in Wellington IA (N2961) of 149 Squadron. Just before 9.30am the crew, piloted by 22-year-old Flying Officer Michael Franklin Briden, took off from their base at RAF Mildenhall and set course. Severely damaged by enemy fighters over the target area, the crew turned for home but were forced to ditch the aircraft when 40-60 miles off Cromer. Although at least three men were seen clinging to a dinghy, and despite an extensive search operation, no survivors were found.[9] For AC2 Leighton's family an anxious wait ensued which was ended when confirmation of the youngster's death was received in February 1940.[10] The tragic events of 18 December led many within Bomber Command to privately concede that the ideas of a self-defending daylight bomber formation was flawed and eventually led to a realisation that a substantial change in policy was necessary.

CHAPTER 2

1940 – The Storm Breaks

Summary of the Year

Following the disastrous results of the daylight raids of September and December 1939 it had become clear to many within Bomber Command that the pre-war assumptions over self-defending bombing formations were dangerously flawed. On the nights between 4-20 January 1940 the command launched several minor leaflet raids with Wellingtons and Hampdens. It was clear that the strategy of Bomber Command was beginning to shift towards night raids. The Whitleys also remained actively involved in leaflet raids and on the night of 12/13 January the range of these raids was extended to Prague and Vienna, with Whitleys taking off from airfields in France.

The pre-war theory that the bomber would always get through had been proven to be an utter fantasy by the disastrous losses suffered on these early daylight raids and the authorities began to realise that, if Bomber Command was to make an active contribution to the war effort without suffering debilitating casualties, a shift in tactics was required. Once again, however, the shift towards night bombing was seriously hampered by a lack of navigational equipment and training for aircrew. Hitherto only the Whitley squadrons and, to a far lesser extent the Hampden and Wellington squadrons, had any extensive experience of night flying.

The early part of the year passed relatively quietly but the night of 11/12 January saw the first night sorties of the war by a few Hampdens and Wellingtons. The following night saw Whitley sorties flying from advanced bases in France launched against Prague and Vienna. There were no losses, but results were probably over-exaggerated. March saw the command have its first success against the U-boats when a Blenheim of 82 Squadron attacked and sank a submarine off Borkum. At the end of the month Bomber Command received a new commanding officer when Air Marshal Sir Charles Portal took over. Despite the change the activities of the command remained largely unchanged until the German invasion of Denmark and Norway on 9 April. Following this several small raids in support of the beleaguered Allied ground forces in Scandinavia were mounted. The greatest change in strategy during the period occurred on 13/14 April when fourteen Hampdens undertook Bomber Command's first minelaying operations of the war, laying the mines in the waters off Denmark in an effort to restrict German shipping.

The invasion of France and the Low Countries in early May resulted in an upswing in activity and the night of 11/12 May saw the first Bomber Command raid of the war on Germany, although the targets remained military in nature. Three days after this raid, and with the German forces making faster progress than anyone had expected, the War Cabinet granted permission for raids to begin against targets east of the Rhine and Bomber Command followed up on this that very night with 99 bombers attacking sixteen oil and rail targets in what was the launch of the strategic bombing campaign. Other activities throughout this period included efforts to support the British Expeditionary Force (BEF) while the operations against oil targets in Germany continued in sporadic fashion.

Following Italy's declaration of war on 10 June Bomber Command launched its first attack of the war on Turin on the night of 11/12. The formal surrender of France and the fact that the Luftwaffe were now poised across the Channel meant that Bomber Command would have to play a much larger role in protecting Britain from aerial attack. As a result of this, the Air Ministry issued a further directive urging the command to attack targets which would reduce the ability of the Luftwaffe to attack Britain. Despite the directive, other targets were also attacked. The command had to fulfil repeated requests from the Admiralty to attack German shipping and on 1/2 July an attack was made on the *Scharnhorst* which saw Flying Officer Guy Gibson of 83 Squadron drop the command's first 2,000lb bomb.

Other targets were also attacked, maintaining its strategic campaign. On 12/13 two squadrons, 49 and 83, attacked the vital Dortmund-Ems Canal aqueduct in an operation which saw the first Bomber Command Victoria Cross (VC) of the war awarded to Flight Lieutenant R.A.B. Learoyd. It was during the Battle of Britain that the first German bombing of London occurred. In reaction, on 25/26 Bomber Command undertook its first raid of the war on Berlin. This was the first indication, even thougb military targets were urged, that the campaign was shifting towards the possibility of a campaign against German cities.

Amongst the many demands at this time were requests from the Admiralty to assist in reducing the potency of the U-boats. In response the first attack on U-boat pens was made on the night of 2/3 September when a force of Hampdens attacked Lorient.

With the Battle of Britain raging, the blitz on London beginning and the invasion of Britain a distinct possibility, the command made repeated attacks on the ports where it was believed the German invasion fleet of barges was being assembled. The attacks were largely successful but there were significant casualties over these targets. Despite the campaign against the invasion barges Bomber Command also made a further retaliatory attack against Berlin on the night of 23/24 September with 119 bombers.

October saw the end of the Battle of Britain and significant changes in Bomber Command. Although Sir Charles Portal had only been in command since the end of March, he was now relieved prior to his promotion to Chief of the Air Staff (which occurred on 25 October) and Air Marshal Sir Richard Peirse became C-in-C of Bomber Command on 5 October. With the blitz against London continuing, the government was increasingly considering an offensive of its own against German towns and cities and at the end of October the Air Ministry issued its first directive sanctioning area bombing of these targets. This was a massive shift from the early war months of insisting only on targets of a military or strategic nature and was to be the main, but not only, tactic of the remainder of the war.

The remainder of the year saw desultory attacks on such targets but the command was clearly feeling its way. One of the largest attacks of the period was in retaliation for the bombing of Coventry on 14/15 November. On 16/17 of that month, Bomber Command dispatched 130 aircraft to attack Hamburg. The year ended with the command beginning to undertake its new area bombing campaign with the first major area attack being made by 134 bombers on the target of Mannheim on 16/17 December. Even though the command had been authorised to make area attacks, the majority of those launched at this stage of the war were made in retaliation for attacks on British towns and cities. In the case of Mannheim, for Luftwaffe attacks on Coventry and Southampton.

The Campaign

February passed fairly quietly with leaflet raids and sea searches but no major operations. This was, perhaps, just as well as it allowed the crews to gain more practice in night flying. March also began quietly but there was a steady stream of casualties caused by flying accidents and so on. On the night of 16/17 March, for example, Hampden I (L4063) of 50 Squadron had taken off from RAF Waddington on a patrol but the bomber did not return to base and wreckage found later confirmed that it had fallen into high ground at Cocklaw Foot in the Cheviot Hills of Northumberland. The four-man crew, led by Flying Officer V.H. Ayres, were all killed. A subsequent enquiry found that faulty direction-finding equipment at Waddington had caused the wrong bearing to be sent to the crew with tragic results.

On 19/20 March Bomber Command carried out a reprisal raid on the German seaplane base at Hornum on the island of Sylt. The raid was in retaliation for the bombs which had dropped on the Orkneys during the Luftwaffe raid on Scapa Flow a couple of nights earlier. Hornum was chosen because it was in a location where there was no civilian housing and a force of fifty aircraft (thirty Whitleys and twenty Hampdens) were sent to bomb the base in two waves separated by two hours, the Whitleys first. Twenty-six of the first wave claimed to have identified and bombed the target and fifteen Hampden crews also claimed to have bombed. Twenty tons of high-explosives and 1,200 incendiary bombs were dropped for the loss of one of the Whitleys. Whitley V (N1405) of 51 Squadron had taken off from RAF Dishforth at 8.35pm with Flight Lieutenant John Edward Baskerville at the controls. The Whitley was shot down into the sea by flak off the coast of Sylt and all of the five-man crew were killed. Flight Lieutenant Baskerville was a 25-year-old Canadian from Manitoba who was serving in the RAF. His co-pilot, Pilot Officer Emery Orville Fennell was also a Canadian serving in the RAF. The five men became the first Bomber Command crew to be killed during a raid on a German land-based target.[1]

On 9 April the Germans invaded Denmark and Norway and the British government scrambled to come up with an adequate response. For Bomber Command the invasion posed a number of serious problems. Firstly, the distance that bombers would have to fly to reach any target was immense and the majority of the journey would be over sea, which would hinder navigation. So great were the distances involved that, with its current equipment, Bomber Command could only hope to bomb targets in southern Norway. The weather was also a factor and even more of a hindrance were the bombing restrictions which were still in place, meaning that Bomber Command could do little to support troops on the ground.

Despite this, the higher command were enthusiastic at the prospect of action and plans were submitted to the new commander-in-chief. Air Chief Marshal Sir Charles Portal had been appointed to take over command from Air Chief Marshal Ludlow-Hewitt on 28 March. Two days after the invasion (and following some reconnaissance flights) the bombing campaign began with a night raid on the airfield at Stavanger/Sola. Two aircraft were lost on this night, 11/12 April. The first was a Whitley from 77 Squadron which was lost while on a shipping reconnaissance operation in the Skaggerak. The pilot, Flying Officer G.E. Saddington and his crew were all killed.[2] The operation to bomb the airfield at Stavanger/Sola cost the command a single Wellington. This was an aircraft from 115 Squadron, based at RAF Marham. Flying Officer F.E. Barber and his crew were shot down in the target area and all the crew were killed.

On the following day Bomber Command launched a heavy daylight attack when eighty-three aircraft took part in an anti-shipping operation. The force, made up of thirty-six Wellingtons, twenty-four Hampdens and twenty-three Blenheims, met with fierce opposition from both flak and fighters and nine of the bombers, six Hampdens and three Wellingtons, were shot down. The victims fell mainly to fighter attack although the Luftwaffe admitted that it had itself lost five fighters.

This was the final proof that to carry on with self-defending formations of bombers operating in daylight would be extremely foolhardy and henceforth the Wellingtons and Hampdens would operate mainly by night.

Within the course of a month the ill-fated Norway Campaign was over. Daylight raids, mainly by Blenheims, had continued but only when the bombers be sure of cloud cover to protect them from the enemy fighters. The latter stages of the campaign saw a shift to night bombing which resulted in far lower casualties, but with unreliable navigational equipment and other difficulties the results of the bombing were invariably poor. Some reinforcement did come to Bomber Command when the Wellingtons of 75 (New Zealand) Squadron participated in their first raid on the night of 17/18 April.

When the German forces launched what was to become known as the Blitzkrieg on France and the Low Countries, the British and French troops were almost immediately put on the back foot and forced into retreat. Bomber Command, still hindered by pre-war thinking and bombing restrictions, had taken no decisive action to stem the German onslaught despite carrying out extensive reconnaissance. The Blenheims of 2 Group were immediately placed under the command of the Advanced Air Striking Force (AASF) and although they continued to operate from their airfields in Britain, they were not controlled by Bomber Command during this period.

The night-bombers, the Whitleys, now joined by the Wellingtons and the Hampdens, were luckier in that they would face far less opposition, but the tasks which they were to be asked to perform brought their own dangers and problems. Although they were not exposed to the ferocious flak and fighter attacks which faced the Blenheim and Battle crews, the problems of navigation, finding their targets and bombing accurately at night, were to prove impossibly difficult to overcome. In the initial days the night bombers were ordered to operate against road and rail communications in the rear, but the small targets which they were asked to find and bomb quickly proved the fact that the vast majority of crews could not hope to locate such targets at night. The bombers were further hindered by the politicians in Britain and France who ordered that no targets across the Rhine could be targeted in case of provoking reprisal raids.

It was not until 15 May that the War Cabinet relented and agreed to allow Bomber Command to attack targets over the Rhine and the command could finally enact its planned strategic bombing offensive against Germany. Portal acted immediately, sending 99 bombers to attack military targets in the Ruhr. With the optimism that marked this stage of the bomber war the aircraft were dispatched to sixteen different targets and the most to attack any one target was nine aircraft. The raids were carried out without loss, but upon return a Wellington of 115 Squadron was blown off course and crashed into high ground near to Rouen. Flight Lieutenant Alec Edward Pringle DFC, and the four members of his crew became Bomber Command's first fatalities of the strategic offensive against Germany. At Cologne, one of the bombers assigned to attack the I.G. Farben Werk missed its target and instead hit a farm, killing a dairyman, Franz Romeike. (The chemical and pharmaceutical company was a key supporter of the Nazi regime, extensively used slave labour from the Auschwitz Concentration Camp and as a subsidiary developed the Zyklon B gas that was used to murder more than one million people.)

Over the next five nights Bomber Command mounted raids against German industrial targets, including Bremen, Cologne and Hamburg but, with the situation in France becoming desperate, was forced to pull its forces back and operate once more against bridges and communications which lay nearer to the battle zone. During this period there was a full moon and Bomber Command attempted to take advantage of this to increase accuracy.

Towards the end of May, however, it was increasingly evident that the Battle of France was going to be lost and that Bomber Command should begin attempts to preserve its forces for a battle in which Britain would have its back to the wall. Despite this, small raids on German industrial targets continued but, demonstrating the wildly optimistic views which commanders had of the possibilities offered by a strategic bombing offensive, it was claimed at the start of June that in just three months Bomber Command could reduce oil production in Germany by 500,000 tons. Overblown claims and hopes such as this were the common theme for the bomber offensive for much of 1940 and 1941.

Through no fault of its crews Bomber Command's part in the Battle of France was slight. The command was, quite simply, in no way strong enough to make any greater contribution at the time. The largest raid of the period involved just 142 aircraft and the bombloads which dropped on the targets, most of which were missed due to navigational or bombing errors, was minimal. Typical of these raids, for example, was the night of 24/25 June when 103 aircraft were dispatched to make attacks on twenty-one separate targets. On this night there were no losses, but accomplishments were also negligible.

With the fall of France on 25 June Britain prepared itself for possible invasion in the knowledge that the Luftwaffe would first have to gain aerial superiority over the southern coast. The period of the Battle of Britain was one of uncertainty for Bomber Command. The commanders were dedicated to maintaining the strategic offensive against German industry, but the realities demanded that airfields in France, now held by the Germans, had to be added to the list of targets (which included, amongst others, German forests). Aircraft factories in Germany also became a valid target.

The greatest contribution of Bomber Command to the Battle of Britain, however, was its campaign against the formations of barges which could be used in the invasion and on the possible invasion ports. Losses during these attacks were substantial for what was still a small force and the lack of attention shown to the efforts of Bomber Command compared to the more easily visible and quantifiable contribution of Fighter Command rankled with many.

On paper, Bomber Command had been strengthened in the build-up to the Battle of Britain with the formation of a Czech Squadron, 311, and two Polish squadrons, 300 and 301, and with the return of the battered squadrons of the AASF. These squadrons, however, had taken such punishment that many had, in all useful terms, been annihilated and needed to be built up and re-equipped. It would be almost a month before the first of them, 103 and 150 Squadrons would be ready to operate in any way.

No advances were made in terms of new navigational or bomb aiming equipment and the efforts of the bomber crews that were sent to attack German targets at night continued to be largely wasted. Reports from German records of the period show that the bombing offensive was achieving very little for an increasing cost. At Munster, for example, fourteen nights of bombing raids saw only one night when more than ten bombs fell in the city, and very little in the way of industrial damage was done in any of the German towns or cities.

On 8/9 September, for example, 133 aircraft of four types made attacks on ports and barges in Hamburg, Bremen, Emden, Ostend and Boulogne. The main effort for the night was at Hamburg where forty-nine Hampdens attempted to bomb the Blohm & Voss Shipyard facilities. The results of the bombing are not available, though it is doubtful any serious damage was done and eight aircraft were lost from the night's efforts. Hampden I (P428) of 50 Squadron was ordered to attack Hamburg but at 11.59pm a wireless transmission was picked up from the bomber stating that the crew were baling out. Squadron Leader F.A. Willan and his crew of three were all later confirmed as being prisoners. Details of the aircraft lost during these raids is often scant with aircraft often being described as having been lost without trace, suspected over the sea. Details, however slight, often only came to light when there were survivors. Wellington IC (P9245, OJ-W) of 149 Squadron was tasked with bombing Boulogne, but the bomber, captained by Squadron Leader Lionel Vincent Andrews crashed onto the sea off Clacton on its return. The second pilot, Pilot Officer C.W. Parish, managed to swim ashore but the remaining five men all perished.

Six nights later came Bomber Command's biggest effort against the invasion ports when 155 aircraft attacked numerous targets. On this night there were no aircraft losses, but one event resulted in the award of the second Bomber Command VC of the war when a Hampden of

83 Squadron was hit over Antwerp. Flying Officer Clare Arthur Connor and his crew were over the target when their Hampden (P1355) was hit by flak and caught fire. The fire spread quickly and the navigator and gunner both baled out. The 18-year-old wireless operator, Sergeant John Hannah attempted to fight the fire with fire extinguishers but when these had been exhausted resorted to beating at the flames with his hands. Hannah sustained terrible injuries from the fire but succeeded in extinguishing it and Connor managed to fly the battered Hampden back to Britain. Connor received the DFC for his actions and Hannah was awarded the VC.[3] His pilot, a Canadian serving in the RAF, lost his life on 4 November 1940 when his aircraft crashed into the sea off the British coast when returning from a raid on Kiel.

On the night of 23/24 Bomber Command launched its second operation against Berlin. The first had been a month previously in retaliation for the first bombing raid on London. On this night, however, the main force of Bomber Command was solely concentrated on this one target. Thus, 129 aircraft made attacks on specified military targets over a three-hour period. Demonstrating the lack of planning which was a feature of this stage of the bombing war, the aircraft selected their own routes and bombed from heights varying between 4,500-16,000 feet.

On 5 October the command changed once more when Sir Charles Portal was promoted to become Chief of the Air Staff and was replaced by Air Vice Marshal Sir Richard Pierse. The new commander was given a directive that his main target was to remain the enemy's oil supplies, but the target list was extended with a long list of specific industrial concerns in both Germany and Italy. Alongside this, the command was to continue with its minelaying operations which the crews referred to as 'gardening' trips.

Pierse faced many problems. Foremost amongst them was the fact that Bomber Command was still woefully understrength for the task facing it. Pierse could field a total strength of no more than 230 serviceable aircraft which were useful for the tasks of Bomber Command and the most he could hope to put into action on any one night was, realistically, no more than 150. The last three months of 1940 were fairly quiet with the same piecemeal attacks aimed, optimistically, at German industrial concerns. There were only two operations of note.

In response to the devastating bombing of Coventry on 14/15 November Pierse sent 130 bombers to attack Hamburg the next night. In the event the weather was poor and only sixty of the crews reported bombing the target.

There was little damage with the authorities in Hamburg reporting only six fires with two dead, thirty-six injured and almost 800 bombed out. This came at the price of the loss of three aircraft while a further five crashed upon return in England.

With the bombing of towns and cities during the Blitz the government took the reins off Bomber Command and relaxed the restrictions which had applied throughout the war so far. On the night of December 16/17 Bomber Command made its first area attack of the war when 134 bombers raided Mannheim. The raid had been specifically authorised by the War Cabinet in response to recent bombing raids upon several British cities including Coventry and Southampton. Operation Abigail Rachel was to involve 200 bombers, but weather forecasts implied poor conditions over some of the bases on return and the number was reduced. Leading the raid were eight experienced Wellington crews who were to start fires in the centre of Mannheim using incendiaries. There was a full moon and the weather over the target was fair, but the raid failed. The leading crews were inaccurate and bombing was scattered over Mannheim. Despite this, 240 buildings were listed as destroyed and there was some industrial damage. Thirty-four people were killed, eighty-one injured and 1,266 were bombed out of their homes. Bomber Command lost just three aircraft although a further four crashed upon return.

CHAPTER 3

1941 – The Doldrums

Summary of the Year

The year began quietly for Bomber Command with desultory minor raids continuing in the same vein as in the latter three months of 1940. However, it also began with bright hopes. Bomber Command was gaining strength, even if slowly, and the recent quiet period had enabled crews to gain experience. Once again, Pierse was instructed that his main target was to be the enemy's oil supplies. A list of nine important facilities was drawn up. They included sites which were at the very maximum range for the aircraft which Bomber Command possessed and, realistically, hopes of finding, far less hitting such targets were small.

The winter of 1940-1941 saw yet another change in tactics with the command urged to mount precision raids on German oil refineries. It was believed in some circles that successful attacks on these small, but vital targets would result in Germany being unable to maintain its war effort. On 15 January the Air Ministry issued a new directive which made the bombing of these oil targets a priority. Despite these attacks on oil targets, the command also continued to make attacks against area targets. One of the problems which had haunted the command throughout the previous year was the number and variety of targets which it was urged to attack and this problem continued into 1941. By March the German U-boat campaign was beginning to have serious repercussion for Britain's supply lines and in that month Peirse was told the matter was a serious crisis and was ordered to switch from targets in Germany to attacks against enemy naval targets. These attacks lasted for approximately three months.

Many grandiose claims had been made for the attacks which had been made so far in the war but by 1941 doubts had been raised in many quarters. The Admiralty, always critical of the amount of funding and resources which were poured into Bomber Command, was one of the main critics, but there were others from those in political office. By the mid-point of the year even some within the RAF were growing increasingly doubtful over the accuracy that was being claimed by both returning crews and the command itself. This is not a criticism of the crews involved. It was incredibly difficult for these men to assess the accuracy of their efforts and intelligence gathering following raids was rudimentary at this stage of the war, as were photographic reconnaissance efforts following the raids. Of far greater concern was the fact that the Prime Minister himself had taken an interest in the criticisms and an inquiry and report had been commissioned to assess the accuracy and effectiveness of the bomber campaign thus far. The Butt Report reported back in August and was possibly a disastrous blow to Bomber Command. The report revealed that very few of the bombers assigned to targets actually located the target and even fewer actually managed to hit the target or even to bomb anywhere near it. The report made no criticism of the crews themselves for it was obvious that the disappointing results were caused by other factors. The vast majority of crews had not been trained to fly at night in wartime conditions, tactics for such raids had not been adequately developed, and available equipment was wholly unsuitable. The conclusions of the report, however, were undeniable. Thus far in the war the efforts of Bomber Command had resulted in negligible results and had cost the country valuable resources and, even more seriously, had resulted in the deaths and losses of hundreds of aircrew for this meagre return.

Despite these massive problems there was some hope for the command in 1941. The year saw the first of the new and far more modern four-engine heavy bombers arrive in service. It fell to 7 Squadron to debut the first of this type, the Short Stirling, on the night of 10/11 February when three of the new aircraft took part in an operation against oil tanks at Rotterdam. Other new types were also on the verge of being ushered into service. On 24/25 February the two-engine Avro Manchester came into service with 207 Squadron when six of its aircraft bombed warships at Brest. The Manchester quickly proved to be a massive disappointment. Problems with the engines resulted in a stream of casualties as it became clear that the aircraft was often incapable of maintaining flight if it lost the use of an engine. In March another four-engine bomber came into service. The Handley Page Halifax was first allocated to 35 Squadron in 4 Group and the squadron first used the type during a raid on Le Havre. Much of the early months of the year were taken up by attacks on oil and shipping targets and a number of small-scale area raids.

Another encouraging sign of technological developments to come arrived on the night of 30 March/1April when Wellingtons from 9 and 149 Squadrons dropped the first two 4,000lb bombs of the war. The target was Emden. These large, high-capacity bombs, quickly nicknamed 'cookies', went on to form the basis of the area bombing main offensive campaign of 1943-1944. This encouraging sign was followed days later when the largest single raid of the war so far saw 229 bombers attack Kiel. At the beginning of May a raid was made by 359 aircraft on the twin targets of Hamburg and Bremen. This period also saw the first real attempt to make a concerted series of raids on the same target with Hamburg being attacked on three occasions in the space of four nights.

The summer was taken up with raids, usually fairly small in size, against naval, oil and power targets, with a number of further area raids also made when conditions allowed. An experiment into a return to daylight bombing began on 8 July when Boeing Fortress aircraft of 90 Squadron made a daylight attack on the docks at Wilhemshaven. The American Fortress had been designed as a high-altitude heavy bomber which would be capable of flying in self-defending formations and the RAF had purchased 20 B-17Cs which had been delivered in May. Named in RAF service the Fortress I, it fell to 90 Squadron to pioneer their use. It was quickly realised, however, that technical issues, losses and other factors meant that the type was judged not to be suitable for Bomber Command service and the experiment ended at the end of September when a final daylight raid was made on Emden (other newer models saw service with RAF Coastal Command and the type G provided decent service from 1944 with Bomber Command's 100 Group). Daylight raids at the time were the province of 2 Group and on 12 August 53 Blenheims attacked power stations at Knapsack and Quadrath. These 2 Group attacks often resulted in heavy losses.

From the start of the war Bomber Command had been a multi-national force and this only increased as the war went on. The majority of squadrons were of mixed nationalities but some Empire governments did ask to form their own squadrons but, despite this, the vast majority of squadrons in the command (barring two Free French Squadrons and the Polish and Czechoslovakian squadrons), even those with national names remained multi-national in character. Mid-June had seen the first operation flown by a Canadian, RCAF, squadron when 405 Squadron dispatched four Wellingtons on an operation to Schwerte. This was followed at the end of

August by the first Australian, RAAF, unit, 455 Squadron sent some of its Hampdens as part of a raid on Frankfurt.

The month also saw the first trial use of a new radar aid in which great hope had been placed. Codenamed 'Gee', the first trial was by two Wellingtons of 115 Squadron on a raid to Mönchengladbach. Gee used radar beams and a lattice network to enable a navigator to establish his position with a fair degree of accuracy. It was highly effective and allowed a crew to successfully navigate to the general area of a target. This was due to the fact that the aid depended upon signals from ground-radar stations and, so, was limited by the curvature of the Earth. Beyond this range, the device was still of value as it gave accurate fixes when in range. Unfortunately, the Germans quickly learned to jam Gee signals and it was used mainly as a navigational aid when outbound from base and when inbound back to Britain.

There were a number of serious question-marks hanging over Bomber Command in the latter half of the year. Questions over the accuracy and effectiveness of the bombing campaign were joined by growing concerns over the losses which were being experienced during the raids. Bad weather was to blame for some of the losses, but it was also increasingly clear that inadequate training and poor equipment was combining with stronger defences to increase the danger of bomber operations.

Overshadowed by the Butt Report the winter opened disastrously for the command. A raid on Berlin by 169 aircraft took place on the night of 7/8 November but twenty-one of the bombers failed to return. Deeply concerned by these losses the Air Ministry, under Churchill's orders, ordered the command to undertake only limited operations for the foreseeable future and the whole future of Bomber Command was hanging in the balance. Amongst these limited operations was an attack on Brest on the night of 7/8 December. This raid was notable in that it involved the first trial of yet another radar aid by the Stirlings of 7 and 15 Squadrons. This aid, codenamed 'Oboe', was a precision bombing aid which allowed individual aircraft to fly along two radar beams until reaching a certain point and allowed, it was hoped, the bomber to bomb with great accuracy. Like Gee, there were high hopes for Oboe despite the fact that its range was again limited by the curvature of the earth and objectives beyond the Ruhr could not be targeted using the new device. The fact that it also depended upon two radar stations meant that only one bomber at a time could use Oboe.

In some respects, the enforced suspension of bombing operations was a blessing in disguise as it allowed the command to assess its needs and its tactical effectiveness so far. The suspension in operations did, however, have other negative connotations as it allowed critics to use the suspension as a justification for its continued fault finding. The Admiralty and the War Office were particularly vociferous in this regard and were just two amongst several groups who were urging the government to drastically reduce the size of Bomber Command to a force which would be used as a support for ground and naval operations.

The Campaign

Air Marshal Pierse, however, was determined to make a statement attack on at least one of these targets during the February full moon period. On the night of 10/11 February, therefore, he dispatched a total of 265 aircraft to two targets. The main target for the night was at Hanover which 222 aircraft were detailed to bomb while 43 aircraft were sent to bomb oil storage tanks at Rotterdam. Of the Hanover force 183 claimed to have bombed their targets in good visibility. Returning crews reported seeing large explosions and fires but no specific report is available from the German authorities. Four of the attacking aircraft were lost. The Rotterdam force, which included three Stirlings from 7 Squadron (the first operational flight by the new four-engined heavy bombers), suffered no losses.

With the introduction of the Stirlings came fresh new hopes for the future. The new four-engined bombers which were being developed, the Stirling, the Halifax and the Lancaster, could carry far heavier bombloads, had better range and, it was hoped, were more robust. Another new type became available to Bomber Command at the end of February when the twin-engined Avro Manchester was made available to 207 Squadron. The Manchester's first operation was when six aircraft attacked German warships in the harbour at Brest on the night of 24/25 February.

With the worries over shipping losses in the Atlantic and the threat of Britain being starved out of the war if such losses continued, the Air Ministry issued new orders to Bomber Command on 9 March when Pierse was ordered to give priority to attacks on the U-boat threat, as well as factories producing long-range aircraft (which were used to locate Allied convoys). Targets included shipyards at Kiel, Hamburg, Bremen and Vegesack, engine factories at Augsburg and Mannheim, aircraft factories at Bremen and Dessau, U-boat bases at Bordeaux, St Lorient, and St Nazaire, and W Kondor air bases at Stavanger and Merignac. Pierse responded immediately with two small raids of just fourteen aircraft each on Le Havre and St Nazaire. The Le Havre raid was a momentous one as it saw the Handley Page Halifax make its operational debut, six of the four-engined bombers, from 35 Squadron, being sent along with eight Blenheims. All of the Halifaxes returned to Britain, but one of them, piloted by Squadron Leader P.A. Gilchrist was shot down by an RAF night-fighter over Surrey. Halifax I (L9489, TL-F) crashed at the village of Normandy at around 10.40pm and only Squadron Leader Gilchrist and his observer, Sergeant R.G. Aedy survived.

Efforts were also to made to sink the *Scharnhorst* and *Gnesienau* which had taken refuge at Brest. The orders to focus on these targets caused something of a disagreement between Portal and Pierse. The latter resented his force being taken off its strategic industrial targets while Portal, who secretly doubted the ability of Bomber Command to hit and seriously damage these targets, welcomed the switch. For the next four months, however, Pierse would have to devote considerable resources to these new targets. Typical of the efforts to sink the two vessels was the raid mounted on the night of 30/31 March when 109 aircraft attacked Brest. Although the majority of crews reported bombing the target no hits were recorded on the two ships.

At the start of April another raid had a more successful result. This was a smaller raid with just fifty-four aircraft taking part, but one of the returning bombers claimed a direct hit on one of the warships and German records later confirmed this. A bomb fell onto the dry dock in which the *Gneisenau* was lying, but failed to explode. The presence of the bomb, however, convinced the captain of the ship to move his vessel and the *Gneisenau* was moored in the harbour instead. It was while here that a Coastal Command Beaufort torpedo bomber manage to score a direct hit which caused serious damage to the ship.[1]

The growing strength of Bomber Command was shown when Pierse was able to dispatch 359 aircraft on 8/9 May. There were several targets with Hamburg and Bremen being the main focus. For Hamburg 188 aircraft were tasked with bombing targets. The raid was a success with considerable damage being done in the city. Much of this was down to the increased use of the new 4,000 lb high capacity bombs which were being used in greater numbers. With typical insouciance the crews referred to the bombs as cookies. Four aircraft were lost. The 214 Squadron crew of 30-year-old Squadron Leader Frank Leslie Herbert Eddison DFC, crashed in Holland with total loss of life. Squadron Leader Eddison was to have been posted to another squadron as a flight commander following the completion of this operation.

The raid on Bremen was made by 133 aircraft and was once again a success, but the main target of the raid, the A.G. Weser submarine yards, were not hit. Five aircraft were lost. Amongst the losses on the Bremen operation was Wellington IC (R1227, GR-M) of 301 Squadron. Sergeant T. Bojakowski and his crew were all killed when their aircraft got into difficulties over the North Sea.

On 24 July Bomber Command made an audacious mass daylight attack on Brest in an attempt to hit the German warships berthed there. One hundred aircraft took part in the raid and, aware of the dangers of daylight operations, a complicated plan was prepared. This would see three RAF B-17 Flying Fortresses bomb from high altitude in the hope of drawing up enemy fighters prematurely. They would be followed by eighteen Hampdens which would have an escort of three squadrons of Spitfires in order to complete the decoy of enemy fighters. The Main Force of seventy-nine Wellingtons, which had no fighter escort, would then attack. Although the plan worked to an extent and six hits were claimed on the *Gneisenau* the fighter opposition was heavier than expected and ten of the Wellingtons and two Hampdens were shot down.

With growing suspicions over the effectiveness of Bomber Command attacks, a report had been commissioned to inquire into the matter. The Butt Report was published on 18 August and it was damning. Its central conclusion was that of every Bomber Command crew which claimed to have bombed on target, only one could be proven to have actually bombed within five miles of the target.

Released from the directive on U-boats, Pierse, for the rest of the year, attempted to hit strategic targets in German cities. Berlin was amongst these targets and it is possible that Pierse wished to hit a hard blow to the German capital in order to provide a useful boost to the prospects of Bomber Command which was in increasing doubt in the wake of the Butt Report. Voices had been raised in high positions within the forces and in government and were questioning the viability of maintaining a large force of bombers. The Admiralty was particularly critical. On the night of 2/3 September the main target for the night was Frankfurt but a separate force of forty-nine aircraft were sent to Berlin. For 61 Squadron the night was disastrous. Only one of its aircraft failed to return, one of five lost on the Berlin raid, but it contained both the commanding officer of the squadron and the station commander of RAF North Luffenham. Manchester I (L7388) was shot down over the target by flak and all of the seven men aboard were killed. Group Captain John Francis Tufnell Barratt DSO and Bar, DFC was 43 and had served in the First World War. The squadron commander was Wing Commander George Engebret Valentine DSO. It would appear that the crew's regular pilot, Flight Lieutenant Alan Bruce Harrison DSO, was also accompanying the two senior officers.

On 7/8 November Pierse sent 169 aircraft to attack Berlin, but in poor weather the raid was scattered and only seventy-three crews reported bombing the target. Disastrously for Pierse, twenty-one aircraft were lost (12.4 per cent of the force). The force had fallen prey to a combination of the fierce flak defences over the German capital and an increased number of night-fighters. The Air Ministry, already concerned over losses for little gain, intervened and in a crushing blow to Pierse and to Bomber Command ordered that only limited operations be carried out for the foreseeable future.

Bomber Command's existence was now in very serious doubt with many advocating the scaling back of the force with air resources dedicated instead to the Battle of the Atlantic and Bomber Command being retained only as a small force which would be used for tactical bombing.

CHAPTER 4

1942 – A Year of Change

Summary of the Year

As 1942 began Bomber Command found its operational opportunities limited by the recently imposed restrictions following the disastrous Berlin raid of 7/8 November 1941. Over the course of January, the command focused largely on the ports of France and Germany, although several raids on towns were made, notably on Hanover and Munster. This unlooked-for pause brought valuable breathing space and allowed recent losses to be replaced.

The year saw Bomber Command transformed from a force which, at the beginning of the war, was under the threat of being dramatically downsized to a force which, by the end of the year, was expanding rapidly with new and modern aircraft and which was increasingly utilising newly developed radar technology and tactics to increase the accuracy of its bombing. The year began, however, with more disappointment. Failed attacks upon the *Gneisenau*, *Scharnhorst*, and *Tirpitz* in January sufficiently worried the Germans into moving several of these vital naval assets in a daring dash through the Channel from Brest to the greater safety of the German ports. The Channel Dash, on 12 February, was a humiliation in which 242 bombers failed to locate the *Gneisenau*, the *Prinz Eugen* or the *Scharnhorst* and they escaped. The incident reflected badly on Bomber Command but neither the Admiralty, nor Coastal Command, could crow as they too shared in much of the blame for the debacle.

Possibly the greatest impetus to this rejuvenation was the removal of the unfortunate Pierse and his replacement on 22 February with the dynamic and committed Air Marshal Sir Arthur 'Bomber' Harris.[1] Harris quickly established himself. On the night of 26/27 February he sent 49 aircraft to attack Kiel and the *Gneisenau* was damaged.

One of the greatest differences in the mentality of Bomber Command came from its new commander. Harris came to Bomber Command with the utter conviction that Germany could be defeated solely by bombing. He had mounted a campaign to convince the government, and particularly Churchill and Portal, that area bombing could destroy Germany's industrial capacity to wage war and, at the same time, erode the morale of the German people to the point that they would force their government to surrender. To this end, Harris had prepared a plan for a grand gesture which would capture the imagination of the public, would influence the government, and silence the command's critics. This was his Thousand Plan which would see the assembly of a force of 1,000 aircraft which would be used to attack several targets over a number of nights.

Harris was a fine and inspiring commander, but he was massively aided by the greater production of the Stirling and Halifax and by the introduction, in March 1942, of the Avro Lancaster. The Lancaster was developed from the hugely disappointing Manchester. It was equipped with four Rolls-Royce Merlin engines (as was the Halifax) and proved to have long range, heavy bomb-carrying capacity, a good service ceiling and decent speed. The Lancaster was first used by 44 Squadron, on a mining-laying trip on 3/4 March and flew on its first bombing raid on 10/11 March when two of the new aircraft joined a raid on Essen. Harris was also substantially aided by the development and refinement of both Gee and Oboe. He demonstrated his ruthlessness to prosecute the bombing campaign with a raid on the Renault lorry factory at Billancourt, to the west of Paris, with 225 aircraft. Despite the fact that 367 French civilians were accidentally killed, Harris justified the attack by claiming, correctly, that the factory was an important target.

Harris also made a highly successful attack on the town of Lubeck at the end of March. In addition to this attack he launched a series of raids aimed at Essen. Results were mixed and there were, as ever, losses on this difficult Ruhr target. These raids saw the first operational use of the Lancaster on Main Force raids when 44 Squadron dispatched some of its new aircraft on the raid which took place on 10/11 March. Meanwhile, 61 Squadron was struggling on with the poor Avro Manchester and one of its aircraft featured in an article in *The Sphere* at the beginning of April. The article focused on the repair work which enabled RAF Bomber Command to quickly and efficiently restore damaged aircraft to airworthiness and enable them to return to the bombing campaign. It featured Manchester L7477 (QR-N) of 61 Squadron. The Manchester was described as having been damaged during the recent raid on the Ruhr but, despite the fuselage and tail being riddled by enemy flak, claimed that the aircraft would once again be airworthy within days.

With the growing awareness of the bombing campaign and the interest in the new heavy bombers which, with their four engines and seven-men crews, seemed to promise a new and more modern way of hitting back at Germany, came increasing press coverage of Bomber Command and many titles ran articles which described the typical day on a bomber station or related stories from the experiences of bomber crews. Such articles almost always found widespread favour with the majority of the general public and the RAF allowed access to not only journalists but, in some cases, photographers. While almost every such article featured a photograph of a bomber and focused on the experiences of aircrew, they also tended to reassure and explain to readers that the work of the RAF groundcrew was also vital to the continued offensive against Germany.

April was a varied month which saw the command's first 8,000lb bomb being dropped over Essen by a 76 Squadron Halifax, an attempt at a daylight precision attack, a return to a sustained attack on one target and further attempts to cripple German capital ships. Probably the most interesting operation of the period was the Augsburg operation of 17 April which saw twelve of the new Lancasters make a daring and low-level daylight attack on the MAN diesel engine factory there. This was a departure for the command and represented an experiment to see if the new, faster, bomber types such as the Lancaster could be used to hit precision targets in daylight. Although hits were scored on the factory the raid proved conclusively that such raids would result in massive casuaties – seven of the Lancasters failed to return. Harris again made his intentions clear with a determine series of raids, over four consecutive nights, on Rostock.

The advent of newer types of aircraft led to the removal of some of the stalwarts of the bomber campaign from front-line duties. The Hampden, Manchester and Whitley were now obsolescent and would gradually be withdrawn as newer types became available. The Wellington, however, would soldier on for some time. The end of April saw the final front-line operational use of the Whitley when two aircraft from 58 Squadron attacked Dunkirk. The final front-line operation by Hampdens was carried out by four aircraft from 408 (RCAF) Squadron in mid-September.

On 30/31 May Harris launched the first of his 1,000-bomber raids when 1,047 aircraft attacked Cologne. To assemble such a vast force, he had been required to beg and borrow aircraft from a number of commands. Most had been extremely co-operative in the venture, but the Admiralty attempted to sabotage the plan in the latter stages by withdrawing its co-operation. Outside of his front-line units the greatest contribution to the plan was made by his training units with some 365 OTU aircraft being sent on the Cologne raid. The raid was a success, but the greatest success of the operation was in the massive public response. It made headlines across the world and was met with massive approval amongst the public and in government circles; Churchill was particularly enthused (as Harris had hoped). The raid also made very positive headlines in the USA as it demonstrated to the American people that Britain was capable of striking such a blow against Germany.

Harris managed to keep his 1,000-force together for a month before he was forced to release the training and other aircraft to their regular duties. Two more thousand-plan raids were mounted in the following days, although both actually involved just under the magic 1,000 figure. On 1/2 June some 956 aircraft attacked Essen, while the night of 25/26 of that month saw 960 aircraft raid Bremen.

In the month following the daring 1,000-bmber raids Harris marshalled his strength and prepared for major developments in the organisation of his command and his tactics. In July the greatest incident of note was another daylight raid, this time carried out by 44 Lancasters on the U-boat yards at Danzig.

The following month saw the formation of the Pathfinder Force (PFF). Initially formed as part of 3 Group the PFF went on to become a separate group, 8 (PFF) Group, which drew resources from all the main force groups. The PFF was something against which Harris had railed but he had been over-ruled and had since thrown his effort behind establishing the force. The idea was that the PFF would be an elite force within Bomber Command which would lead the way to the target using superior navigational skills and equipment and then accurately mark the target using flares and specially developed incendiary devices. Harris had despised the idea of an elite force and the debates over the formation of PFF had been rancorous.

August was another month of change. The PFF launched its first attack on 18/19 August when 31 of its aircraft led the way for a total force of just 118 bombers to Flensburg. The following day saw Bomber Command once again take part in a combined operation when 62 Douglas Bostons of 2 Group assisted the Dieppe raid by dropping bombs and laying smoke. At the end of the month there was a daring operation in which nine Lancasters from 106 Squadron flew 950 miles to bomb the German aircraft carrier, *Graf Zeppelin*, at Gdynia. Unfortunately, the raid was called off as haze meant that bombing was not possible.

Throughout the following months PFF continued to develop its techniques and at the start of September it introduced several different duties to its crews. Illuminators were to go in to attack the target first and drop flares to light up the target for the pathfinder crews who were following. They were followed by the visual-markers who identified the target and dropped coloured markers. Finally, backers-up were spread throughout the raid with heir duty being to ensure that the target point continued to be marked throughout the raid. The first use of these techniques was on a raid on Bremen on 4/5 September. Just five nights later the PFF dropped the first 4,000lb incendiary target marker during a raid on Dusseldorf.

The final three months of 1942 saw Harris continue to develop tactics while attempting to marshal his resources and further strengthen his command. Several interesting and daring attacks were launched during the period. They included a daylight attack by 94 Lancasters of 5 Group on the Schneider armaments factory at Le Creusot on 17 October. This was followed a week later by a daylight raid on Milan by 88 Lancasters from both 5 and 8 (PFF) Group. The operation was mounted to coincide with the campaign at El Alamein. Raids in Italy were a feature of the period with the first involving over 100 aircraft taking place on 22/23 October, with the target being Genoa. At the end of November Bomber Command dropped its first 8,000lb bomb on Italy, over Turin. Other attacks in these final months of 1942 included a low-level daylight attack using the newly introduced de Havilland Mosquito. This was an attack by six Mosquitoes of 105 Squadron on a German ship in the Gironde estuary.

At the start of December every available 2 Group aircraft was involved in a raid on the Philips radio and valve factory at Eindhoven. Demonstrating the dangers of such daylight attacks, some eleven aircraft failed to return. The Mosquito, with its exceptionally high service ceiling and its speed, was the ideal candidate to house the Oboe equipment which was now coming on stream and the device was first used operationally in a Mosquito on 20/21 December when a small number of aircraft from 106 Squadron attacked the Lutterade power station in Holland.

The Campaign

On 2/3 January ninety-four aircraft of five different types were dispatched to bomb the ports of Brest, St Nazaire and to lay mines off the Frisians and various French ports. Hampden I (P5328, UB-Q) of 455 (RAAF) Squadron took off from RAF Swinderby tasked with laying mines off La Rochelle. Upon its return the Hampden crashed at 1am at Folly Farm, Buckinghamshire. The aircraft burst into flames on impact and debris was scattered across a large area. The four-man crew of the Hampden were all killed.

The pilot was 30-year-old Aberdonian, Pilot Officer Charles Ludwig. He had been educated at Aberdeen University where he had excelled and had graduated as a Bachelor of Medicine, Bachelor of Surgery. He had also developed a reputation for his daring practical jokes such as when he placed a skeleton, complete with a top hat, on top of Mitchell Tower of Marischal College. The prank had utilised his considerable skill as a mountaineer, having climbed extensively in the Cairngorms, Dolomites and Caucasus. It was said that he had also crossed Rubislaw Quarry hand-over-hand on a wire rope. Pilot Officer Ludwig had embarked upon a fine career and was lecturing at Leeds University when war broke out. Anxious to do his patriotic duty, he resigned and joined up as an aircraftman before being commissioned in 1941. At the time of his death he was shortly to have been married.

Just an hour after the Hampden crashed, Whitley V (Z6656) of 78 Squadron crashed on moorland while descending on approach to its base at RAF Croft. The Whitley, piloted by Sergeant A.J. Attwell, RCAF, came down on Woogill Moor in Nidderdale but on this occasion, thankfully, the crew managed to escape, although all were injured to some degree.

The attacks on ports and mining operations provided valuable experience to crews but they came at a steady, if relatively low cost, in aircraft and crews. Sometimes these operations cost the lives of proven and experienced airmen. On the night following the loss of the Hampden and Whitley mentioned above, Bomber Command sent another force to bomb Brest and to lay mines off the Frisians. Two aircraft failed to return; 106 Squadron lost Hampden I (AT123) which disappeared without trace whilst engaged upon a 'gardening' operation. Two of the crew, pilot and gunner, had been decorated with the DFM during previous service with the same squadron.[2]

At the beginning of the year Churchill was in Washington but, in the face of rising Bomber Command losses and growing evidence of a lack of effectiveness, he took the decision to remove Sir Richard Pierse as the commanding officer. On the face of it this was a rather harsh decision which failed to take into account the facts that Pierse had, from his appointment in October 1940, been struggling to build up his command despite the slow arrival of the much-promised four-engined bombers and a lack of effective navigational aids. It seems from an analysis that Pierse had achieved as much as any commander could have with Bomber Command during this period. In spite of the limitations placed upon operations, the crews still faced immense dangers which were only exacerbated by the ferocious winter weather.

The man chosen as Pierse's replacement was the former commanding officer of 5 Group Sir Arthur Harris. There was, however, a period between the announcement of this appointment and the time it took for Harris to hand over the reins at 5 Group and take over at High Wycombe. During this period command fell to Air Vice Marshal Sir John Baldwin of 3 Group. Raids organised during this period consisted largely of operations against ports, with Brest being targeted particularly as it was known that the *Gneisenau* and the *Scharnhorst* were berthed there. The port attacks were interspersed with a small number of raids against Emden, Hamburg, Munster and Wilhelmshaven.

On two consecutive nights beginning 14/15 January Bomber Command launched attacks on the city of Hamburg. In line with the restrictions placed upon the force, these attacks were small in numbers with ninety-five aircraft involved on the first attack and ninety-six on the second. The first attack saw just forty-eight of the attacking crews claim to have bombed Hamburg (which recorded some minor damage and fires with six people killed).

The raid cost the command six aircraft that night. Wellington IC (X9742) of 40 Squadron had taken off from RAF Alconbury under the command of Pilot Officer E.G. Broad, RAAF, and was last heard of calling for help shortly after 7.30pm. Nothing further was heard and no trace of the bomber was ever found.

Meanwhile, 50 Squadron at RAF Skellingthorpe lost two of its Hampdens without trace. Pilot Officer E.V. Hore and crew had taken off aboard AE431 while Sergeant R.A. Baddeley and crew were aboard AE420. Based at RAF Bottesford, 207 Squadron also lost two aircraft and crew that night. Avro Manchester I (L7309, EM-O) took off under the command of Flying Officer G.B. Dawkins DFM. The Manchester was shot down, but five of the six crew managed to safely bail out to be taken prisoner. The one fatality was air gunner Sergeant J.W. Cadman.[3] The second loss was Manchester I (L7523, EM-M) which crashed at Cliff House Farm near Withernsea. All seven crew, all of whom were NCOs, were killed.[4] The crew of Flight Lieutenant W.J.W. Kingston of 144 Squadron had a lucky escape after their Hampden ran out and crashed after hitting a chimney stack while trying to land at RAF Langham.

Several Wellingtons of 99 Squadron were dispatched to attack Emden but Z8947, LN-J, with Sergeant Carter and his crew was badly shot up by night-fighters and Sergeant Carter crash-landed the bomber at Hopton, Suffolk. One of the air gunners, Sergeant Norman, suffered a badly broken elbow which ended his flying career. He was an experienced airman and had flown in the region of thirty operations.[5]

The final Bomber Command loss of the night was that of Blenheim IV (V6391, RT-V) of 114 Squadron. The Blenheim, piloted by Flight Lieutenant B.J. Adam, RAAF, had taken off from West Raynham as part of a force of Blenheim intruders sent to attack Dutch airfields which housed night-fighters. At 8.42pm the Blenheim was shot down by flak and crashed in the sea off Holland, killing all three of its crew.[6]

The second raid resulted in fifty-two aircraft claiming to have bombed the target, but once again damage was limited and there were only three fatalities on the ground in Hamburg. Three Wellingtons and a Hampden were lost but bad weather upon return saw another eight bombers crash in England. At a time when Bomber Command was attempting to conserve its strength and when results were under very close scrutiny, especially from those who believed that the command should be hugely scaled down and its resources diverted elsewhere, such losses were a blow.

The severe weather curtailed operations throughout much of January, but training continued and some crews were sent on what were viewed as less dangerous sorties to give them operational experience. The weather and these training details both came at a cost. Sergeant Walter Chantler Williams, RAAF, was a 33-year-old navigator who had just been posted with his crew to 50 Squadron at RAF Skellingthorpe. The squadron was flying Handley Page Hampdens with Bomber Command and Sergeant Williams was part of a mixed crew consisting of two Australians and two British airmen. Sergeant Williams was from South Shields but had emigrated to Australia where he had married Constance Bertha Williams of Hazlewood Park, South Australia.

On the night of 21 January Sergeant Williams and his crew were flying Hampden I (AE381) on an unspecified mission when they became lost in severe blizzard conditions. The squadron records do not record what task the crew were embarking on with most accounts suggesting that it was a night navigation exercise, but one eye witness to the subsequent crash stated that the crew were carrying propaganda leaflets suggesting that they were on a 'Nickel' operation. Shortly after 8.30pm the crew made contact with and overflew RAF Ringway before asking for assistance. Ringway's controllers ordered the pilot to turn through 180 degrees and to make another pass over the airfield. Nothing more was heard until the local police rang up to say an aircraft had crashed into Cluther Rocks on Kinder at 8.38pm All four of the crew were killed. The body of Sergeant Williams was brought back to his hometown by his parents John Henry and Lena Williams. Amongst the service graves in Harton Cemetery at South Shields is that of this lone Australian airman.

In a further attempt to demonstrate how Bomber Command could be used against German naval assets, a small force consisting of nine Halifaxes and seven Stirlings were sent from Lossiemouth to attack the *Tirpitz* which was lying-up at Trondheim on 29/30 January. This was an extremely audacious and optimistic plan which failed utterly. Only two aircraft reported reaching the Norwegian coast and they could only report that they had bombed ships but had not positively identified the great battleship itself. Little resistance was encountered, however, although two aircraft were lost. Halifax I (L9851, MP-Q) of 76 Squadron had taken off shortly after 2am but ditched four miles off Aberdeen at around 10am after the aircraft, skippered by Sergeant J.W.H. Harwood, lost power in the port inner engine. The crew had been in difficulties for some time as they had experienced severe icing, which no doubt resulted in the engine failure, and had lost wireless communications. The crew were all picked up uninjured from the sea. The second loss of the night came when Stirling I (W7462, OJ-T) of 149 Squadron, piloted by Flight Lieutenant R.W.A. Turtle, slid off the icy runway upon return to Lossiemouth. As was typical of such events occurring to Stirlings, the massive undercarriage collapsed and the bomber was damaged beyond repair. The *Tirpitz* would continue to elude Bomber Command for some time.

On the following night seventy-two aircraft were sent to have yet another crack at Brest. No substantial results were reported and a further five aircraft (three Manchesters and two Hampdens) were lost, with nineteen airmen being killed and eleven taken prisoner. One airman, Sergeant A.L. Wright, successfully evaded capture after escaping from his Manchester when it was shot down by flak.

The three Manchesters which were lost were all from 61 Squadron based at RAF Woolfox Lodge. The squadron had only dispatched nine of the unreliable and widely disliked Manchesters on the raid; the loss rate of 33 per cent must have struck deeply at a squadron which had been given a poor aircraft with which to fight. Manchester I (L7396) took off at 6.50pm with Flight Lieutenant Henry Charles Shaw Page DFC (27) at the controls and was last heard sending distress signals while fifty or so miles south of Plymouth. Despite an extensive search by two destroyers, no trace of the Manchester or its crew was found but the body of Flight Lieutenant Page was later washed ashore on the Scillies. A married man who lived at Retford in Nottinghamshire, Flight Lieutenant Page had previously served in the Army with the Middlesex Regiment. The bodies of the other seven men aboard were never recovered. They included 35-year-old Squadron Leader Thomas Noel Challoner Burrough DFC who, as a 5 Group staff officer, had accompanied the crew as an official observer.

Manchester I (L7472), under the command of Flight Lieutenant R.D. Fraser had taken off shortly before the above aircraft. Over Brest the Manchester was coned by searchlights before being hit by flak. On fire, the bomber then clipped a balloon cable and some of the crew baled out before Flight Lieutenant Fraser ditched the stricken aircraft off the French coast. Unfortunately, one of the gunners, 20-year-old Sergeant Stephen Joseph MacLean, RCAF, became trapped in the escape hatch and, despite the best efforts of Fraser, was drowned when the aircraft sank. Another of the crew, Sergeant Geoffrey Herbert Marshall, was also lost. Both men are commemorated on the Runnymede Memorial. The remaining six men of the crew were all taken prisoner.

The final Manchester to be lost from the squadron was Manchester I (R5787, QR-M). Captained by 20-year-old Pilot Officer John Robert Bruno Parsons, the bomber had taken off shortly after 6pm but was hit by flak and crash-landed north-west of Brest. Two of the crew, including Pilot Officer Parsons, were killed in the crash while two more died of their injuries.[7] Two men were taken prisoner while Sergeant Wright evaded capture.

Following the series of raids on Brest, however, the Germans decided that the two battle cruisers, along with the cruiser *Prinz Eugen*, were not safe in the port and the decision was made for the ships to make a dramatic and dangerous dash through the English Channel to Germany. Under the cover of very poor weather and with extensive air cover the ships made the attempt on 12 February. British Intelligence was unaware of this development until the ships were spotted late in the day off Le Touquet. Because of the poor weather most of Bomber Command had been stood down and only 5 Group was at readiness and, even for this group, four hours would be required. Frantic efforts were made to bomb up aircraft and to hurriedly brief crews and get them off before darkness made the operation impossible. Bomber Command launched its aircraft in three waves and, along with aircraft from Coastal Command and the Fleet Air Arm, began searching for the ships. In what was its largest daylight operation of the war so far, Bomber Command flew 242 sorties through the course of the day using 92 Wellingtons, 64 Hampdens, 37 Blenheims, 15 Manchesters, 13 Halifaxes, 11 Stirlings and 10 Bostons from 2 Group. Due to the weather most of the bombers failed to find their targets and even those that did failed to achieve any hits.

Many of those bombers which did locate their targets fell victim to the extensive fighter cover which the Luftwaffe had been ordered to provide. Sixteen Bomber Command aircraft failed to return. The victims were ten Hampdens (including four from 49 Squadron), four Wellingtons, and two Blenheims. Amongst the losses were two squadron commanders. Wing Commander Geoffrey Frederick Simond MiD (35) was the commanding officer of 144 Squadron. His Hampden I (AT175) was lost without trace and he and his four crewmates are commemorated at Runnymede. Wing Commander Richard Denis Barry MacFadden DFC was the commanding officer of 214 Squadron. His Wellington IC (Z1081) was ditched in the North Sea but six of the seven crew lost their lives. Amongst the dead from this crew were three men who had been decorated with the DFC. Aside from Wing Commander MacFadden they were Squadron Leader Martin Tyringham Stephens and Flight Lieutenant Patrick Roderick Hughes. Squadron Leader Stephens was a 40-year-old qualified air gunner who was on the strength of Station HQ Stradishall but was attached to the squadron.

Two flight commanders were also lost on Operation Fuller. Squadron Leader Ian Kingston Pembroke Cross DFC MiD, was flying Wellington IC (Z8714) of 103 Squadron and was also forced to ditch in the North Sea. Squadron Leader Cross and four of his crew survived to be taken prisoner, while two crew died.[8] Squadron Leader George Lawlor Bernays Harris (28) was flying Hampden I (AT134, PT-K) of 420 (RCAF) Squadron and was presumed lost over the sea. Harris was a New Zealander from Wellington City and had married an English woman from Sutton Coldfield.

The only redeeming feature for Bomber Command was that it was later revealed that the two battle cruisers had been damaged after striking mines which had been previously laid off the Frisians by Hampdens of 5 Group. The reporting of the escape of the ships caused consternation and questions were asked of the abilities of both the RN and of Bomber Command in the light of their failure to prevent what became known as the Channel Dash. Once again, this was poor publicity for the command at a time when it least needed it. Officialdom also knew that in recent months Bomber Command had dropped 3,413 tons of bombs aimed at destroying these ships and had lost 127 aircraft in the effort. Less well known was the fact that these efforts had achieved some success with both battle cruisers being struck by bombs and badly damaged. Perhaps even more crucially, the constant attentions of Bomber Command had prevented any further Atlantic raids and had successfully persuaded the Germans to remove the ships to German ports where they might be safer but were also far less of a threat.

The press reporting was largely critical. The account given in the *Daily Mirror* the following day attempted to portray a far more organised effort than had been the case. The report admitted to the losses but also claimed that at least one of the ships had been torpedoed while all had been hit by bombs. It also claimed that escorting RAF fighters had shot down fifteen enemy fighters during the operation. Even so, the leader in the *Mirror* was critical, stating in bold type that Britain could lose the war. Other newspapers were far more critical. The *Sketch*, rather unfairly given the efforts over Brest, asked why the Air Ministry had only tried to destroy the ships after they had left port. More seriously for Bomber Command was the impact which the escape of the ships had upon public attitudes. The Ministry of Information's Home Intelligence Weekly Report for the period stated bluntly that the majority of the public believed it was the worst week of the war since Dunkirk.

There was a mood of bitter recrimination in some parts of the country. In Lincolnshire, home to many bomber squadrons, the local press in the form of the *Lincolnshire Echo* asked whether or not the recent series of raids on Brest had been worthwhile. While the newspaper pointed out that the 'daring, determination and skill of the men who have carried out the attacks is not, and never could be, held in question', it also added that the main issue was 'whether the high policy which they so bravely implemented was justifiable' and asked whether it 'could be claimed that their loss was not in vain' if, as had happened, the ships had now been made seaworthy and had escaped to be able to slip into the Atlantic to raid shipping lanes at a later date.[9]

We have already seen how the Manchester was coming under some suspicion as losses amongst the type were higher than average and there were severe doubts over the mechanical and technical defects which were affecting both availability and reliability. Efforts were made, however, to keep such doubts from the general public and some publicity was given to the type in the form of press accounts which gave the impression that it was a reliable and rugged design. On the day after the disastrous Channel Dash the *Lincolnshire Echo* gave an account of one crew's experiences on a recent raid on Brest. The pilot reported how on the approach to the target they had been hit by flak and the rear gunner injured, but that the Manchester was still flying perfectly and they bombed the target successfully before setting course for home. The pilot told the press that he 'had absolute peace of mind the whole way home' despite the fact that later inspection showed that the Manchester had been badly damaged. The piece concluded with the pilot testifying that this 'only goes to show that Manchesters can take it!'[10]

Sir Arthur Harris had missed the Channel Dash and took over in the days that followed. He inherited a command which was under a very significant cloud. Bomber Command took up a large amount of Britain's limited wartime resources and, with the conclusions of the Butt Report, the recent heavy losses over Berlin and Brest and the disastrous humiliation of the Channel Dash, there were many voices in high places which were urging that the command be massively downsized to provide a tactical force and that the resources be diverted elsewhere. The Admiralty was particularly vociferous in its criticism and there was a real risk that Bomber Command would be scaled back or even disbanded. Harris knew this and was determined to prove his belief that Bomber Command could end the war through the bombing of German towns and cities. He also knew that to do this he would need to make a grand statement which would build up support for the command and convince those in power that Bomber Command was an effective force and could be built up to be a potential war-winning force.

In many ways Harris was the ideal man for the job. Forceful, bullishly determined and obstinate, he balanced these qualities with vast experience of air operations and of the Air Ministry. Many have claimed that he was no politician, and in many ways this is true, but he was also savvy and fiercely committed to his new command. In terms of strategy Harris was the ultimate pragmatist and had a clear, though sometimes overly simple, view of the bombing war. His experiences in the RAF had convinced him that it was impossible for Bomber Command to mount a precision bombing campaign, but he did not see the bombing campaign as a no-alternative option, but as a possible war winning strategy in and of itself. Recent shifts in policy had given him leeway to pursue his beliefs with the Air Ministry, ordering that henceforth Bomber Command's main priority would be to focus on destroying the morale of the German population and particularly the morale of industrial workers. Harris would later deny that this was his prime aim, stating that he saw the area campaign more as causing severe disruption to German industry.

The beginning of Harris's period of command began quietly. He was quite aware of the losses suffered after Pierse had sent bomber forces off in poor weather and he was determined not to be rushed into making the same mistake during his tenure. Marshalling his still limited forces – as squadrons were still being drawn off for service in other theatres or with Coastal Command – he bided his time. Many of the operations carried out during this period were mine-laying expeditions ('gardening' sorties). Harris firmly believed that these operations were not only militarily important, but also that they gave his crews very valuable night-flying experience under operational conditions but with smaller risks.

In response to government urging to make an attack on one of several French factories which were known to be producing matériel for the German war effort, Harris decided to send a large force to attack the Renault factory at Boulogne-Billancourt. It was estimated that this factory was producing 18,000 lorries per year for the use of the Germans. Harris undoubtedly saw this as an early attempt to show that Bomber Command could be effective (even though this was not to be an area attack, but more of a precision raid) in disrupting important industrial targets. On 3/4 March Harris dispatched the largest single force that Bomber Command had ever sent to a single target; 235 aircraft in total departed for Billancourt. The force consisted of 89 Wellingtons, 48 Hampdens, 29 Stirlings, 26 Manchesters, 23 Whitleys and 20 Halifaxes in three waves. Several experienced crews were placed at the front of the waves and others were ordered to drop flares in order to guide the force into the target.

Other important lessons were being learned. The concentration of bombers over the target was increased to a rate of 121 per hour and the fact that there were no collisions bore this decision out. Although the four-engined bombers were available in only small numbers, the force also carried a greater weight of bombs than had ever been dropped on a target with the total tonnage being put at between 412-470. The raid was judged a complete success with an estimated 40 per cent of the factory being wrecked, production halted for at least a month and repairs not being completed for several months. On the downside, casualties amongst the French civilian population, many of whom were housed in blocks of workers' housing close to the factory, were high. Many of the civilians, assuming that the sirens were sounding only as bombers passed overhead bound for Germany, failed to take shelter and 367 French people were killed (this was more than had ever been killed in a raid on Germany) with a further 341 injured. Reports at the time and after the war seem, however, to show that the French people of

Billancourt were largely accepting of their fates, seeing those who had been killed as being victims of the Germans rather than of Bomber Command.

Four aircraft were lost as a result of the Billancourt operation although only one of these crashed over enemy territory. This was a Wellington IC (Z1070, KX-Y) of 311 (Czechoslovak) Squadron piloted by Sergeant Bohuslav Hradil. He and his crew were all killed when their bomber crashed near to Creil. Halifax II (R9445, TL-T) of 35 Squadron which had been hit by flak, made an emergency landing at RAF Oakington during which the aircraft was irreparably damaged, but the crew were uninjured. Wellington II (Z8441, NP-K) of 158 Squadron suffered engine trouble shortly after taking off from RAF Pocklington and crashed while attempting to land back at base, injuring three crewmen. The final loss of the raid was Stirling I (N3712, HA-Y) of 218 Squadron. Flying Officer D.W. Allen and his crew were landing back at base when a bomb which had apparently hung up dropped from the aircraft and exploded. All of the crew were injured to some degree and the wireless operator and mid-upper gunner died as a result of their injuries.[11]

One other bomber was lost on the night. Four Wellingtons had been sent to Emden and one of these, from 311 (Czechoslovak) Squadron, was lost without trace. The night also provided another landmark as four Lancasters from 44 Squadron were sent to lay mines off the north-west coast of Germany. This was the first operation of the Lancaster and all returned safely to RAF Waddington.

There were several interesting operations during this period. On 8 March 2 Group sent a force of twenty-four of the American-built Bostons to carry out raids against a number of targets in France. Many of these operations had fighter cover provided by Fighter Command but twelve of the Bostons, from 88 and 226 Squadrons, undertook a low-level attack on the Ford factory which was at Poissy. This target, near Paris, was out of range of fighter cover but, nevertheless, eight of the Bostons managed to successfully bomb the factory, although one was lost. Unfortunately, the Boston which was lost was flown by the commanding officer of 226 Squadron. Boston III (Z2209, MQ-G) became the first of the type to be lost on Bomber Command operations. Wing Commander Vernon Stanley Butler DFC and his crew were killed when their Boston was damaged by flak and then crippled by its own bomb blast. Butler attempted to put the Boston down, but it hit a tree and exploded.

On the night of 8/9 March Harris sent a large raid consisting of 211 aircraft to attack Essen. The leading aircraft on this night were fitted with the radar navigation device codenamed Gee but despite this aid (which could only guide an aircraft to the general vicinity) and clear conditions, the permanent industrial haze which hung over Essen defeated the best efforts of the crews and the raid was a disappointment which caused only minor damage in Essen for the loss of eight bombers. Harris followed this raid up with a further raid on Essen on the next night. This time 187 aircraft were dispatched but, again, thick haze led to poor results with only two buildings being reported destroyed in Essen although this time losses were lighter with only three aircraft failing to return. The crowded nature of the Ruhr along with the industrial haze always led to targeting problems and twenty-four other towns in the Ruhr reported being bombed on this night. Harris tried once more the next night although only 126 aircraft were available to him. Once again results were disappointing and only sixty-two crews reported bombing the target. Just two bombs fell on industrial premises and only one house was reported as having been destroyed. A total of four bombers were lost.

Although the Gee raids on Essen had been a disappointment Harris determined that the new aid might be of more help on a target which was more easily visible and on the night of 13/14 March he dispatched 135 aircraft to bomb Cologne. The leading crews on this operation carried flares and incendiary loads and many successfully located and illuminated the target for those following. Several important industrial facilities were badly damaged while 237 separate fires were recorded in Cologne. Even more encouragingly losses consisted of just one Manchester.

After a period of minor operations Harris decided to have another go at Essen on 25/26 March and sent the biggest raid of the war so far with 254 aircraft, including seven Lancasters, to attack this important target. Visibility was good and initial intelligence gathered from the crews upon their return seemed to give the impression of a successful attack, but photo-reconnaissance later proved that much of the bombing had fallen on a decoy site and only nine high-explosive bombs fell on Essen itself. Nine bombers were lost and the Manchester, once again, showed its vulnerability. Twenty Manchesters had been dispatched on the raid and five of these failed to return.

Briefing the next day must have been a notably tense occasion when the main target for the night was again revealed to be Essen. This time only 115 aircraft, consisting of 104 Wellingtons and eleven Stirlings, were sent. The raid was yet another failure and heavy resistance was encountered with night-fighters a constant menace and heavy flak over the target itself. Eleven aircraft (ten Wellingtons and a Stirling) failed to return, a loss rate of 9.6 per cent.

Although success at Essen was proving impossible, Harris was absolutely determined that Bomber Command should be seen to have a notable success over a German target. On the night of 28/29 March he sent 234 bombers to attack the old city of Lübeck. This was Harris's first real attempt to demonstrate the true possibilities of his theories on area bombing. The aiming point for the bombers was given as the heart of the Altstadt. With its closely packed wooden buildings, it was hoped that fires would quickly spread out of control. To increase this possibility approximately two-thirds of the bombloads would consist of incendiaries. Although Lübeck was beyond Gee range the device could be used in initial navigation and the first bombers over the target consisted of experienced crews flying bombers fitted with the device. Conditions were very good and almost 200 crews reported bombing the target successfully. Intelligence and German reports later confirmed that damage was very extensive with 190 acres of the old town being destroyed, which was 30 per cent of the built-up area of Lübeck. It was calculated that 62 per cent of all buildings in Lübeck were either destroyed or damaged, including 256 which were classed as either industrial or commercial properties. Amongst the industrial targets to be hit and destroyed was the Drägerwerk factory which manufactured oxygen equipment for U-boats. Many buildings of historical interest were also destroyed during the raid and approximately 320 people were killed (this was the heaviest loss of life in a German target).[12]

This hugely successful raid cost Bomber Command twelve aircraft (a further one was written off upon return) and fifty-three airmen lost their lives. At Oakington, 7 Squadron lost three of its Stirlings. There were several unusual losses on the night. The rear gunner of one of 7 Squadron's lost Stirlings (W7466, MG-B) was 23-year-old Captain John Frimston Wyn-Griffith, Royal Artillery. The Army officer was serving on attachment to the squadron at the time.

Stirling I (W7507, HA-P) of 218 Squadron, with Flight Lieutenant A.G.L. Humphreys at the controls, returned to RAF Marham with severe battle damage caused by a combination of flak and night-fighters. Flight Lieutenant Humphreys made a successful crash-landing and all the crew survived, although the rear gunner, Sergeant Stronnell, had been very badly wounded in the knee during one of the night-fighter attacks and the Stirling was subsequently stricken off due to the damage it had sustained. Flight Lieutenant Humphreys was awarded an immediate DFC for his actions and his wireless operator, Sergeant K. Wheeler, the DFM.[13]

There was one further loss; 109 Squadron was a special operations squadron which fell under the aegis of Bomber Command and 109 Wellington IC (X9913), captained by 20-year-old Pilot Officer Gordon James Maygothling, was engaged on wireless signal investigation work during the Lübeck raid when it was lost without trace.[14] Amongst the eight-man crew was Leading Aircraftman Robert Frank Rendell. It was extremely unusual for a non-NCO airman to be serving aboard an operational bomber and it can only be surmised that LAC Rendell was some sort of specialist in his field.

Harris, while pleased with the results of the Lübeck raid, was determined to obtain several successes and news of the successful raid was withheld from the press for several weeks. During this time Harris launched several large raids on a variety of targets including Cologne, Dortmund, Hamburg and Essen, but the results were largely disappointing and Essen in particular proved to be a difficult target to hit. In the recent series of eight raids against the city some 1,555 aircraft had been dispatched and 1,006 had reported bombing successfully. With the difficult weather conditions photographic assessment was difficult and only 212 bombing photographs were suitable for assessing ground details and of these only twenty-two could be accurately located within five miles of the target.

One raid during this period stood out as it was a departure from the typical area raid using large forces. It was another attempt by Harris to achieve concentrated and accurate bombing on a vital target using a small force flying the new Lancaster bomber at low level. Harris selected the large M.A.N. factory at Augsburg as his target and crews from 44 and 97 Squadrons were given a week of special training and low-flying practice. On 17 April twelve crews, six from each squadron, were dispatched on the operation. Leading the operation as a whole was South African Squadron Leader John Nettleton, an experienced flight commander on 44 Squadron who was nearing the end of his first tour. Leading the 97 Squadron contingent was another flight commander, Squadron Leader John Sherwood, a pre-war officer who was very experienced having flown with 144 Squadron, earning the DFC, before joining 97 Squadron, where he earned a Bar to his DFC.

As part of the diversionary plan thirty Bostons along with extensive fighter escorts raided targets in northern France. This effort to draw off enemy fighters was not wholly successful and four of the Lancasters, all from 44 Squadron, were shot down before reaching the target. As the formations crossed the French coast Squadron Leader Sherwood had noticed that Nettleton's formation had strayed north of the chosen course. Of the remaining crews all reported successfully bombing the target, although a further four were shot down in the target area after bombing. Of the five aircraft which returned to their bases, one was damaged beyond repair and the remaining four had all suffered damage to some extent. Despite the success of the bombing, the loss rate of 59 per cent led Harris to conclude that, even in the Lancaster, such operations were too costly and, except for exceptional targets, were discontinued. The raid resulted in the loss of 37 airmen killed and a further twelve taken prisoner. Many of these airmen were very experienced bomber crew with those lost possessing three DFCs, four DFMs and six MiDs between them. The surviving crews were described as having been left numb at the losses and were given three days leave to recover.

Squadron Leader Sherwood's Lancaster had been hit by flak while bombing the target and one wing burst into flames before the bomber crashed into the ground and exploded. Sherwood had successfully led his formation almost 600 miles over enemy territory at very low level and had arrived bang on target, a remarkable feat of both flying and navigation. After hearing the debriefing and looking over the intelligence notes, Harris immediately recommended both Nettleton and Sherwood for the VC. Nettleton's VC was duly gazetted on 24 April and he became the first South African of the war to be awarded this medal. The Air Ministry, somewhat harshly, refused to award Sherwood with the VC, but did agree to the award of the DSO in the unlikely event that he had survived. Miraculously, he had. When his Lancaster hit the ground and exploded Sherwood, still in his seat, was catapulted out of the aircraft and survived to be taken prisoner. Sherwood was subsequently notified of the award of his DSO, dated 30 June 1942, while in Stalag Luft 3 at Sagan.[15]

Aircraft Lost on the Augsburg Operation.

Aircraft	Code	Squadron	Captain
L7536	KM-H	44	Sgt G.T. Rhodes
L7548	KM-T	44	W/O H.V. Crum, DFM
L7565	KM-V	44	W/O J.F. Beckett, DFM
R5506	KM-P	44	F/Lt R.R. Sandford, DFC
R5510	KM-A	44	F/O A.J. Garwell, DFM
L7573	OF-K	97	S/Ldr J.S Sherwood, DFC and Bar
R5513	OF-P	97	W/O T.J. Mycock, DFC

On consecutive nights between 23 and 27 April Bomber Command launched four raids on Rostock. These were raids reminiscent of the attack on Lübeck but multiplied and once again the damage was very significant indeed. The raids, of which the final one was the most successful, destroyed 1,765 buildings and damaged more than 500 with an estimated 60 per cent of the main town being destroyed, largely by fire. Some 204 people were killed in Rostock but many people had fled the town after the first raid. A feature of all of the raids was the detachment of part of the force to attempt to precision bomb a Heinkel factory on the outskirts of the town. During the four raids 520-523 sorties had been flown to Rostock and only eight aircraft were lost, a rate of 1.5 per cent.

Following the Rostock raid the news of the recent operations was released to the press. With two German towns having suffered devastating attacks and the raw courage and verve of the Augsburg operation, the news was incredibly well received by a public and press, which was desperately waiting for positive war news. The *Daily Mirror* of 25 April carried an unambiguous headline stating, 'We Smash Their Towns One By One'. Not only was this a triumphalist headline, it was also an unambiguous statement of approval and acknowledgment of the change in British bombing policy. Other papers published similar articles, often accompanied by aerial reconnaissance photographs of the damage inflicted upon German towns. Another popular point with the press was Goebbels' description of Bomber Command as terror fliers, claiming that Lübeck and Rostock were not military targets and were chosen simply because they were old and architecturally important towns. This, of course, conveniently ignored the fact that both towns were important ports, used as supply hubs for the Eastern Front and that Rostock also housed a large Heinkel factory.

There was clearly a new mood within Britain with politicians expressing Britain's determination to continue to carry the war to the enemy by whatever means were effective. The new attitude was well received. Typical of the press coverage of the recent raids was that found in the *Daily Record* of 28 April. Several pages were devoted to the recent raids with particular focus on Rostock, Lübeck and the Augsburg raid. The editorial praised the efforts of the RAF and assured readers that the raids had made Hitler realise that this was 'but the prelude to a fugue of raids on the Reich' and that 'Britain's air offensive is on the move, and it will not stop at Berlin. Wherever Germany is producing guns, 'planes, tanks or ships – there will be the British bombers also'. This was all a long way from the doldrum days coverage of the winter of 1941-1942. The editorial continued to reassure readers that the Bomber Command offensive 'will be relentless and the bomber forces the RAF will use will be as powerful – if not more powerful – than those which raided the home of the Heinkel works'. Clearly, Harris had made a bright start.

Not everyone was pleased with the raids. There were a small number of letters to newspapers and journals which expressed opposition to the raids on Rostock and Lübeck. One letter to the *Spectator* from an F.L. Jackson argued that the Lübeck raid had focused solely on the old town which contained few military targets. The writer concluded by stating his belief that either the RAF had descended to the level of the Nazis or was highly inaccurate. This harsh and, frankly, stupid claim was in a very distinct minority and far more common were letters in support of the recent raids. Some readers, indeed, went further. A letter to the *Gloucestershire Echo*, published on 28 April, for example, stated clear support for the recent raids on Rostock, Lübeck, the Skoda works at Pilsen and other industrial targets, but went on to ask whether, 'While not relaxing for a moment our policy of bombing industrial objectives, could we not now spare a few bombs for the important political centres, and thereby attack the enemy's morale? Such places as Berlin, Munich, Leipzig and Nuremberg immediately come to the mind.'[16] In reinforcing his argument, the author, a Mr W.N. Parry, then related how Berlin had suffered approximately 50 raids compared to 500 or so suffered by London.

Such support, while welcome, also highlighted some of the problems facing Harris. Many members of the public, seeing the successful attacks, then let their imaginations run away with them without giving thought to the problems which faced Bomber Command. The targets which Mr Parry so heartily recommended were all on Harris's list, but they were also at very long range for the aircraft which he had at his disposal and were amongst the best defended in Germany. To attempt to launch large raids on such targets at this moment would have resulted in incredibly high casualties and penetrating so far into Germany in the lightening nights was an impossibility anyway. Such targets were generally left for the longer, darker, winter nights.

The rash of press releases in the wake of this series of raids stoked public fervour with the tales of heroism of the Augsburg raid. The press could speak of the gallant sacrifice made by half the formation on this daring daylight operation flown at very low level in the face of tremendous odds.

There was a lack of focus on whether or not the raid could be justified in the face of the losses suffered and, instead, much was made of the flurry of decorations which were awarded in its wake.

At around the same time as the raids were announced Bomber Command received some more good publicity with the release of the film *One of Our Aircraft is Missing*. The film had an interesting plot in that the actual raid was simply a backdrop to the real story of how a shot down Wellington crew managed to evade the Germans with the help of a series of courageous Dutch civilians. In one of the final scenes the airmen are put aboard a vessel to smuggle them back to England when they hear the drones of bombers overhead and nearby Germans start running to the shelters. One of their rescuers, a Dutch woman portrayed by Googie Withers, tells them that the Dutch people are not antagonistic towards the men of Bomber Command despite civilian casualties. Indeed, she asserts the sight of the Germans running for cover and cowering and the sound of the droning engines every night gave the Dutch people and the people of all the occupied countries hope and renewed courage. The film was very well received and provided another useful boost for Bomber Command. The very last shot of the film features the crew of B-for Bertie standing in front of their new Stirling bomber, a clear hint of things to come.

The next few weeks passed relatively quietly with small forces sent to a variety of targets. Several unsuccessful attempts were made to once again hit the *Tirpitz*. On the first of these, on 27/28 April, thirty-one Halifaxes and twelve Lancasters were sent to Trondheim. Although they found their target no hits were recorded and four Halifaxes and one Lancaster were lost. One of the Halifaxes contained the commanding officer of 10 Squadron. Wing Commander Donald C.T. Bennett was flying Halifax II (W1041, ZA-B) when the bomber was hit by flak and later crash-landed in Norway. Bennett and two of his crew were able to evade capture and make their way back to Britain but the other four were taken prisoner.

Readers will recall Flight Lieutenant A.G.L. Humphreys of 218 Squadron being awarded the DFC for successfully crash-landing his battle-damaged Stirling following the Lübeck operation. With a new crew Flight Lieutenant Humphreys took off at 11.16pm on 17 May on a 'gardening' operation but his Stirling I (N6071, HA-G) was hit by flak off the Danish coast and Humphreys ordered the crew to abandon. All seven men successfully got out of the aircraft, but the flak continued to fire and three of the crew were injured while bomb-aimer Flying Officer Eliot Ralph Barnfather, RAAF, was killed when struck in the stomach by shrapnel. The remaining crew, including Flight Lieutenant Humphreys were taken prisoner.

The reason for the seeming pause in the campaign was because Harris had his mind firmly set on conserving his forces for something special. He was determined to strike while the iron was hot and to make sure that Bomber Command retained the support and good publicity which it had attracted. The recent raids had been a good start, but Harris was too wily to think the battle for the future of Bomber Command was won. He had the idea of launching a series of raids on German cities using a bomber force of 1,000 aircraft. Such a feat was sure, if successful, to capture the public's imagination and to ensure that support for Bomber Command in political circles would be insurmountable. To this end, and with the successes of recent weeks still large in the public consciousness, he approached both the Prime Minister and Sir Charles Portal to gain their support for his plan.

Both men were immensely impressed and enthused by the idea and Harris was told to go ahead with the planning for Operation Millennium. With his front-line strength at approximately 400 aircraft and crews Harris knew that he would depend to a large extent upon his training units to provide aircraft with crews made up of a mixture of instructors (many of whom were veterans) and crew who were in the latter stages of their training. The commanding officer of Coastal Command immediately volunteered 250 aircraft, but Flying Training Command could only provide a handful. At this point Harris also decided on Hamburg as the primary target, with Cologne as secondary in the event of poor weather over Hamburg.

Harris had his 1,000 aircraft but there remained much to do to make sure that Operation Millennium was a success. Never before had so many aircraft been routed to the same target. One innovation was the use of what became known as the bomber stream. This entailed all of the bombers flying on the same route and the same speeds to and from the target. To lessen the chances of collisions each aircraft was given a specific height band. It was hoped that, as well as aiding navigation, the sheer number of bombers passing through the enemy radar boxes at the same time would reduce the amount of night-fighter interceptions. One result of this decision was that the number of bombers passing over the target at the same time would have to be greatly increased. As discussed earlier, some thought had already been given to this tactic, but it was really stepped up for Millennium with only 90 minutes being given for the 1,000 aircraft to bomb. It was hoped that this would cause grave problems to the defences by overwhelming them and once again Gee would play a role. The experienced crews of 1 and 3 Groups whose aircraft were equipped with the device were chosen to lead the raid.

As Harris neared the end of his planning there was a calamity. The Admiralty, never a friend of Bomber Command and despite earlier reassurances, refused to let Coastal Command aircraft participate in the raids. Now in danger of falling short of the magical 1,000 total, Harris ordered his own units to redouble their efforts in order to make as many aircraft as physically possible ready for the raid. Although the main force squadrons did indeed redouble their efforts, it was his training units which came to the rescue. The decision was taken to let trainees who were not advanced on their courses to take part where necessary. These inexperienced trainee crews would be extremely vulnerable and efforts were made to ensure that they at least were assigned an experienced pilot. Despite this, some forty-nine aircraft of the 208 provided by 91 Group took off on the first 1,000 bomber raid with an inexperienced trainee at the controls. As a final measure forty-nine Blenheims of 2 Group and fifty-four aircraft from Fighter Command and Army Co-operation Command were assigned to fly Intruder raids against enemy night-fighter airfields. By 26 May Harris and his force were ready, now the weather would decide matters.

In the event the weather over Hamburg was poor for several days and, knowing that time was running out, on 30 May Harris took the decision to send the force to Cologne. Operation Millennium was underway. The crews were no doubt astounded when they were briefed for the first ever 1,000 bomber raid and there was no doubt some trepidation about the feasibility of having that many aircraft over the target at once. On the night some 1,047 aircraft, of seven different types, were dispatched for Cologne. To make up the total Harris had had to authorise the use of twenty-eight Whitleys despite the fact that the type had officially flown its last operation as part of the main force on the night of 29/30 April. One can hardly imagine the strain at High Wycombe as Harris awaited results. Although Churchill had told him he would accept the loss of 100 bombers, Harris thought such a result would be a disaster and this was undoubtedly the greatest risk taken by Harris at this early stage in his command.

Aircraft Dispatched for Cologne.

Group	Aircraft Dispatched	Total
1	156 Wellingtons	156
3	134 Wellingtons, 88 Stirlings	222
4	131 Halifaxes, 9 Wellingtons, 7 Whitleys	147
5	73 Lancasters, 46 Manchesters, 34 Hampdens	153
91 Group	236 Wellingtons, 21 Whitleys	257
92 Group	63 Wellingtons, 45 Hampdens	108
FTC	4 Wellingtons	4

In the event the raid was a success beyond what Harris could have hoped. The number of aircraft which actually bombed Cologne was between 868-898 and the total tonnage of bombs stood at 1,455 (again two-thirds were incendiaries). Cologne was a modern city which did not burn as easily as Lübeck or Rostock, but the damage done was severe with 3,330 buildings destroyed and over 10,000 damaged. Some thirty-six large industrial firms suffered damage which led to complete close-down of production, seventy suffered between 50-80 per cent production loss and 222 up to 50 per cent. Deaths in Cologne amounted to 469-486 with 5,027 injured and over 45,000 bombed out of their homes. Estimates claimed that in the immediate aftermath of the raid between 135,000-150,000 of the population of Cologne fled from the city.

Casualties, unsurprisingly, were a record high for Bomber Command but were far below the expectations of many. Forty-one bombers failed to return but the losses pointed to some unusual and interesting conclusions. Of the three distinct waves the first two suffered losses of 4.8 and 4.1 per cent respectively while the third wave suffered just 1.9 per cent. This was clear evidence that the defences of Cologne became overwhelmed as the raid progressed. Interestingly, the OTU crews who flew suffered a loss rate of 3.3 per cent which was lower than that of the regular bomber group crews which stood at 4.1 per cent. Even more surprisingly, those crews that took off with pupil pilots suffered lower casualties than those which had taken off with instructors at the controls.

Enthusiasm for the operation, however, was high amongst many airmen. At 3 Group, Air Vice Marshal Baldwin decided that he wished to fly on the operation and he hitched a ride with the commanding officer of 218 (Gold

Coast) Squadron, returning safely. Harris would have been somewhat displeased as he disliked his senior officers flying on operations as their experience was too valuable to lose.

There were many examples of courage during the raid but the stand-out was that which earned 20-year-old Flying Officer Leslie Thomas Manser of 50 Squadron the VC. Manser and his crew were aboard a Manchester I (L7301, ZN-D) which had been borrowed from 106 Squadron and took off from RAF Skellingthorpe just after 11pm. They almost immediately ran into problems when it became clear that the engines of the Manchester were running badly and the aircraft would not climb above 7,000 feet. This was more than enough reason for Manser to abort the sortie, but the decision was taken to press on in the hope that the bulk of the flak would be aimed at the bombers flying higher. Unfortunately, this was not the case and the Manchester was coned over the target before being badly hit by flak and set on fire. In a dive and with the fuselage on fire, Manser managed to recover the aircraft at just 800 feet. With an injured rear gunner and a severely damaged aircraft, Manser manged to gain height to 2,000 feet before the port engine exploded in flames which spread along the wing before burning out. Despite a valiant attempt to make for Britain, it became clear that the Manchester did not have sufficient height and Manser gave the order to abandon the aircraft. He struggled to hold the battered Manchester steady while they did so and when his co-pilot attempted to clip a chest-pack parachute onto him, told him to get out. No sooner had the co-pilot baled out than the aircraft turned onto its back and crashed, killing Manser instantly. Coming down in Holland, five of Manser's crew managed to evade capture and return to England where their testimony was key in securing their courageous pilot's award.

Sergeant Sidney Godfrey Falconer (who as a 19-year-old agricultural student had joined the RAF two days after the first bombs fell on his home town of South Shields) had completed his training as a pilot and been posted to 218 (Gold Coast) Squadron in early 1942. Falconer undertook his first operation as second pilot, under Sergeant Lamason, RNZAF, as part of a fifteen-strong attack on Le Havre. After flying ten operations with the New Zealander he was given command of his own crew and flew his first operation as captain on 29 May in an attack on Gennevilliers in the north western suburbs of Paris. The 1,000 bomber raid was just his second as skipper of his own crew but his twelfth overall. He would prove himself a remarkably able and determined captain.

Two aircraft from 218 (Gold Coast) Squadron were lost on the raid. The first got into trouble shortly after taking off. The Stirling I (R9311, HA-L) of Sergeant Sidney Godfrey Falconer clipped some high ground with its port wheel. The pilot maintained control of the Stirling, despite the wheel being ripped off, and pressed on to successfully bomb the target. Upon return shortly before 6am he successfully made a wheels-up landing. Sergeant Falconer had a second-pilot with him but so skilfully performed was his crash-landing that none of the crew were injured. Sergeant Falconer was a native of South Shields and had joined the RAF in response to the bombing of his hometown in 1940, telling his father that someone had to pay the Nazis back for what they were doing. He went on to become a skilled and very resolute bomber captain. He was awarded an immediate DFM for his actions on a raid a few days later and was later commissioned. The other was W7502, HA-N, piloted by Pilot Officer Arthur Wilfrid Davis. The Stirling was badly shot up by flak and crashed at Huppenbroich. Mid-upper gunner, Sergeant Tate, RCAF, baled out with the observer, Flight Sergeant Joseph Lewthwaite Borrowdale, clinging to his back (presumably Borrowdale's parachute had been destroyed) but Borrowdale, who was from Whitehaven, was killed when he slipped and fell to his death after Tate's parachute deployed. Tate was the only survivor from the crew.

The vagaries of fate always played a part in the lives and deaths of aircrew and it was far from uncommon for one squadron to have a relatively quiet night with no losses while a neighbouring squadron lost several aircraft on the same raid; the first 1,000 bomber raid was no different. One of the heaviest losers on the night was from 12 Squadron. Four of its Wellington IIs failed to return to RAF Binbrook. Three were shot down over enemy territory but the fourth was possibly a victim of the rushed attempts to get as many aircraft as possible into the air. Wellington II (Z8598, PH-B) took off at 10.55pm with 22-year-old Sergeant George Hamilton Everatt at the controls, but at 11.32pm the Wellington exploded in mid-air and crashed near Lexham Hall in Norfolk. The aircraft had recently undergone repairs to damage suffered in operations earlier in the month and had only recently been accepted back on charge by the squadron.

Four Wellington ICs from 22 OTU were also lost on Operation Millennium. The crews all contained men of some experience with every missing crew possessing at least two decorations; the loss of such experience was a blow. R1235 was lost with all of its crew, including rear gunner, Pilot Officer Dudley Arthur Ronald Tallis DFM (who had previously served with 102 Squadron), and wireless operator, Pilot Officer William Frazer Caldwell (who received a DFM in 1943 for his previous service with 9 Squadron). The crew of R1714 possessed a DFC and Bar and a MiD. DV701's crew held a DFC and a DFM and reflected the multi-national nature of Bomber Command with one British airman, a Royal New Zealand Air Force pilot and three Royal Canadian Air Force airmen. The crew of DV843 held two DFMs.

The other unit to suffer four losses was 26 OTU. Amongst these losses was Wellington IC (DV709) which made it back to Britain but overturned and crashed while the crew, captained by Sergeant John James Dixon, were attempting to make an emergency landing in a field near Soham. Three of the crew survived, although they were all injured, but Sergeant Dixon (20), from Southport, and his rear gunner, Sergeant Brian Buchanan Camlin (23) of Belfast, were killed. The crew had been posted to join 57 Squadron and were awaiting the completion of paperwork when they were sent to Cologne.

Amongst the more unusual losses was the last Wellington IA to be downed on a bombing operation. N2894 had taken off from RAF Feltwell with a crew drawn from the Central Gunnery School (CGS) but was shot down by a night-fighter over Klarenbeek, Holland, with only the rear gunner, Flight Sergeant G.J. Waddington-Allwright baling out to become a PoW.[17]

The new tactics were largely borne-out with no collisions known to have occurred over the target. Indeed, the only collision which did take place was between two aircraft upon their return to Britain. Hampden I (P5321, GL-P3) of 14 OTU had taken off from RAF Cottesmore shortly after 11pm and was on its way home. Emerging from a rain cloud over Cambridgeshire the pilot, Squadron Leader D.B. Falconer DFC, saw an aircraft with its navigation lights on but there was no time to take avoiding action and the two bombers collided and crashed. In P5321 Squadron Leader Falconer was able to bale out but his three crewmates were all killed. The aircraft with which the Hampden had collided was Halifax II (W1013) of 78 Squadron. The Halifax was flying with a crew of only six and there were four survivors. The pilot, Pilot Officer G.C. Foers, survived along with two others, all injured, but wireless operator/air gunner, Sergeant George Bolton of Gateshead, and rear gunner, Sergeant Andrew Caie of Aberdeen, were both killed.[18]

Harris kept his thousand bomber force together and sent 956 aircraft to Essen on 1/2 June. The force employed a very similar plan to that which had been used at Cologne with the exception that, given the haze problems at Essen, the experienced raid leaders carried a higher proportion of flares than on the previous raid. Despite this and a fair weather forecast the target was, once more, obscured with a ground haze and bombing was therefore scattered with Essen reporting only minor damage. Eleven other nearby towns were also hit, including Duisburg, Mülheim and Oberhausen. A total of thirty-one Bomber Command aircraft were lost on the raid along with three aircraft on intruder operations.

The moon period was now ending and the thousand force was dispersed as the training units could no longer be held from their correct duties, but Harris wanted to have one more go at a thousand bomber raid. Throughout June Emden and Essen were each targeted several times by smaller forces. The largest attack during this period was one made by 233 aircraft on Emden on the night of 6/7 June. This was successful and caused damage to property and the dock facilities, but cost nine bombers.

On the night of 25/26 June Harris reassembled his thousand force, although only 960 aircraft were actually available. Even to get to this figure Harris was forced to utilise the day bombing Bostons and Mosquitos of 2 Group. Churchill had heard of the shortfall, however, and intervened by telling the Admiralty that Coastal Command would be permitted to take part in the operation. This added 102 aircraft (Wellingtons and Bostons) to the force and Army Co-operation Command also contributed five at the last minute, meaning that 1,067 aircraft were dispatched making this the biggest raid of the three thousand-bomber operations. This time there was a different plan which included portions of the force being tasked with bombing specific targets. The largest of these precision forces was made up of the entire contribution of 5 Group which was ordered to attack the Focke-Wulf factory. Other targets included the A.G. Weser Shipyard and the Deschimag Shipyard. The main force was ordered to make an area attack as before.

Unfortunately, the target was completely cloud covered but the glow of early fires enabled 696 crews to successfully attack. The results were not as dramatic as those at Cologne but were better than the Essen attack with many fires and almost 7,000 houses destroyed or damaged. The Focke-Wulf factory was damaged and there was damage of varying degrees at a number of shipyards, a refinery and in dockside warehouses.

The raid brought another record loss for an RAF raid with forty-eight aircraft failing to return. The losses suffered by the OTU crews this time were heavy; 91 Group had dispatched 198 aircraft (Wellingtons and Whitleys) but had lost twenty-three of these, some 11.6 per cent.

Harris was determined to maintain the pressure on the German port targets and three further raids on Bremen were dispatched up until 3 July. On the night of 27/28 June a force consisting of 144 aircraft was dispatched to attack Bremen once again. Heavy cloud was encountered but 119 of the bombers claimed that they had bombed the target after obtaining Gee fixes showing they were over Bremen. At 11.40pm Stirling I (N3751, BU-P) of 214 (Federated Malay States) Squadron lifted off from RAF Stradishall with Sergeant Frank Morton Griggs, RAAF, at the controls. Griggs and his crew bombed the target, but their Stirling was hit by flak and badly damaged with one of the starboard engines being put out of action. Almost immediately afterwards the Stirling was attacked by a fighter and was damaged further. A second fighter then opened fire and the wireless operator, Sergeant William Wildey, was badly wounded in the arm. During the attacks the rear gunner, Sergeant Horace Arthur William Sewell (20) of Eastbourne was killed. As one of the fighters again approached the mid-upper gunner, Sergeant James Ian Cunningham Waddicar of Clitheroe, opened fire and shot down the fighter. In addition to the other damage the electrical systems had been knocked out, including the crew intercom.

The battered Stirling continued its return journey over Holland while the injured Sergeant Wildey was attended to by bomb aimer, Sergeant Ronald Watson. The navigator, Sergeant Arthur O'Hara, then reported two approaching Bf 109 fighters and Sergeant Watson managed to shoot down one of the fighters despite his turret being jammed. Sergeant Waddicar's turret had also been damaged but he managed to repair one of his guns and shot down the second fighter, which exploded over the sea. Yet another fighter then opened fire but was driven off by Sergeant Waddicar. In evading this fighter, the pilot temporarily lost control of the Stirling which went into a steep dive. Sergeant Grigg desperately pulled out of the dive and Sergeant Waddicar reported that the tail actually struck the sea. At this point the Stirling came under sustained fire from several flak ships. At 5am the battered Stirling arrived back over Stradishall and the crew must have breathed a sigh of relief, but while circling base the remaining starboard engine burst into flames. Sergeant Griggs extinguished the fire and feathered the engine before skilfully making a wheels-up crash landing. The crew clambered out of the Stirling and it was at this stage that Sergeant Waddicar realised just how badly damaged the aircraft had been in the repeated attacks. This must have been a truly horrific ordeal for the crew and it resulted, most unusually, in all of the six survivors being awarded the DFM.

Sergeant Waddicar was a very experienced airman having joined the RAF in May 1940. He had at first flown as a gunner in Lysanders before being posted to fly in night-fighter Boulton-Paul Defiants. Waddicar explained to his local newspaper that he had then been posted to Bomber Command and had flown around sixteen operations with 214 Squadron and had experienced some lucky escapes, but he told the reporter that the crews took their jobs philosophically and just got on with it.[19]

Readers will remember the experiences of Sergeant Sidney Godfrey Falconer during the first 1,000 bomber raid. On the Bremen raid of 27/28 June Sergeant Falconer and his crew were briefed for a follow-up operation on the same target, Bremen. The raid was far smaller, consisting of just 144 aircraft and was to take place despite a full moon. An estimated 119 aircraft successfully hit the city, although the bombers had to drop their bombloads through cloud using the limited radar aid known as Gee. Losses totalled nine aircraft. There were just twenty-six Stirlings operating on this raid and only one was lost. For Sergeant Falconer and his crew it was a harrowing night and one in which the young airman (aged just 21) proved both his courage and his ability as a pilot.

Shortly after crossing the Dutch coast Falconer's bomber was attacked by three enemy night-fighters (two Ju-88s and an Me 110). The rear gunner and the Me 110, attacking from directly astern, opened fire at the same time and the night-fighter's fire put the rear turret out of action. The mid-upper gunner then took control of the action but his turret too was hit by fire and put out of action. At the same time, one of the Ju-88s attacked from directly ahead (very unusual at night and showing how bright the conditions must have been) and its fire knocked out the remaining front turret. The remaining Ju-88 was also making a determined attack from the starboard quarter. Sergeant Falconer was desperately taking evasive action and during the 20-minute fight had descended from 15,000 feet to sea level. Indeed, the Stirling was so low that its trailing radio aerial had been torn away after it hit the Zuider Zee. Just when Sergeant Falconer and his crew thought they had eluded the fighters a single-engine fighter appeared which raked the battered Stirling from nose to tail before it too was shaken off.

Sergeant Falconer now found himself having to evade fire from light anti-aircraft guns on the coast before he and his crew could take stock of their position. Two of the crew were wounded, all of the gun turrets were out of action, the flying controls and control column were damaged, the brake system was also rendered useless, the intercom and radio had been destroyed, the oxygen system (not needed at low level) had been shot away during the attacks, as had both the astrodome and the blind flying panel. The situation was indeed dire, but showing incredible determination and skill Sergeant Falconer managed to bring the battered bomber back to England and landed safely. The aircraft had to be sent away to be repaired and was not able to fly again until the next year.

Sergeant Falconer was recommended for an immediate DFM for his actions with the commendation stating that he had shown 'daring and adroitness of the highest order. His cool courage and command of the situation were remarkable. His expert and stout-hearted captaincy undoubtedly saved the lives of his crew … His loyalty, fearlessness and sense of duty are outstanding.' The DFM was subsequently gazetted on 17 July at which point Falconer had completed twenty operations. He continued on operations and completed his operational tour of thirty ops on 24 August with a raid on Frankfurt. He was one of the few to complete a tour that summer with 218 (Gold Coast) Squadron, and on 18 September was posted as an instructor to 21 OTU. Sergeant Falconer not only received the DFM but also a commission to Pilot Officer (backdated to 20 June).

The idea of forming a dedicated force within Bomber Command which would fly at the head of the bomber stream and would be charged with illuminating and marking aiming points was one which met with much opposition from Harris. Ironically, it was Harris who had pioneered the use of such a force, albeit in an informal way, by placing experienced Gee-equipped crews at the head of raids loaded with flares and incendiaries. Higher forces than Harris, however, were determined on the idea and, as ever, when given a direct order Harris, despite his misgivings, followed it with dedication.

The commander of his new Pathfinder Force (PFF) as it was to be known, Harris had absolutely refused to call it by the name recommended – the Target Finding Force – was a man who had recently evaded capture and returned to the UK after an raid on the *Tirpitz*. Group Captain Don Bennett was the ideal choice, although younger than most senior officers in the command. He was a skilled pilot and navigator, had a brilliant mind and a good grasp of operational conditions. In addition to these qualifications, he was a determined commander who gave everything he had and expected no less from those under him.

During one meeting with Harris at which his new appointment was discussed, Harris told him bluntly that he bitterly opposed the creation of PFF, believing that it would weaken the command overall by taking away the best crews from the Main Force, and because he automatically believed that the official formation of an elite within the command would cause antagonism amongst the other Groups. He had, he informed Bennett, done everything that he could to stop the formation of PFF. However, he had been given a direct order from no less than the Prime Minister and he had therefore selected Bennett to command the PFF himself. The original conception of the PFF was as a force within Bomber Command but subordinate to Bomber Command HQ. It was not a Group and Bennett did not hold the equivalent rank as those officers commanding Groups. This could have presented Bennett with some difficulties in the recruitment of suitable crews, but here again Harris helped. Although he told Bennett that he himself would waste no effort on the PFF he would give Bennett every support.

Despite his antipathy towards the creation of an elite, it was Harris's idea to award a special badge for members of PFF. The crews themselves would initially consist of those squadrons from each group which had the record for the most accurate bombing photographs. The crews of PFF would face a period of initial training, but both Harris and Bennett realised that in order to make the most of a crew's expertise, a longer tour of operations would be required. Thus, PFF crews were faced with an initial tour consisting of forty-five operations, extendable to sixty (which would count as two tours).

At the outset the PFF was faced with many operational difficulties. Not all the crews had the necessary skills, the force was equipped with a mishmash of aircraft types and had little in the way of dedicated armaments to illuminate or mark a target. On top of these difficulties was the fact that Bennett, quite correctly, insisted that each crewman become an expert in his area. This applied especially to the pilots, navigators and bomb-aimers who would be key to the success of PFF, and therefore Main Force, operations. Bennett, himself a skilled navigator, was aware that the tools available to Bomber Command navigators were woefully inadequate and that Gee, while useful, was easily jammed and not accurate enough for target identification.

One of the first tasks which Bennett undertook was to investigate progress on a new radar navigation and bomb aiming device which had the codename of H2S. Bennett visited the Telecommunications Research Establishment (TRE) at Great Malvern College and was appalled at what he found. The staff at TRE and its aerodrome at RAF Defford were maintaining peacetime standards with no sense of urgency, while the maintenance staff were not capable of maintaining aircraft which would have to be regularly flown if H2S was to be successfully developed. Bennett quickly got in touch with Bomber Command and had several groundcrew from 4 Group posted to Defford. The scientists, led by Professor Dee, were revitalised and work went on apace with Bennett himself often flying the Halifaxes which were equipped with the developmental H2S sets. Within weeks H2S was a workable proposition, but although it could be used to identify ground features in order to navigate and, indeed, bomb, the sets were very complex, had poor serviceability and required some degree of skill to operate correctly.

While Bennett helped with the work on H2S another radar device was being worked on completely separately and independently of the authorities. R.H. Reeves and Dr F.E. Jones were working on a device codenamed Oboe and this new device, which relied on radar beams from ground stations and a corresponding set in a high-flying aircraft, enabled a very high degree of accuracy in bombing but, like H2S, there were problems with reliability.

Bennett also worked extensively with various pyrotechnic experts to develop workable target marking devices. New, more powerful, flares and hooded flares were quickly worked on, barometer fuses were utilised. High-powered candles were developed which were quickly named target indicators. Bennett had requested the development of these indicators and they were produced in a variety of base colours with some ejecting stars of varying colours. The target indicators were a huge success and remained in service throughout the war.

Despite the promise of co-operation from wider Bomber Command, the creation of the PFF was certainly not straightforward. Bennett described how the commander of 4 Group (Bennett's old group), Air Vice Marshal Roddy Carr, was very helpful and enthusiastically promised to encourage his best crews to apply for postings to 35 Squadron, which was to be 4 Group's contribution to the PFF. At 5 Group, however, it was a very different story. Air Vice Marshal Alec Coryton was absolute in his disapproval of PFF and proved to be, in Bennett's own words, 'antagonistic'. Under orders, however, he agreed to transfer 83 Squadron to the PFF on the day required. The commanding officers of 1 and 3 Groups were non-committal although Air Vice Marshal Rice of 1 Group at least agreed to allow volunteers to be posted to 156 Squadron. Thus, the PFF was established with five squadrons flying different aircraft and four of them being affiliated to Main Force Groups. The exception to this was 109 Squadron which was equipped with specially adapted pressurised Wellingtons which were being used to test Oboe.

Original PFF Squadrons.

Squadron	Aircraft	Group Affiliation
7	Stirling	3
35	Halifax	4
83	Lancaster	5
156	Wellington	1
109	Wellington (pressurised)	None

The first PFF operation took place on 18/19 August when a force of 118 aircraft attacked Flensburg. PFF dispatched thirty-one aircraft to locate and mark the target. Flensburg was chosen because its location, on an inlet of the Baltic, was in theory an easy target to identify for the PFF crews. The forecast winds were incorrect, however, and much of the force drifted north of the target. Sixteen of the PFF crews claimed to have marked the target while seventy-eight Main Force crews claimed to have bombed on target, but Flensburg was not hit at all while the Danish towns of Sonderborg and Aabenraa did receive bombs on this night. The first operation for the PFF had been a shambles and the PFF also suffered their first loss on this night as Halifax II (W1226, TL-J) of 35 Squadron was amongst the four aircraft which failed to return. Sergeant J.W. Smith and his crew had taken off from RAF Graveley for Flensburg only to be attacked twice by a night-fighter, one of which they claimed to have destroyed, and were forced to ditch. All seven men were taken prisoner, but the rear gunner, Sergeant Arthur John Owen Leo was killed on 20 August 1944 when a working party of which he was a member was attacked from the air.[20]

The second operation for PFF was mounted on 24/25 August when 226 aircraft were sent to Frankfurt. Once again, however, there were severe problems for the PFF crews who had difficulty identifying the target in cloudy conditions and much of the attack fell in open country, although there was some damage in Frankfurt itself. More worryingly, five PFF crews were amongst the sixteen reported lost or missing. No 7 Squadron lost three of its Stirlings, including that of its commanding officer, Wing Commander John Morland Shewell, who was killed along with three of his crew. At Graveley, 35 Squadron lost another Halifax when 18-year-old Pilot Officer Frank Edward Gardiner and his crew failed to return. The final PFF aircraft to go missing on this night was Lancaster I (R5610, OL-G) of 83 Squadron. Flight Lieutenant Oliver Rayner Matheson DFC and his crew were shot down by a night-fighter with four of the crew being killed, two being taken prisoner and one, Flight Lieutenant Matheson, evading capture. Flight Lieutenant Matheson was a very experienced pilot who had joined the RAF in January 1937 and had been awarded the DFC for his prior service with 75 (New Zealand) Squadron.

Just two days later, however, the fortunes of the PFF improved when they successfully marked the town of Kassel and the 306 aircraft which had been dispatched caused heavy damage throughout this manufacturing town. Included amongst the damage were three Henschel factories.

Although the public were largely given the most positive accounts of Bomber Command activities as was possible, it was increasingly clear that the casualties suffered by the aircrews were severe. In light of the government's new policy of being more open to the general public, the Secretary of State for Air addressed the subject of casualties in the House of Commons in October 1942. He stated that during the year until the end of September Bomber Command had carried out raids on 140 nights and 79 days. This period included the thousand bomber raids and a large number of raids which involved between 300-500 bombers. During this period some 1,082 aircraft had been lost. Although this was a large figure the Secretary of State was at pains to point out that this period had seen at least 14,000 bombers utilised on operations and that the loss rate could not 'be considered unduly high, especially in view of the non-stop, continuous nature of our bombing offensive'.[21] It has been suggested in the press that the cost of lost bombers stood at approximately £54,000,000 but this figure could not be considered excessive when compared with the amount of damage which had been done to German industry and Germany's war effort. The Secretary then outlined how the newer, bigger, four-engined bombers which were now replacing those which had started the war, were more robust allowing even heavily damaged aircraft to return to base to be repaired and that these new bombers were carrying far larger bombloads to Germany and in greater numbers than ever before.

Once again, the press were eager to support the command and this statement was supported by claims over the effectiveness of the new bombers. Reporting on the Secretary's speech, for example, *The Sphere* featured a photo of three Short Stirling bombers alongside claims over the aircraft's performance. While not far off the truth, the piece did overestimate both the speed of the Stirling and its maximum bombload. *The Sphere* piece also answered some of the perceived criticisms of the costs of the bomber campaign. While admitting that the Stirling (and other heavy bombers) used a huge amount of petrol and oil, stating that each of the four 1,600 hp engines consumed a gallon of fuel every minute while cruising and more on take-off, this had to be counterbalanced by the fact that the Stirling was 'capable of carrying a very heavy load of bombs for very long distance'.[22]

Despite increasingly positive reports in the press and the growing support for Bomber Command amongst both the general public and the government, losses during Harris's first months in charge had been high and there was evidence that morale was slipping in several squadrons. An aircrew member of Bomber Command had to fly a first operational tour of thirty operations before a period of leave and a spell away from operations, usually as an instructor. An airman who had completed a tour could then be called back to complete a second tour of twenty operations. This straight rule of fifty operations could be impacted by many factors, including the fact that minelaying operations and those to France or the Low Countries could sometimes count as only a third of an operation and 'Nickel' raids generally did not count at all.

Despite the massive strain which airmen were under – most were well aware of casualties amongst their own squadron – cases of airmen refusing to go on operations remained relatively low. This was possibly due in part to the rather harsh way in which such men were treated. They were quickly branded as Lacking Moral Fibre (LMF), stripped of their rank, posted away and given menial ground duties.

CHAPTER 5

1943 – Main Offensive

Summary of the Year

The year 1943 was, in many ways, a watershed and possibly the most important and interesting one of the war for Bomber Command. By this point in the war the command was largely becoming equipped with the modern four-engine heavy bombers with which it would continue until victory. The main exception to this were the squadrons which were still soldiering on with the Vickers Wellingtons. Even here, however, newer marks of the veteran aircraft were becoming available. The command was expanding rapidly with new squadrons coming into being and in January an entirely new group, 6 (RCAF) Group, began operations.

Crew training had improved with several new categories of aircrew now being the norm. These included dedicated navigators and air bombers (commonly called bomb aimers) replacing the multi-role observer and the new category of flight engineer being introduced to remove the need for second pilots. Air gunners were now specially trained for their duties rather than being volunteers drawn from airmen as had been the case at the start of the war. Radar technologies such as Gee and Oboe also became more widely available with every main force and PFF aircraft being equipped with the former device (although it was almost always jammed over enemy territory). Another device, codenamed H2S, also entered service in January. It was hoped that H2S, which was a ground scanning radar, would be invaluable both in navigation and bombing, but there were many teething problems. The radar was never as accurate as was hoped and was sometimes difficult to use. Shortly after the introduction of H2S an aircraft carrying it was shot down and the radar equipment salvaged and analysed. This allowed the Germans to, amongst other things, develop the FuG 350 Naxos Z radar set which, when fitted into a night fighter, allowed the fighter to home in on H2S emissions. This fact was not discovered for some time and led to the destruction of a large number of bombers.

'Bomber' Harris was given his freedom to demonstrate his commitment to area bombing as a war-winning tactic when the Combined Chiefs of Staff issued the Casablanca Directive in January. This gave Harris permission to mount a sustained strategic bombing campaign against Germany's towns and cities. Buoyed by the success of the Thousand Plan in 1942, Harris once again intended to mount an offensive which would capture the imagination. This time it would be a sustained offensive against the industrially vital Ruhr. Harris was well-aware that there was still doubt over his strategic bombing plan and the Ruhr, with its industrial importance, was the perfect target to demonstrate the growing potential of his command in a manner which would, if successful, allow him to demand more resources in order to further build his war-winning force.

January saw 8 (PPF) Group reformed to take over the previous Pathfinder Force. It drew on the resources of all the other groups for its personnel and aircraft and was at first equipped with multiple types of aircraft. At the end of the month Oboe Mosquitoes carried out their first ground-marking raid with an attack on Dusseldorf and H2S was used for the first time on operations by PFF Halifaxes and Stirlings over Hamburg.

Between March and July the airmen got used to entering their briefing rooms to see that the target was yet again one in the Ruhr (which was quickly and bitterly nicknamed 'Happy Valley'). During this period Harris mounted 31 major raids (and many minor ones) against the Ruhr. The Battle of the Ruhr was a huge success but came at the cost of 1,045 aircraft and the loss of more than 5,500 aircrew killed or missing, with many others taken prisoner.

Raids were also made on other targets. It was impossible to attack solely Ruhr targets as the Germans would quickly concentrate their forces in the area. A number of high-profile and specialised raids were also carried out during the period, the most famous being that mounted against the Ruhr dams by the specially assembled and trained 617 Squadron, led by Wing Commander Guy Gibson.

A number of other developments took place during the Battle of the Ruhr period. One of the greatest problems facing Bomber Command was in determining what the weather conditions would be over the target, on return to base and en-route to the target. At the beginning of April the newly-formed 1409 Met Flight (part of 8 (PFF) Group) mounted its first operation, to Brittany. The Met Flight, equipped with the high-flying and speedy Mosquito, would go on to become a vital part of bomber operations.

The daylight operations of 2 Group continued in sporadic fashion throughout the period although the group would shortly be removed from Bomber Command and transferred to 2nd Tactical Air Force (2TAF). One of its final operations as part of Bomber Command clearly demonstrated the risks of such operations. On 3 May eleven Venturas of 487 Squadron attacked a power station near Amsterdam but all but one of the Venturas was shot down. Even the Mosquitoes were not immune during these daylight attacks and on 27 May five from fourteen Mosquitoes were shot down during an attack on the Jena Zeiss optical factories by 105 and 139 Squadrons. In June another unusual operation was undertaken. The first shuttle raid saw 60 Lancasters attack the Zeppelin works at Friedrichshafen before flying on and landing at Allied airfields in North Africa. On their return to England the Lancasters mounted an attack on La Spezia.

Buoyed by the success of the Battle of the Ruhr, Harris was determined to press home his advantage. He was aided by the fact that permission was given to use the radar disruption device known as 'Window' for the first time over Germany and Occupied Europe. Window consisted of metal strips, painted black on one side which, when released in clouds from aircraft, swamped the enemy radar screens with false returns and greatly hampered their ability to home in on individual bombers. In July and August Harris authorised the use of Window during the Battle of Hamburg which consisted of four Bomber Command attacks (aided by further attacks in daylight by the US Eighth Air Force) in quick succession upon the port city.

The attacks coincided with very hot weather and the disruption caused by Window, the concentrated and accurate bombing aided by Hamburg's coastal location and the meteorological conditions, resulted in a phenomenon never seen before – a firestorm. It occurred when the fires started in the city joined together and were further whipped up by the hurricane force winds caused by the blazes. The result was the almost total destruction of Hamburg and the deaths of 41,000 people. The Battle of Hamburg was a massive success for Bomber Command, but Harris did not adequately grasp the fact that the repeated attacks on such a target were the reason for the success. Even if he had, repeated attacks on the same target would quickly become too expensive in terms of losses for Bomber Command. Quite simply, Harris did not yet have the resources to mount attacks such as those of the Battle of Hamburg on a regular basis. (After the war, Hitler's armaments minister,

Albert Speer, commented that if six such raids had been made in quick succession it would have been extremely difficult for Germany to have stayed in the war.)

Although Harris had made substantial progress there were still problems within his command. With his dedication to strategic bombing it should come as no surprise that he was appalled by the Pointblank Directive which modified the earlier Casablanca Directive, stating that the German aircraft industry should be the first priority during the autumn of 1943. Harris viewed this as a diversion from his main campaign and maintained a healthy disgust at what he referred to as panacea targets which were the brainchild of scientists and politicians. Although he did not, and could not, ignore the directive and did dispatch some raids to targets on the directive's list, Harris continued to assign priority to his strategic bombing of Germany's towns and cities.

During this period Harris was also ordered to make several raids on Italian targets to hasten the withdrawal of that country from the war. The attacks on Italy had begun in 1940 but on the night of 16/17 August the final Italian operation took place with the bombing of Turin. One of the most interesting Bomber Command missions of the war took place on the next night when 596 bombers were sent in a complex precision raid on the rocket research facilities at Peenemunde. This was the first operational use of the Master Bomber technique which saw a highly experienced pilot and crew designated to guide and control the raid over the target.

In August he began feeling his way into his next, and greatest battle, the Battle of Berlin. Harris had insisted that Bomber Command and the US Eighth Air Force between them could, for a high cost, destroy Berlin and he believed that this would force the Germans out of the war. The Battle of Berlin had begun in August but the main operations against the German capital began in November and continued until March 1944.

Why did Harris insist on making the distant and extremely well-defended capital his next target? There were several reasons. He did firmly believe that a severely damaged or destroyed Berlin would result in Germany capitulating, but he was also very much aware that his time to prove his theory was running out with the invasion of Occupied Europe increasingly likely to take place in 1944. Harris' initial plan for the Battle of Berlin had been conceived of as a joint offensive involving both Bomber Command and the US Eighth Air Force but the Americans were not yet in a place to take part in a sustained campaign against Berlin and so the responsibility fell solely to Bomber Command. Harris must have known that mounting a sustained campaign against the German capital in the depths of winter and with the forces currently available to him was stretching the capabilities of his command, but he decided to press on anyway.

One of the problems facing the command was that the German night fighter force had changed its tactics in the face of the problems caused by Window. The previous tactics, which involved night fighters being vectored onto individual bombers by ground controllers had been severely disrupted by the use of Window. Two complementary tactics, named *Zahme Sau* (Tame Boar) and *Wilde Sau* (Wild Boar), had been introduced. *Zahme Sau* saw the use of single-engine fighters being used over the target city while *Wilde Sau* saw the twin-engine night fighters released from the ground controlled Himmelbelt defences and instead ordered to locate and infiltrate the bomber stream with the aid of a running commentary. The *Wilde Sau* tactics, in particular, proved very successful and were extremely difficult to counteract. German tactics developed in other ways with the use of night fighter flares to aid the *Wilde Sau* and *Zahme Sau* fighters to find the bomber stream.

As a result of these new tactics, bomber losses began to mount rapidly. The 1943 attacks on Berlin were hindered by atrocious weather conditions, by the range to the target and by the city's sheer size and defences. These factors and the new German tactics resulted in heavy losses. The first attack of the Battle of Berlin took place on 23/24 August when Harris sent 727 bombers to the German capital. The raid resulted in the loss of 56 aircraft, the highest total yet in a single raid.

Despite the focus on the area campaign of strategic bombing, the command continued to make precision attacks where viable; 617 Squadron continued to be the precision bombing specialists of Bomber Command (later they were joined by 9 Squadron) and undertook a number of raids on important targets. The squadron received new bombs with which to carry out these precision attacks and, on the night of 15/16 September, 617 Squadron attacked the Dortmund-Ems Canal with the newly developed 12,000lbs High Capacity bombs.

The new tactics of the German night fighters saw the planners at Bomber Command begin to develop their own new tactics in the hope of reducing losses. At the end of September there was an attack on Hanover with 711 aircraft (this was the first of four heavy raids on the city during September and October) but on this night 29 aircraft from 8 (PFF) Group carried on in a feint to Oldenburg and made a spoof attack to try to draw off enemy night fighters. Another development in the ongoing technological battle took place at the start of October when the first bombers equipped with the device known as 'Airborne Cigar' (ABC) took part in a raid. The device equipped the Lancasters of 101 Squadron in 1 Group and necessitated the inclusion of an eighth, German-speaking, crewman in the Lancaster. ABC was designed to monitor the higher bandwidths for German ground-to-air transmissions, specifically the running commentaries which guided night fighters into the bomber stream. Once a broadcast was detected by the German-speaking set operator he switched on one of the three transmitters which overwhelmed the German broadcast with a warbling note.

The speed of technological developments in the bomber offensive was extraordinary and the first of the four-engine bombers, the Stirling, was now considered obsolescent due to its poor ceiling and bomb-carrying capacity. As a result, it had been gradually phased out. On 22/23 November the Stirlings of 3 Group mounted their last bombing operation over Germany with a raid on Berlin. Other technological developments during this period include the first use of 'G-H' which was a combination and development of Gee and Oboe. G-H was able to be used by up to 100 aircraft at a time but was limited in range like its predecessors. It was allocated largely to those squadrons of 3 and 6 Groups which were re-equipping with Lancasters. The former group, which was re-equipping with the Lancaster was the main user of the device and the group later pioneered the use of a G-H leader (in the lead position of a 'vic' formation of three aircraft) to carry out accurate daylight raids through heavy cloud. It was hoped that the new G-H device would enable very accurate bombing through cloud when target indicators were ineffective. The first operational use of the device was on 7/8 October by Lancasters of 3 and 6 Groups during a night raid on Stuttgart.

Losses, however, continued to mount despite these developments and Bomber Command formed a group tasked with supporting bomber operations. In November 100 (Bomber Support) Group became operational, equipped with a mix of heavy bombers and night fighters. Its duties were to use a variety of homing devices, radar and radio countermeasures to deter, frustrate and disable the German defences. In the final month of the year the Bristol Beaufighters of 141 Squadron operated as intruders for the first time. The intruders were night fighters fitted with the new 'Serrate' radar equipment which allowed them to home in on the radar used by German night fighters. They were ordered to patrol along the route of the bomber stream and to engage German night fighters.

The public were kept informed about the progress of the bomber campaign against Germany but the information which was disseminated was often presented through the lens of propaganda. In some cases photographs of bomber aircraft were accompanied by captions which attempted to support the narrative of a successful and ever-heavier bombing campaign regardless of the actual facts surrounding the photographs. *The Sphere* of 27 November 1943, for example, featured a spread entitled 'The Bomber Offensive by Day and by Night'. Part of this article, which came at the beginning phase of the Battle of Berlin, featured a photograph of a Handley Page Halifax shortly after take-off. The accompanying caption assured readers that the bomber, R-for Robert, was on its way to 'carry on with the task of wiping out German centres of industrial production'. In fact, as is made plain by the identification code on the fuselage, it was in fact Halifax V Series I (Special) (EB151, OO-R) of 1663 HCU based at RAF Rufforth. The picture had in fact been taken as the bomber took off from RAF Holme-on-Spalding Moor during a training flight.

Sometime the information given was either out of date or gave an incorrect impression of an aircraft or its operational capabilities. In the same article as mentioned above there appeared a picture of a WAAF working in the Perspex nose of a Halifax bomber. The caption assured readers that this was a gun turret in the aircraft and that it was occupied by the front gunner and bomb aimer. In fact, the front position was not a turret (it had a fixed mounted single machine-gun) which was operated by the bomb aimer (or air bomber as they were officially termed) but proved to be so underused that many squadrons with the earlier marks of Halifax (I, II and V) removed the Perspex nose and had it faired over completely. The more streamline Perspex nose was retained in the later Mk III Halifax which, in November 1943, was just coming into service. The caption goes on to state that all of the crew positions in the Halifax were armoured, a claim which was blatantly untrue.

The Campaign

This would be a pivotal year in Bomber Command's war and would see a variety of battles and innovations fought out by the men of the command along with several more specialised operations. The year opened with a highly experimental raid on the night of 31 December into 1 January when eight Lancasters and two Oboe-equipped Mosquitos of the PFF made an attack on Düsseldorf to test the Oboe equipment. The raid was accurate, but one Lancaster was lost. Two nights later the experiment was continued when three Mosquitos and nineteen Lancasters attacked Essen. The raid was repeated (interspersed with a raid on Duisburg) on several occasions in the next few nights.

There was a useful boost in January when 6 (RCAF) Group became operational with its first operation being to send fifteen aircraft as part of a force raiding the French U-boat port of Lorient. The attack on Lorient involved 122 aircraft and took place on 14/15 January. The Pathfinder marking of the target, the U-boat pens, was accurate, but bombing by the Main Force became inaccurate and there were some recriminations between 8 Group and the Main Force Groups. On this raid 6 (RCAF) Group lost its first aircraft when Wellington III (BK165, OW-F) of 426 Squadron failed to return. The aircraft, piloted by Pilot Officer George Milne, RCAF, was lost without trace. The six-man crew (five Canadians and the British rear gunner) are all commemorated on the Runnymede Memorial.

We have already seen how Canadian and Australian squadrons had been formed in Bomber Command and this was typical of the command's multi-national make-up. Possibly no other military command in modern history has had the make-up of Bomber Command. While there were national squadrons, such as those mentioned above, the squadrons of Bomber Command remained multi-national throughout the war. Canadians and Australians always made the greatest contribution after the British, but there were New Zealanders (and 75 Squadron bore the additional name New Zealand), South Africans, Rhodesians and men from all over the Empire. In addition, there were significant numbers from several of the occupied countries such as Poland, Czechoslovakia, France and Norway. Throughout the war there were also smaller, but significant, numbers of men from the USA who served in Bomber Command and they were joined by some men from neutral Ireland.

There appear to have been no problems incorporating men from such a wide variety of backgrounds and nationalities and, despite some resistance at higher levels, the black volunteers who came from the Caribbean and from Africa were also easily accepted and appreciated at squadron level. The numbers of black airmen who served in Bomber Command is not known but at least 495 black airmen were killed while serving with the RAF, the majority with Bomber Command.[1]

This mixture of nationalities worked well for Bomber Command with many veterans claiming that mixed squadrons and crews were more efficient because of the friendly sense of rivalry and competition which they engendered. The majority of those who flew the most operations were British. This was solely down to the policy of the Australian and Canadian governments in requesting that their airmen be returned after successfully completing a tour of operations. This applied especially to Australia after that country itself came under threat of invasion from Japan. Harris believed that British airmen were better educated and some thought that Canadian crews, and especially pilots, could be ill-disciplined but, against this, were the many who believed that the 'foreigners' had distinctly positive qualities such as the belief that Canadian gunners had sharper eyesight.

The decision to form a dedicated force in Bomber Command to lead the way for the Main Force and to illuminate and mark targets was taken in 1942 but it would be 1943 when the Pathfinders would face their sternest test.

On the night following the Lorient raid the PFF dropped its first specifically designed target indicator bomb over no less a target than Berlin. This was also the first ever raid consisting solely of four-engined bombers and in many ways was the curtain opener for what was to follow during the rest of Bomber Command's war. Just nine days after this the contribution of the PFF was recognised as the PFF became 8 (Pathfinder Force) Group with the now Air Vice Marshal Bennett retained in command. Bomber Command then made attacks on Berlin on two consecutive nights. The first raid, on 16/17 January, saw 201 aircraft from 8, 1, 4 and 5 Groups. It had been planned initially that Stirlings of 3 Group would also take part, but it was then decided that only the higher flying Lancasters and Halifaxes would be sent. The vast majority of aircraft on the raid were Lancasters – 190 of them – and 5 Group made up the bulk of the force. The raid, however, was a disappointment. Thick cloud made navigation a problem (Berlin was well beyond Gee range and H2S was not yet ready) and the city was covered by haze which made accurate bombing difficult. On the other hand, the German response was oddly muted and only one Lancaster failed to return. This was Lancaster I (ED332, QR-D) of 61 Squadron which had taken off from RAF Syerston at 4.30pm with Squadron Leader Edward Donald J. Parker GC DFC, at the controls. Nothing further was heard from the crew but they were later confirmed as having been killed and the seven men are all buried in the Berlin 1939-1945 War Cemetery. Squadron Leader Parker had previously served with both 40 and 49 Squadrons and had earned his GC for saving the life of his wireless operator following a crash on 8 January 1940.

The second attack involved 170 Lancasters and seventeen Halifaxes but once again the Pathfinders failed to mark the centre of the city and most of the bombing fell onto the southern areas. This disappointing raid resulted in the heavy loss of nineteen Lancasters and three Halifaxes (an 11.8 per cent loss rate) after the enemy night-fighters managed to successfully infiltrate the bomber stream. This was also the final experimental raid on the German capital using the Pathfinder marking techniques, with Harris being reluctant to continue the experiment until H2S became widely available to the Pathfinders. An odd passenger on this raid was BBC reporter Richard Dimbleby, who accompanied Wing Commander Guy Gibson in a Lancaster of 106 Squadron.

Throughout January Harris sent small forces to attack Essen as part of an experiment to test the new Oboe blind marking equipment which, it was hoped, would dramatically increase bombing accuracy. From 9-14 January, Bomber Command targeted the city on successive nights with small forces of bombers ordered to drop bombs on the Pathfinder markers dropped by Mosquitos. On the final raid of this series the command dispatched sixty-nine aircraft (three Mosquitos and sixty-six Lancasters). The planned Oboe trial went wrong on this night with two of the Mosquitos having to abort their sorties due to technical problems, while the third dropped its markers which failed to ignite above the cloud base. Despite this, it would appear that the small force of bombers did indeed bomb accurately, but four Lancasters were lost in the raid.

One of the bombers which failed to return was Lancaster I (R5690, ZN-T) of 106 Squadron. After taking off from RAF Syerston nothing further was heard from the bomber and it transpired that it had been shot down by a night-fighter over Holland and all of the crew were killed. The flight engineer was 22-year-old Edinburgh man, Sergeant Alexander Dunbar.[2] This crew was very experienced and had four decorations to their names. The pilot, 24-year-old Flight Lieutenant Everard Frank Gray Healey DFC DFM, had joined up at the start of the war and had been awarded the DFM in April 1942 and then the DFC in November of the same year. His navigator, Flying Officer John Ray Pennington DFC, had also been awarded his DFC in November 1942 as had the bomb-aimer, Pilot Officer David MacLeod Crozier DFM, RCAF.[3]

That night 106 Squadron lost two aircraft with Lancaster I (W4261, ZN-C) also failing to return. The aircraft had taken off with Flight Sergeant Maurice Andrew Phair, RCAF, at the controls. It is not known how ZN-C was shot down, but the wreckage and the remains of the crew were found near Düsseldorf. Flight Sergeant Phair had come a long way to die in Bomber Command's war as he was an American citizen from Limestone, Maine. Five of the crew were members of the RCAF while the flight engineer and wireless operator were both Englishmen. The mid-upper gunner in ZN-C was Flight Sergeant Russell Zavitz, RCAF, of Ilderton, Ontario. Zavitz was unusual in that, at 39 years of age, he was much older than most Bomber Command aircrew.[4]

The remainder of January passed fairly quietly for the Main Force squadrons with 'gardening' operations and minor attacks on Lorient and Düsseldorf. On 27 January a successful and daring daylight attack was made on a diesel engine factory at Copenhagen by just nine Mosquitos. Two of the Mosquitos were lost. DZ407, GB-R, of 105 Squadron flew into high-tension cables and crashed killing the pilot, Sergeant James George Dawson of Southampton, and his navigator, Sergeant Ronald Harry Cox. DK336 belonged to 105 Squadron but was borrowed by 139 Squadron for the operation. The aircraft took part in the attack successfully but on return suffered an engine failure and crashed at East Dereham, Norfolk, after hitting a balloon cable and a tree. Both crewmen were killed. They were Sergeant Richard Clare and Pilot Officer Edward Doyle.

That night also saw a further development which heralded much for the future accuracy of Bomber Command. During a raid on Düsseldorf in the Ruhr, Mosquitos from the command which were equipped with Oboe carried out ground marking duties over a major target for the first time. Pathfinder Lancasters then backed up the target indicators which had been dropped by the Mosquitos. As was usual over the Ruhr there was a ground haze, but the new technique ensured that the bombing remained concentrated and there was widespread damage for the loss of six aircraft.

The Mosquitos of 105 and 109 Squadrons concluded what had been a busy month by dispatching six of its aircraft on the first ever daylight raid on the German capital on 30 January. The raids were timed to bomb the capital at the same time as Goering was expected to be speaking on the wireless. The first raid by three Mosquitos of 105 Squadron interrupted Goering's morning speech and then three more from 139 Squadron repeated the attempt during his afternoon speech. By this time, however, the defences had been alerted and one of the Mosquitos was shot down by flak, becoming the first Bomber Command Mosquito to be lost over Berlin. Squadron Leader Donald Frederick William Darling, DFC, and his navigator Flying Officer William Wright, were both killed.

The first month of the year ended with the debut of yet another new technological development when H2S was first used operationally by Pathfinder Halifaxes and Stirlings on a raid on Hamburg. The attempt was not a success. There had been scant time to train the operators on the new devices effectively and bombing was therefore widely scattered although some damage was done.

Just days after H2S had first been used came a potential disaster when a Stirling carrying the new device was shot down over Germany and the set salvaged by the Luftwaffe. The raid in question was on Cologne on the night of 2/3 February and involved 161 aircraft. Results were again disappointing and five aircraft were lost. Included amongst them, however, was Stirling I (R9264, MG-L) of 7 Squadron which was shot down by a night-fighter over Holland and it was from this aircraft that the Germans salvaged the H2S set. The crew was a very experienced one. The pilot was Squadron Leader William Arthur Smith DFC MiD and between them the seven-man crew possessed two DFCs, two DFMs and a MiD. Five were killed but the two gunners survived to be taken prisoner.[5]

On the following day the men of Bomber Command were once again called to their briefing rooms where they were told that they would be launching an attack consisting of 263 aircraft against Hamburg. The raid got off to a poor start when icing conditions were experienced over the North Sea causing many aircraft to abort the sortie and return to base. As a result, bombing was sparse and scattered and the raid judged a failure despite forty-five large fires being started (including two in oil refineries). To make matters worse for the airmen the German night fighters were active and sixteen bombers (6.1 per cent of the total dispatched) were lost. The Stirling I (BF408, HA-T) of 218 (Gold Coast) Squadron had taken off from Downham Market at 6.47pm with Flight Sergeant S.L. Treves at the controls. The flight engineer in the crew was 25-year-old Sergeant Ronald Hargreaves, a married man from Newcastle. It would appear that the aircraft suffered a catastrophic navigational error and it was reported as having crashed in the Straits of Dover with total loss of life.[6] Sergeant Hargreaves left behind his widow Olga and his parents, James and Nellie, in Newcastle.

On the night following the death of Sergeant Hargreaves the command launched a raid by 188 aircraft against the Italian city of Turin. This time the mission went according to plan and the bombers caused severe damage to the city for the loss of three Lancasters. Amongst the three was Lancaster I (ED352, DX-Q) of 57 Squadron. The bomber had taken off from Scampton shortly after 6pm under the command of Pilot Officer A.F.G. Ritch, RCAF but nothing more was heard. It was later reported that the bomber had crashed in mountains just to the north-east of Bourg-Saint-Maurice in France. All of the seven-man crew were killed and are buried in the local churchyard. After the war their remains were moved to the Saint-Germain-au-Mont d'Or Communal Cemetery Extension. The rear gunner in the crew was Flight Sergeant Ronald Shears, the son of Ellis and Florence Shears and the nephew of Ann Gordon of Jesmond. It would appear that, like many, Ronald had volunteered for aircrew duty out of a strong sense of patriotism and duty as his relatives had the following inscription placed upon his headstone: 'THE WORLD WAS HIS COUNTRY, TO DO GOOD WAS HIS RELIGION'.

The start of February was a relatively quiet one for the many Geordies serving in Bomber Command but even so there was a further casualty before the first week was out. On the night of 5/6 February the command did not mount any major bombing operations but it did dispatch nineteen Stirlings to lay mines in the vicinity of the Frisians. Two of the aircraft failed to return and one of these was the Stirling I (BK644, WP-T) of 90 Squadron. The bomber had taken off from Ridgewell but was, like so many, lost without trace. The second pilot, Pilot Officer Albert Carr, was a 19-year-old from Fenham.[7]

Demonstrating the command's growing strength, the raid on Lorient on 13/14 February saw the Main Force squadrons drop 1,000 tons of bombs for the first time, the greater bomb-carrying capacity of the four-engine bombers presaging ever heavier raids on German and occupied towns and cities in the future. The raid was carried out in good weather and considerable damage was done in the target area.

Although much of 1943 would be dominated by Harris's main offensive over German towns and cities, there were numerous raids on smaller and more specialised targets during the year. We have already seen how Mosquitos had successfully attacked a factory in Denmark during January.

On 3 March several Molybdenum mines at Knaben in Norway were the targets for ten Mosquitos of 139 Squadron. The attacks were made successfully but one of the Mosquitos was shot down by enemy fighters.

That night Harris launched a large attack on Hamburg using 417 aircraft. Unfortunately, and despite good visibility, the Pathfinders made a mistake on this night and the majority of the bombing took place some 13 miles from Hamburg on the small town of Wedel, causing massive damage. Some bombers did successfully attack Hamburg, however, and 95 people were killed here. The erroneous bombing at Wedel also caused important damage with several industrial concerns being destroyed. Ten aircraft were lost during the raid.

Although Bomber Command suffered severe casualties, its activities caught the imagination of the general public and found widespread support. The public welcomed the news that at least one part of the armed forces was taking the attack to Germany itself and few had any moral qualms after the Blitz and the hardships of the previous years. Newspaper reports of raids were constant throughout the war, especially after Bomber Harris began his main offensive in 1943. The reports always endeavoured to put a positive spin on the news of RAF raids even though, at times, they had to admit that there had been casualties. The reports were widely read and increased the support for the bombing campaign.

On 23 February The *Newcastle Journal* carried a headline of '100 "Big Bombs" fell on Bremen'. The story referred to a raid launched on the night of Sunday 21 February.[8] Although only a medium sized raid consisting of 143 aircraft (mainly Lancasters but accompanied by seven Stirlings and six Halifaxes), the report informed readers of the glow of fires being seen through thick cloud. The newspaper was also at pains to point out the industrial importance of Bremen citing the number of aircraft and engineering plants, oil refineries and shipbuilding facilities in the city. The official report also confidently told of how over 100 of the 4,000lb bombs known to aircrew as 'cookies' had fallen on the city during the attack and triumphantly declared that no aircraft had been lost in the raid, despite heavy anti-aircraft fire over the target. Indeed, no aircraft were lost but the bombing through thick cloud meant that there were no bombing photographs to assess the success of the raid.

At the end of February there were several changes in the upper echelons of Bomber Command. Sir Robert Saundby became Deputy Commander-in-Chief, Air Vice Marshal E.A.B. Rice took command of 1 Group, Air

Vice Marshal R. Harrison became commander of 3 Group, Air Vice Marshal the Hon. R. Cochrane took over at 5 Group and Air Vice Marshal G.E. Brookes commanded the Canadian 6 Group. Harris, though, was aware that 2 Group would shortly be leaving his command. He understood this decision but, typically, demanded that the two Mosquito squadrons, 105 and 109 remain with Bomber Command and be transferred to 8 (PFF) Group.

Throughout the spring the press continued to highlight the growing strength of Bomber Command and in both the national and regional press articles praising the activities of the RAF's bombers and their crews were commonplace. No matter how isolated, every community in Britain was treated to descriptions of the operations of Bomber Command and how the bomber boys were hitting back at Germany with ever growing confidence and strength.

Although Orkney was just about as geographically isolated as anywhere in Britain, the residents had no doubt of the growing strength of the Bomber Command campaign. The air correspondent of the *Orkney Herald* told readers how the nightly raids were growing in strength and intensity and were causing an increasing level of devastation in German towns and cities. The campaign was having a serious impact on the German economy and its industry. The reporter stated that a 'neutral estimate of the direct and indirect effect of this bombing is a drop of 30 per cent in German output'.[9] What was more, the heavy and persistent raids by both British and American bombers were seriously disrupting the transport systems of Germany, with the dislocation causing great concern amongst the Nazi commanders.

Some Orcadians had been questioning why there had been no further 1,000 bomber raids such as those which had taken place in the previous year. The answer was two-fold. Assembling a fleet of 1,000 bombers had been a tremendously taxing undertaking which had involved the use of not just the whole of Bomber Command's frontline strength, but also the aircraft of the training units, day-bomber squadrons and even some which were donated by other commands. Secondly, the improving equipment and aircraft of the command now meant that a higher tonnage of bombs could be dropped by fewer aircraft, while the creation of 8 (PFF) Group had also enabled the force to achieve greater accuracy. The reporter informed his readers that the 1,000 bomber raids had been a successful experiment, but that subsequent attempts to build up Bomber Command quickly had been frustrated by the need for some of its aircraft to be diverted to Coastal Command duties.

Nevertheless, the reporter stated that the introduction of the new four-engine bombers, the Stirling, Halifax and Lancaster, meant that a force of just 300 bombers was able to deliver a bombload equivalent to that delivered during a 1,000-bomber raid. The reporter illustrated this point by comparing the Whitley (a main part of the force from 1939-1942) to the newly introduced Lancaster. While the Whitley had a cruising speed of 160-180 mph and could carry 6,000lbs of bombs, the Lancaster could carry three times the bombload, could fly at greater altitude and was faster than the Whitley. The 1,000 bomber raids might be repeated once again, assured the reporter, but the tonnage of bombs would be far greater than the 1,500 tons of bombs dropped on Cologne by 1,000 bombers in 1942 and many of the bombs would be the new 8,000lb bombs which had recently caused great destruction in Germany. Thus were the people of Orkney kept informed about developments in the air war while also being subtly encouraged to back the efforts of the RAF.

On 5/6 March Harris opened what was to become the Battle of the Ruhr with an attack on that hard to hit target, Essen, by 442 aircraft. This was the launching of what Sir Arthur Harris would later call his Main Offensive, which would last until the end of March 1944 and in addition to the Battle of the Ruhr would involve a campaign against Hamburg and Berlin and culminating in the disastrous Nuremberg raid. Harris had chosen the Ruhr as the target for this first battle for a variety of factors – its many and closely packed industrially important towns and cities, a shorter flying time than many other German targets and the fact that it was within range of Oboe. No doubt his intention was eventually to knock out Berlin itself, but he recognised that his Command was not yet ready for that particular task.

The force which Harris commanded was undoubtedly far more powerful than that which he had inherited back in the previous year. In March Bomber Command had almost 600 aircraft and by the end of May this had increased to over 800, the vast majority of which were the newer four-engined bombers.

Of course, the Battle of the Ruhr was spread out over four months and Bomber Command launched numerous raids which were not in the Ruhr area. This was vital if the Germans were not to be able to concentrate their defences around the Ruhr. During this four-month period Bomber Command would mount forty-three major raids, of which approximately two-thirds would be on Ruhr targets. Over the course of the period the crews of Bomber Command would ruefully ascribe the moniker of 'happy valley' to the Ruhr, so often were they to see a Ruhr target marked at briefing. The undertaking of the Battle of the Ruhr was not one which Harris entered into lightly. He was well aware that the defences there were amongst the most ferocious in Germany and that the night-fighter units which his men would face were amongst the most experienced in the Luftwaffe. The Battle of the Ruhr would be a dangerous proposal.

Harris was, despite his earlier misgivings, also placing great hope in the abilities of the Pathfinders to accurately mark the targets in the Ruhr. They had had time to develop their tactics earlier in the year and there was great hope that Oboe would enable the Mosquitos of the Oboe-equipped 109 Squadron (and, later, 105 Squadron) to accurately mark the targets at the beginnings of the raids, but much would still depend upon the heavy bomber Pathfinder squadrons to maintain the marking of targets. The Pathfinders had also learned that casualties could be alleviated to some degree by increasing the numbers of aircraft accompanying the early marker aircraft and thus new Pathfinder crews could expect to fly operations, all carrying high-explosive loads, alongside their more experienced colleagues in the first wave in order to help overwhelm defences. The Pathfinders also received reinforcement during the period with the newly formed 6 (RCAF) Group contributing their 405 squadron to 8 (PFF) Group.

The opening raid of the Battle of the Ruhr saw 442 aircraft take off for Essen (it was also Bomber Command's 100,000th sortie of the war). The raid got off to a bad start when Wellington III (BJ755) of 429 Squadron crashed on take-off at RAF East Moor killing the navigator, Sergeant Ernest Maxwell Bell, RCAF, and injuring the pilot, Flight Sergeant R.F. Conroy, and the other three crewmen. Flight Sergeant Conroy, together with three of his crew from the Essen operation, would be shot down on 11/12 July on an operation to Düsseldorf. Conroy was the only survivor on this occasion and he managed to successfully evade capture and return to Britain.[10]

Another setback occurred when fifty-six aircraft turned back claiming various mechanical defects (this was almost 13 per cent of the total on the raid) including three of the eight Oboe Mosquitoes. The remaining five Mosquitoes marked accurately and on time and the Pathfinder backers-up performed well in reinforcing and maintaining the marking of the centre of

Essen. The Main Force was split into three distinct waves with Halifaxes in the first, Stirlings and Wellingtons in the second wave and Lancasters in the final wave. Some 362 of the aircraft claimed to have bombed on target and subsequent post-raid reconnaissance showed that this had been by far the most successful attack on this elusive target. Fifty-three buildings within the Krupp works were destroyed and over 3,000 houses destroyed. It was assessed that 160 acres of Essen had been destroyed.

In one of the raids away from the Ruhr, Bomber Command followed up the Essen raid with an attack on Nuremberg on the night of 8/9 March. This time 335 aircraft took part in the raid on this distant target, but ground haze once again thwarted the Pathfinders and bombing became stretched over a 10-mile line stretching back from the aiming point. Important damage, however, was done to both the M.A.N. and Siemens factories in the town. Eight of the attacking aircraft were lost from the force. A peculiar tale of tragedy and survival emerged from this raid. The 7 Squadron crew of 23-year-old Sergeant Lionel Louis Victor Toupin found themselves in difficulties as they approached the British coast upon their return from the raid and, possibly because of fuel shortage, Toupin gave the order to abandon the Stirling. The mid-upper gunner, Sergeant D.R. Spanton, did not hear the order and after the Stirling crossed the coast was surprised to discover that he was the only man left on board. The gunner promptly baled out, but the rest of his crew had fallen into the sea and all were drowned. Unfortunately, like so many, this turned out to be a temporary reprieve for Sergeant Spanton was killed when his aircraft crashed into the sea off the Dutch coast while engaged on an operation to Wuppertal on the night of 24/25 July.

This was followed by another long-range attack on the night of 9/10 March when 264 aircraft attacked Munich. Although bombing drifted from the centre of the city there was a great deal of damage done. Bomber Command losses on Munich amounted to eight aircraft.

At RAF Elsham Wolds 103 Squadron was hoping that one of its senior crews might shortly reach the end of their tour and thereby lay something of a jinx in which no crew had successfully completed a tour for several long months. This hope had received a blow when the most senior pilot, Flight Sergeant William Frank Austin DFM, and his crew had been lost without trace on their penultimate operation to Berlin on 1/2 March. This was followed by the loss of another senior crew when Sergeant Alexander Greig and his crew failed to return from Hamburg the next night. Known to his RAF colleagues as Jock, 22-year-old Sergeant Greig was from Aberdeen. He and his crew took off from Elsham aboard Lancaster I (W4788) shortly before 7pm. Along with his regular crew, Sergeant Greig had a second pilot on board on this night (known in RAF terms as a second dickie). Flight Sergeant James Mead (24) was going with Greig in order to gain his first experience of a Bomber Command raid before he would be allowed to take his own crew on operations.

Nothing more was heard of Sergeant Greig and his crew and back at Elsham Wolds the crew were listed as missing. His parents, John and Margaret Esther Greig, were notified of their second son's failure to return from operations at their home, 7 Printfield Terrace, Woodside. It was later revealed that Sergeant Greig's Lancaster crashed at Hohenaspe and all aboard were killed. On 8 March the crew were buried at Hohenaspe and their bodies were later relocated to Kiel War Cemetery.[11]

On the Munich raid the squadron would receive another shattering blow to its morale when the third of its most senior crews failed to return. Flight Sergeant John Victor Roper (19) and his crew had taken off aboard Lancaster I (W4860) but had been shot down near Lavannes, France and all but his navigator were killed. Two of 77 Squadron's Halifaxes at RAF Elvington were lost on the Munich raid. One of them was piloted by Squadron Leader R.J. Sage in Halifax II (DT734, KN-J). He and his crew were forced to turn back after experiencing a glycol leak, but the aircraft was shot down by a night-fighter over Belgium. The rear gunner was killed in the attack, but the remaining crew baled out. Sage, his wireless operator and his mid-upper gunner were captured, but the remaining three crew evaded and returned to Britain.[12]

A common part of night operations now was for numbers of bombers, often Wellingtons or Stirlings, being sent on 'gardening' or other diversionary operations while the Main Force was attacking German targets. On this night, for example, eight Mosquitoes were sent to bomb targets in the Ruhr while sixty-two aircraft were sent to lay mines off the Frisians. Three of the minelaying Wellingtons were lost. Two of them, from 426 and 429 Squadrons, disappeared without trace, while the remaining Wellington III (BK368, AS-P) came from 166 Squadron. The bomber was hit by flak and crashed in Denmark. The pilot, Flight Sergeant John Patrick Kavanagh, RCAF, and three of his crew were killed, but his bomb-aimer, Sergeant J. Sandilands survived despite being unconscious for two days with a head injury.

On the day that Sergeant Greig and his crew were buried, another Aberdonian airman lost his life in a flying accident while training in Britain. Sergeant Alexander Bruce Cowie (20) was an air gunner flying in the rear turret of Wellington IC (X3219) of 21 OTU. The crew of Sergeant Alexander McDougall (a 20-year-old fellow Scot, from Glasgow) had taken off from Moreton-in-Marsh on a night cross-country flight, but the aircraft crashed at 9.25pm. After hitting the ground at Barton St David, Somerset, the Wellington burst into flames and the five-man crew were all killed. Subsequent investigations concluded that the probable cause of the crash was engine failure but, somewhat mysteriously, the debris of the starboard engine was found to contain no less than 50 yards of wire. His parents, Alexander and Annie Guyan, were notified at their home, 12 Fonthill Road, that their son had been killed on active service.

Five days after Bomber Command's offensive against the Ruhr began, the command attacked Stuttgart with 314 aircraft (152 Lancasters, 109 Halifaxes and 53 Stirlings). It was important that locations outside the Ruhr also be attacked so that the Germans could not concentrate their defences. For 405 (RCAF) Squadron it was a bad night with four Halifax bombers failing to return to their base at Topcliffe. Halifax II (W7803, LQ-B) crashed at La Malmaison in France killing all eight men aboard. The navigator in the crew was Pilot Officer William Watson Kirkpatrick, RAFVR. Kirkpatrick (29) was a married man from Edinburgh and was one of four RAF men in this crew. His widow Mary had a moving inscription placed on his headstone in La Malmaison Communal Cemetery: 'HIS MEMORY, TO US A TREASURE; HIS LOSS, A LIFETIME'S REGRET. MARY.'[13] The raid was not a success as the main force was late and bombing was not concentrated.

The Mosquitos of Bomber Command gradually extended their attacks and on 15/16 March sixteen of these remarkable aircraft launched an attack on railway workshops at Paderborn, some 200 miles inland from the coast.

Harris had recognised as soon as he took over Bomber Command that one of the main enemies facing his bombers was poor weather and that in the past errors in the weather forecasts had sometimes resulted in poor bombing or, in some cases, heavy casualties. One idea to ameliorate this problem was to send specialised aircraft and crews to assess weather conditions over Europe before operations were planned. It was hoped that the results of these meteorological flights, combined with more traditional forecasts, would enable Bomber Command to avoid the worst effects of weather. Thus, a specialised unit had been gradually formed as more Mosquitos became available. The Mosquito was the ideal aircraft for this purpose. Its ability to fly at very high altitude at remarkable speeds and at extreme range would, it was hoped, allow it to evade enemy defences, while the two-man crew would allow accurate assessment of weather. Numbered as 1409 Met Flight and based at 8 Group HQ at RAF Wyton, this specialised unit flew its first sortie on 2 April.

On 3/4 April Bomber Command made yet another attack on Essen with 348 aircraft. The weather forecast was far from perfect, but the bombing was well concentrated and widespread damage was again done. On the next night Harris launched what was the largest, non-1,000 force, raid of the war so far when Bomber Command dispatched 577 bombers to attack Kiel. Thick cloud and high winds led to poor marking and decoy fires drew off much of the bombing. Twelve bombers were lost. Amongst the airmen killed on this raid was Squadron Leader the Hon. B Grimston DFC. The 29-year-old pilot was the son of the 4th Earl of Verulam. He was flying Lancaster I (ED615) of 156 Squadron on this raid and the Germans later reported that the aircraft had crashed in the target area, killing all eight men on board.[14]

As the Bomber Command main offensive got underway the list of targets grew. Amongst them were several in Italy. Most of the crews looked forward to these raids with less fear than they did targets in Germany as it was felt that Italian defences were far weaker. However, the distance involved was sobering as was the fact that the bomber stream had to fly over occupied France to reach the target and this exposed crews to the risk of night-fighter attack. Despite being referred to as 'an ice-cream operation' (the ground crews even painted an ice-cream cone instead of the traditional bomb on aircraft which returned from an operation to Italy) a great many aircrew were to lose their lives on such raids. On 13/14 April the target was La Spezia and 103 Squadron at Elsham Wolds contributed several Lancaster bombers to the effort with two failing to return. One of these was a Lancaster I (W4318, pm-G) piloted by Flight Lieutenant E.C. Lee-Brown. After taking off at 8.20pm the crew began the long journey to Italy but while over Le Mans the aircraft crashed with the loss of all seven crew. Amongst them was flight engineer Sergeant George Watson Houliston. The 31-year-old married man was from Edinburgh where he left his parents and his widow, Mary.[15]

Above left: P/O Cyril Joe Barton, VC. (Public Domain)

Above middle: P/O Larry Slatter. Killed on a minelaying sortie. (Gloucestershire Echo)

Above right: P/O T.A. Sheen. Experienced Pathfinder taken prisoner. (Cheshire Observer)

Above left: Sgt Charles McAllister Jarvie (r) with his wireless operator, Sergeant John Wilkinson. Both were killed on the Dam Busters raid.

Above right: F/O Begbie (seated on the left) and crew. (Unknown)

Above left: *Squadron Leader P.A. Haggerty, DFC, killed on operations.* (Evening Chronicle)

Above right: *Sgt Andrew Ridley, killed on operations to Munich.* (Evening Chronicle)

F/O Rodger (2nd from front, behind his pilot). Photographed at RAF Scampton in the days after the dam busters raid. (Public Domain)

Thus far the spring months had been reasonable ones for the command; although there had, of course, been losses these had been counterbalanced by new developments and a string of achievements. Despite the bombing raids the command had also continued with its valuable maritime mining contribution. On the night of 28/29 April, however, came a blow when twenty-two aircraft failed to return from such a sortie. This was the heaviest loss of the war so far by a Bomber Command force engaged on 'gardening' operations.

May opened with a 2 Group daylight attack on a power station near Amsterdam. The operation was carried out by Lockheed Venturas of 487 Squadron on 3 April but demonstrated just how dangerous such missions were over occupied Europe. In a disastrous operation all but one of the eleven Venturas which set out were shot down.

Given Bomber Command was one of the few forces directly hitting back at the Germans it is unsurprising that the force was popular with the public. The Wings for Victory campaigns which were held across Britain raised fortunes for the purchase of aircraft and the maintenance of the RAF, and Bomber Command often had a leading role in the campaigns. On 5 May, for example, the *Shields Evening News* in the North East of England carried on its front page several accounts of bombing raids. One of the main headlines related how 'Bomber Command's Very Heavy Raid on Dortmund' had been undertaken. The report related how visibility was good, aside from ground haze, and that early reports indicated that concentrated bombing had led to heavy damage in the city. The report did admit that thirty of the British bombers had failed to return and were missing. The report then highlighted the industrial importance of Dortmund telling readers that the city of 500,000 people contained several important synthetic oil plants.

The raid had consisted of 596 aircraft in what was the 'largest "non-1,000" raid of the war so far and the first major attack on Dortmund'.[16] In fact some of the backing-up marking by the Pathfinders went astray and a large decoy fire site also fooled several bombers into attacking. Having said that, over 50 per cent of the force did bomb within three miles of the specified aiming point and severe damage was indeed inflicted with more than 1,200 buildings destroyed and twice that number heavily damaged, including several important factories and industrial concerns. At least 693 people were killed in the city (including 200 PoWs). The reporting in the newspaper was fairly accurate although thirty-one bombers had been lost in the attack with a further seven crashing in England due to poor weather.

The Dam Buster Raids – Operation Chastise

While the Battle of the Ruhr was going on, Wing Commander Guy Gibson had been tasked with forming the elite and specialised 617 Squadron for a special operation requiring low flying and using a specially designed bomb (actually a mine) against, what was to him, an unknown but undoubtedly dangerous target. The original intent had been to form the squadron from the best bomber pilots and crews available from 5 Group. Initially, it had been intended to select crews from those who had already completed a tour of operations or who were nearing the completion of their tours. The urgent need for crews, however, soon saw this intention fail and several of the crews were in fact very inexperienced. For at least one member of the aircrew who would take part the operation it would be his first. Clearly this was far from ideal, but Gibson trained his men hard and the vast majority performed very well during the short but intensive training period. It could be argued that the decision to restrict crew selection only to those from 5 Group squadrons was incorrect and smacked of inter-command jealousies. It may well have resulted in a more experienced selection if the crews of the Lancaster-equipped 1 Group had been included (possibly along with members of the Lancaster squadron of 8 Group).

The lack of experience of some who would fly on the Dams Raid was typified by the crew of Vernon Byers. Charles McAllister Jarvie was born in Glasgow in 1922, the son of Charles and Nellie Jarvie. Like many young men of the time he had become fascinated with the RAF and shortly after his eighteenth birthday in July 1940 he joined up. After waiting to be called up he was finally selected for aircrew training in 1942 and underwent training as an air gunner. Having completed his training Sergeant Jarvie joined up with the crew of Sergeant Herbert Vine and in November 1942 the crew were then posted to the Lancasters of 467 Squadron at Bottesford to undertake their first tour of operations with Bomber Command. After flying on five operations with his crew, Sergeant Jarvie and his friend and crewmate Pilot Officer Arthur Whittaker were transferred to the newly arrived crew of Canadian pilot, Pilot Officer Vernon Byers. Sergeant Jarvie then flew another three operations with Byers before the crew were transferred to the newly-formed 617 Squadron.

The arrival of the Byers crew must have come as something of a shock to the commanding officer of 617, Wing Commander Guy Gibson. Pilot Officer Byers had flown just four operations and whilst Sergeant Jarvie and Pilot Officer Whittaker had flown on eight, just three of these had been with Pilot Officer Byers and his crew. They were therefore amongst the least experienced of the crews on the squadron and there must have been considerable doubt over their abilities to cope. No doubt adding to Jarvie's confusion, was the fact that he had flown his previous operations as a mid-upper gunner, but the specialised Lancasters of 617 Squadron had had their mid-upper turrets removed and Jarvie was to fly in the front turret.

The crew, no doubt aware of their inexperience compared to many others on the squadron, seem to have thrown themselves into the training programme with Byers and his crew amassing over fifty hours of daytime practice (compared to a squadron average of 25-40) and 10-15 hours night-flying practice.

On the night of 16/17 May the training was over for 617 Squadron. The crews, briefed earlier in the day amidst great secrecy, now knew their targets were several dams in the Ruhr and that, if they succeeded, the raid which they were about to set out on would make headlines across the world. They were also keenly aware that the mission was extremely dangerous requiring incredible flying skills along with superb navigation and bombing accuracy. On the face of it, flying at night at extremely low level into the heart of the German defences to carry out an innovative attack with an untried weapon must have seemed to many, Harris included, the height of folly and, in many ways, a disaster waiting to happen. Nevertheless, nineteen specially adapted Lancasters from 617 Squadron took off in waves from RAF Scampton and set course to make history.

The first wave, led by Gibson, successfully crossed the coast, but the second wave ran into trouble immediately. First, the Lancaster of New Zealander Flight Lieutenant Les Munro was hit by flak off the coast and too badly damaged to continue. Meanwhile another Lancaster, piloted by Flying Officer Geoff Rice, had struck the sea and had its mine wrenched off. Miraculously, Rice maintained control and staggered back to RAF Scampton. Shortly afterwards Pilot Officer Vernon W. Byers and his crew were shot down. The formation suffered another loss when Pilot Officer Barlow's Lancaster hit high-tension wires and crashed in flames. These losses spelt disaster for the proposed attack on the Sorpe dam with only the Lancaster of American Flight Lieutenant Joe McCarthy making it to its target from the second wave. McCarthy and his crew had taken off late after their original aircraft had proven unserviceable. Ken Brown's was the only other crew to drop a mine on the Sorpe.

The first wave had encountered flak as it passed over Dulmen and the Lancaster of Flight Lieutenant John Hopgood DFC and Bar, was damaged and at least one of his crew, and possibly Hopgood himself, wounded. The second three aircraft of this wave also ran into trouble here and Flight Lieutenant William Astell and his crew were killed when their Lancaster hit high-tension wires and crashed.

Arriving over the Mohne Dam, Gibson made the first attack. His mine exploded but the dam wall remained intact. He then called in Hopgood to make his attack. Aboard the damaged Lancaster, Hopgood and his crew roared towards the dam in the face of heavy anti-aircraft fire. AJ-M was hit in both wings and the port wing caught fire. The Upkeep mine was dropped seconds too late and cleared the dam wall, detonating underneath the stricken Lancaster. Hopgood fought desperately to gain height to allow his crew to bale out. His rear gunner and bomb-aimer managed to bale out and the injured wireless operator was also pushed out. Only the gunner and bomb-aimer survived from AJ-M; the Lancaster made it to 500 feet before the wing came off and the bomber crashed. Martin aboard AJ-P then attacked, while Gibson flew across the dam to try to draw off fire. AJ-P was hit but not seriously damaged and the mine appeared to be on target.

The next Lancaster to attack was AJ-A piloted by Squadron Leader Young. Martin in AJ-P flew alongside him firing at the flak positions while Gibson turned on his lights and again flew across the dam. Once more the mine was dropped accurately and, it was thought, damaged the dam. The fifth attack was made by Flight Lieutenant Maltby in AJ-J. Once again Martin, this time joined by Gibson, flew alongside him. An accurate attack was made and a massive plume of mud, stone and water erupted into the night sky. Gibson called in the next aircraft but, as he did so, the dam wall collapsed as a massive breach appeared in it. The Lancasters circled for a short time observing the incredible sight of the water pouring down the valley.

Gibson then led the remaining Lancasters of the first wave to the Eder reservoir. There, after several initial abortive attempts by Flight Lieutenant David Shannon and Squadron Leader Henry Maudslay, Shannon successfully dropped his mine, but with no noticeable effect on the dam. Maudslay then made another attempt but the mine was dropped too late and hit the lip of the dam wall and exploded while the Lancaster was directly overhead. It was believed at the time that this had caused Maudslay to crash, but in fact his Lancaster had been badly damaged by the blast and he was struggling to get home. Shortly after 2.30am, however, Maudslay's Lancaster III (ED937, AJ-Z) was hit by flak over Emmerich and crashed killing all aboard. Back at the Eder Flight Lieutenant Les Knight in AJ-N made his attack. Knight's crew made a well-executed and highly accurate attack and the dam wall collapsed.

On the afternoon of 16 May Byers and his crew were briefed for the raid on the dams and found that they would form part of the second wave which was to attack the Sorpe Dam (using a technique they had never practised). Along with them in this wave were some experienced pilots, but the second wave also included the very inexperienced pilots Rice and Byers. Although these two crews were 'very under-experienced, [they] had done well enough during training'.[17]

That night, Byers and his crew climbed aboard their Lancaster (AJ-K 'King'). Taking off shortly before 9.30pm the crew set course, unaware that the meteorological forecast they had been given was incorrect. An un-forecast wind blew the Lancaster off-course and the crew found themselves to the south of where they should have been. We shall never know for certain, but it appears that the crew realised they were off-course and, at approximately 11pm, climbed to 300 feet to ascertain their position. Unfortunately, their course took them over the heavily defended island of Texel and the Lancaster was quickly hit by anti-aircraft fire plummeting into the sea ablaze, killing all seven men aboard, including Pilot Officer Byers and Sergeant Jarvie.[18]

Of the third, reserve wave AJ-C under the control of Pilot Officer Warner Ottley was hit by light flak. The rear gunner, Sergeant Fred Tees, heard his skipper say 'I'm sorry boys they got us', as the Lancaster plunged to the ground. The bomber exploded when it hit the ground, but Tees was miraculously thrown clear and survived. AJ-S flown by Pilot Officer L.J. Burpee DFC, RCAF, had drifted off-track and flew over a night-fighter base. Burpee was apparently blinded by searchlights and flew into trees causing the Lancaster to crash with total loss of life.

The remaining three crews of the reserve wave were ordered to other targets, but their attacks were unsuccessful. As the Lancasters made their way home the aircraft of Squadron Leader H.M. Young DFC and Bar, was hit by flak while it was crossing the Dutch coast and the Lancaster crashed into the sea killing everyone on board.

The Dams raid was over and 617 Squadron had pulled off a remarkable feat in destroying two of their three main targets. The details made available to the press and public resulted in a massive reaction with the public imagination being fired by the sheer daring of the raids' accomplishments. The attack, however, had come at a terrible cost with eight of the nineteen Lancasters failing to return to RAF Scampton. Although some have questioned the military value of the attacks, it cannot be denied that the success of what became known as the Dam Busters provided a huge boost to morale in Britain and abroad in the USA. Furthermore, the Mohne reservoir contained almost 140 million tons of water and was a key source of supply for the vital industries of the Ruhr. The water which was released as a result of the raid resulted in widespread flooding which caused devastation. Communications and the supply of electricity were badly affected across a wide area, while mine-workings and factories were ruined or badly damaged by the flooding. The Eder was an even larger reservoir than the Mohne but was further away from the Ruhr than the Mohne. The Eder, however, was a key supply source for the city of Kassel and that city and its hinterlands were badly affected for some time.

One of the criticisms of the raid was that the aircraft which had been allocated to the Eder Dam should instead have been directed to attack the Sorpe (which was more closely connected to the Ruhr) but this ignores the fact that Barnes Wallis had informed Bomber Command that the earthen construction of the Sorpe would be more resistant to his mine. Another criticism has been over the command and control exercised by Gibson. Once again this ignores many of the realities of the situation. Some have questioned why Gibson chose Hopgood as second in command on the raid instead of one of his flight commanders. This is possibly justified to a certain extent, but it probably reflected the trust that Gibson had in Hopgood. After all, Hopgood had come from Gibson's old squadron and the two had known each other for some time and had flown on several special operations together. Nevertheless, it did ignore the fact that Hopgood's crew were relative unknowns to one another and had not been amongst the best performers in training.

This criticism leads on to another that has been levelled at Gibson's decision making during the raid. That is the decision to have Squadron Leader Young continue on to the Eder even though he had already dropped his mine at the Mohne. This action did result in the death of Young and his crew, but this could certainly not have been foreseen. In all likelihood, following the death of Hopgood, and being unaware of whether or not there would be anti-aircraft guns defending the Eder, Gibson merely wanted one of the squadron's leadership present to take over the operation in the event of Gibson himself being shot down or otherwise being unable to exercise control. Young's death, along with his crew, was simply one of those tragic turns of fate in the bomber war.

The crews of 617 had performed admirably considering the short period of training which they had been afforded and the lack of experience which some possessed. Gibson, however, could be particularly unforgiving of error, or what he perceived as error. Immediately after the raid he asked the pilots who had returned early the reasons for aborting the operation. Flight Lieutenant Munro was particularly rankled when Gibson merely commented that he must have been flying too high. This was, in all likelihood, unfair and it was mere misfortune which had seen Munro's intercom knocked out by a lucky hit. Gibson was more forgiving of Geoff Rice, probably in the knowledge that he had almost done a similar thing himself during training. It was simply part of Gibson's character to, at times, be extremely judgemental.

A complex character, Gibson could be an extremely harsh taskmaster, someone who was determined to have his own way and he could be a snob when it came to rank. Many of the NCOs on 617 Squadron could recall that Gibson never bothered with them, saving his time for the officers. As the crews trained feverishly there came a blow when Squadron Leader Young reported that Flight Sergeant George Lancaster's navigator, Flight Sergeant Cleveland, was not performing adequately. Gibson was away at the time but, when he returned, he immediately sacked the unfortunate navigator. Lancaster, a Canadian who had come from 57 Squadron, complained, telling Gibson that if the navigator went the rest of the crew would follow. Gibson was not the type to back down and Lancaster and his crew were posted back to 57 Squadron. This was unfortunate because Lancaster's bomb-aimer, Flight Sergeant Clifford, had proved himself the most accurate on the squadron. It is not known how hard Gibson might have attempted to urge Lancaster and his crew to accept his decision regarding their navigator. There were certainly arguments on both sides. Accurate navigation, as was to be proven later, was an absolute necessity so a navigator who was underperforming or was not up to the task was an exceptionally dangerous liability and a risk to both his crew's survival and the success of the operation. On the other hand, many crews were notoriously faithful to each other and Gibson must have known, or at least suspected, that Lancaster's reaction would be to side with his navigator and the accuracy of Lancaster's bomb aimer was a factor which should also have been taken into account.

We have already seen how dangerous daylight attacks could prove and on 27 May fourteen Mosquitos from 105 and 109 Squadrons mounted an attack on the Jena Zeiss optical factories and suffered the loss of five aircraft. Just days after this attack 2 Group made what was to be its last operation as part of Bomber Command before it departed for the 2nd Tactical Air Force (TAF) which was to fly operations in preparation for D-Day.

When a Bomber Command airman had completed his first tour of operations, he could usually rely on a period of rest for a minimum of six months which was often spent as an instructor at an OTU or Heavy Conversion Unit (HCU). After this they could be recalled for a further tour of operations – a daunting prospect. Many who had completed a tour of operations lost their lives in flying accidents whilst training others or signed on for a second tour and were subsequently killed. Pilot Officer Albert Edward Gray was a 22-year-old wireless operator/air gunner from Whitley Bay, Northumberland. He had flown his first tour in 1941 with 83 Squadron completing thirty-two operations including two to Berlin. On one operation he and his crew had sunk a 7,000-ton enemy ship off the Frisian Isles, whilst on another occasion the navigator's equipment had been lost due to enemy action and the then Sergeant Gray had been responsible for navigating the aircraft home using his visual loop indicator. He had enjoyed a high reputation on the squadron and had been important in helping to instruct new wireless operators on the squadron. For his actions Sergeant Gray was awarded the DFM in October 1941.

By June 1943 he was assigned to 515 Squadron which was engaged on highly secret operations to attempt to jam German radar. The squadron was equipped with the obsolete Boulton-Paul Defiant as an interim measure. On 8 June Pilot Officer Gray was flying in Defiant II (AA435) when the pilot became disorientated in foggy conditions and crashed into the cliffs at Beachy Head, killing both himself and Pilot Officer Gray. He is buried in Hartley (South) Cemetery, Whitley Bay, where his headstone bears the poignant inscription:

'We sing his songs
And miss his love.
Now he is safe
With God above.
Dad and all.'[19]

On 20/21 June Bomber Command launched another innovative attack when sixty Lancasters took off from Britain to attack the Zeppelin works at Friedrichshafen before flying on to North Africa to Allied air bases. This was the first of what were to become known as shuttle raids. Two nights later the Lancasters returned to Britain after bombing La Spezia on their way home.

The following night the weary crews of Bomber Command were briefed for an attack on the Ruhr town of Krefeld. The plan was to send 705 aircraft (made up of Lancasters, Halifaxes, Stirlings, Wellingtons and Mosquitos) but for the men being briefed there was a greater degree of concern as they were aware that the full moon period (during which they usually did not operate) was not finished and they feared greater exposure to the enemy night fighters in such conditions. The sky was clear when the bombers reached Krefeld and a very concentrated raid developed resulting in severe damage to the city centre. The cost, as the aircrew anticipated, was high with forty-four aircraft (6.2 per cent of the force) being lost. Amongst them was Stirling III (BK815, LS-V) of 15 Squadron. This aircraft had taken off from Oakington shortly before midnight but failed to return and it was later revealed that it had been shot down by anti-aircraft fire over Belgium. Seven of the eight men who were aboard were killed, with only the mid-upper gunner surviving to be taken prisoner. The crew, skippered by Pilot Officer E.F. Curtis, had an inexperienced pilot along with them to gain experience of operations; this was Flight Sergeant Francis Dennis McQuillan. A native of Gosforth, Northumberland, Flight Sergeant McQuillan was just 21 when he was killed, leaving behind his mother, Margaret.[20]

With Bomber Command having managed to gain the upper hand in the technological bombing war in recent months, the Luftwaffe came up with new tactics to destroy enemy bombers at night. One of these was the use of single-engined fighter aircraft as night-fighters over the targets of raids. The technique, known in the Luftwaffe as Wild Boar, was first used over Cologne during a raid on 3/4 July. Proposed by Major Hajo Hermann, the technique called for both skill and courage as the single-engined fighters were not designed to be flown or landed at night and the pilots had to co-ordinate their activities with the searchlight and anti-aircraft defences over targets while making effective attacks on enemy bombers.

On 12/13 July Bomber Command suffered a blow when Wing Commander John Nettleton, VC, failed to return from an operation to Turin.

Alongside the accounts of bombing raids in local and national newspapers were the publication of local casualties sustained during them. This demonstrated that the bombing war was very dangerous and increased the respect most people had for the men of Bomber Command. Given the nature of bomber operations it sometimes took a great deal of time to provide any clarity to anxious relatives who had received a bald telegram notifying them that a loved one was missing after an operation. The family of Mr and Mrs W. Armstrong of Woodhorn Road, Ashington, Northumberland faced a wait of several months after their 21-year-old son, Chester, was posted missing following a raid on 13/14 July. It was not until December that they received word that their son was now 'believed to have lost his life as a result of air operations'. Flying as navigator in a Lancaster II of 115 Squadron, based at RAF East Wretham, Pilot Officer Armstrong had taken off just after midnight for a raid on the town of Aachen. The Lancaster (DS660 KO-P) was shot down over France by a night-fighter and crashed in the Pas-de-Calais. Six of the seven-man crew of Flying Officer R.B. Larson, RCAF, were killed with only the pilot surviving.[21]

P/O Armstrong had been educated at Bedlington Secondary School, Bede College and St John's, York and had been going on to a career as a teacher before volunteering for aircrew duties.

At least one other airman from the same area of south-east Northumberland lost his life on this raid; 19-year-old Sergeant John Foggon of Blyth was the flight engineer in a Halifax II (DT769 EQ-J) of 408 (Moose) Squadron, RCAF, based at RAF Leeming. Shot down by the night-fighter of Leutnant Rolf Bussmann of Nachtjagdgeschwader I, five of the Halifax crew were killed whilst the navigator and air bomber became prisoners of war.[22]

At last, the authorities had given their permission for Bomber Command to pioneer the use of the anti-radar technology known by the codename Window. Harris resolved to use what he hoped would be an effective device to disrupt enemy defences to launch a concerted attack on a single target over a number of nights in order to, once again, prove what the now mightier Bomber Command could do if given the opportunity. The target he chose was Hamburg.

On the night of 16/17 August came the final RAF Bomber Command raid on Italy when 154 bombers attacked Turin. Although a concentrated raid was reported (this is doubtful as there were only five people killed in Turin) there were four bombers which failed to return from the attack. Amongst them was Halifax II (HR880, TL-K) of 35 Squadron. The experienced pathfinder crew of Squadron Leader Patrick Archibald Haggarty DFC, had taken off from Graveley shortly after 8pm but failed to return to base and it was subsequently reported that the bomber had been shot down in the Milan area. Five of the crew had been killed in the crashing aircraft but the navigator (Flight Lieutenant R.D. Ferguson) and the wireless operator (Sergeant R.L. Hooper) had successfully escaped from the bomber and were taken prisoner.[23] Squadron Leader Haggarty, however, was dead. Aged 29, Haggarty was a native of Heaton, Newcastle, where his parents, Thomas and Janet, lived at 40 Heaton Road. Tragically, the announcement of the award of his DFC was published in the press the day after he had been killed.

Two days before he set out on his fatal mission Squadron Leader Haggerty had managed to speak to his father, a dentist, on the telephone and had confirmed the news of his DFC which his father had been told of in advance. The modest officer had refused to talk about the circumstances of his award merely telling his father that it had been 'a piece of cake'.[24] Squadron Leader Haggerty had joined the RAF in the summer of 1939, qualified as a pilot in 1940 and flown several operations during that year before he was posted, because of his ability, to Canada as an instructor under the new Empire Air Training Scheme. After spending a year as an instructor, he had been brought back to Britain and had volunteered for front-line duties once more. He also had a younger brother, John, who was a leading aircraftman in the RAF.

On the night following the Turin raid came one of the most interesting and specialised attacks made by Bomber Command during the war. The rocket weapon development site on the Baltic island of Peenemunde was attacked by 596 aircraft in three distinct waves and with three distinct aiming points. The raid also saw the first use of a master bomber – a specially selected pilot and crew who, along with a deputy, would be responsible for guiding the Main Force and ensuring that the target was correctly marked and that, on this night, the aiming points were effectively moved at varying stages of the raid. It also saw 5 Group attempt to use its own bombing technique.

Forty aircraft were lost but this was considered acceptable given the importance of the target. RAF Wickenby-based 12 Squadron lost just one aircraft: Lancaster III (DV168, PH-F) flown by Squadron Leader Fraser Burstock Slade DSO, a Glaswegian. The Lancaster was shot down by a night-fighter and all seven crewmen were killed when it crashed into the sea off Denmark. The wireless operator was an Edinburgh man, Pilot Officer John Francis Bell MacIntyre (21). He is commemorated, along with the rest of the crew, on the Runnymede Memorial.

The opening of the attack went well but by the time the bombers of 5 and 6 Groups had arrived at the end of the raid, resistance had stiffened and casualties were disproportionately large in these groups. For 49 Squadron at Fiskerton the night was a poor one with four Lancasters failing to return from the twelve which it had sent. Amongst these was that of one of the flight commanders. The experienced Squadron Leader R.N. Todd-White and his crew had taken off shortly before 10pm aboard Lancaster III (ED805) on what was the second operation of their second tour. It became the sixteenth bomber to be shot down, crashing into the Baltic killing the entire seven-man crew. The mid-upper gunner was 19-year-old Geordie Sergeant George Humble. His parents, George and Margaret, were told of their son's death at their Newcastle home and afterwards were informed that his body had been recovered from the sea and was buried at Poznan Old Garrison Cemetery. Sergeant Humble had been a keen member of 5th Newcastle Boys' Brigade and his grieving parents had the motto of this group placed on his headstone.[25]

We have already seen how the Wings for Victory campaigns helped to support Bomber Command's war effort. Part of the success of the campaign lay in the fact that the RAF was seen as the most glamorous of the services, carried a certain mystique and had bolstered this with its performance in the fateful summer of 1940. Service with the RAF possessed a certain glamour for many young men and women, especially after the Battle of Britain had made heroes of the pilots of Fighter Command. Flying itself was still viewed with a certain mystique and many preferred to serve in the RAF rather than what they viewed as the miserable and, at times, boring life in the Army. However, the majority of men who passed the stringent medical required for duties as aircrew found themselves not as pilots, and certainly not as fighter pilots, but were instead trained for other aircrew roles such as gunners or navigators and were posted to Bomber Command (or Coastal Command) which was, from 1942, engaged upon its grand offensive designed to crush Germany.

Amongst those who had joined the RAF were two brothers from North Shields in Northumberland. The Goulden family was well-known in local sporting circles with Mr Thomas C. Goulden being the groundskeeper for Tynemouth Cricket Club and his eldest son, Thomas, the opening batsman for the club as well as playing for Northumberland. He was also a good rugby player who played at stand-off half for Percy Park and, again, represented the county in the sport. At the outbreak of the war he had decided to give up his engineering job and join the RAF. A younger son, Donald, had also joined the RAF and was flying as an air gunner with Bomber Command. By the time of the Peenemunde operation Donald knew that his eldest brother had been posted missing.[26]

Amongst the Halifax force despatched was the 10 Squadron Halifax II (JD200, ZA-S) of Flight Sergeant A.J.E. Long, one of eighteen aircraft sent by the squadron that night; the mid-upper gunner was Sergeant Donald Goulden. Taking off from RAF Melbourne just after 9pm, nothing further was heard from the aircraft or its crew and it failed to return to base. It seems probable that the aircraft was the thirty-ninth to be shot down over Peenemunde and its eight-man crew (the crew were carrying an inexperienced second-pilot to give him his first operational experience) were all killed. The Long crew had an average age of just 23 and had already flown eight operations.[27]

Once again the Goulden family received a telegram informing them that another son had been posted missing whilst involved in aerial operations; the second in just over three months. The family would receive little comfort as neither brother's body was found and they are both commemorated on the Runnymede Memorial to the missing.

At least one other Newcastle airman lost his life on 17 August. Sergeant Leonard Alan Bell (20) was an under-training navigator based at 4 Observer Advanced Flying Unit at West Freugh in Wigtownshire. At approximately 9.40pm on 16 August Sergeant Bell had taken off along with four other airmen aboard Avro Anson I (DG755) for a night navigation and bombing exercise. After completing the exercise, the Anson came into land but aborted and overshot to go around again. Shortly afterwards, however, the aircraft stalled and crashed to the ground at 12.50am killing three of the crew, including Sergeant Bell, instantly and mortally injuring the remaining two.[28]

After the Battles of the Ruhr and Hamburg the popular press were stoking public enthusiasm for a committed campaign against Berlin. Harris too, was eager for a campaign against the German capital and he believed that Bomber Command, aided by the USAAF Eighth Air Force, could wreck Berlin and that this would force the Germans to sue for peace. However, he also knew that Berlin was a difficult target to attack. It was a huge and modern city which lay at extreme range and was very heavily defended. Thus, Harris determined to feel his way gradually towards a Battle of Berlin. The first step took place on the night of 23/24 August when 727 aircraft were sent to the capital.

On the night of 31 August and early hours of 1 September the raid on Berlin saw the Luftwaffe use fighter flares to illuminate the air over the target for the first time. The Stirlings of Bomber Command had been struggling against heavy losses for some time and on this night the Stirling force suffered a 16 per cent loss rate.

As Bomber Command built its strength for the Battle of Berlin which was to take place over the winter, raids were still maintained, although in many cases with smaller forces. On 6/7 September a force of 257 Lancasters and 147 Halifaxes took off bound for the distant target of Munich. Amongst them was Halifax II (JB921, DY-B) of 102 Squadron based at Pocklington. The mid-upper gunner in the crew was Sergeant Andrew Ridley (21), the son of Joseph and Grace Ridley of 165 Sutton Dwellings, Barrack Road, Newcastle. It appears the crew fell victim to a night fighter attack as one of the four survivors from the crew reported that everything was normal until the fuel tanks suddenly burst into flames.[29] As on most occasions this airman was originally posted as missing and it was not until November that his parents were informed that their son was believed to have been killed.

Yet another first was reached on 15/16 September when Lancasters of 617 Squadron dropped the first 12,000lb bombs of the war during an attack by eight bombers on the Dortmund-Ems Canal. This was one of two precision attacks on this night. When they reached the target area they found it was shrouded in mist and defended by light flak batteries. Only three aircraft returned to Coningsby. One of the Lancasters which was shot down by light flak, was that of Flight Lieutenant H.S. Wilson (JA898, KC-X). Wilson's navigator was Edinburgh-born Flying Officer James Alexander Rodger. A 32-year-old married man, Rodger left behind his widow, Muriel, in Edinburgh, where they lived at 56 Cowan Road.[30] The crew had been trained for the Dam Busters raid but had missed out as one of the crew was ill on the night of the operation.

In the second raid, 369 aircraft (209 Halifaxes, 120 Stirlings, 40 Lancasters, and 5 American B-17s) were tasked with bombing the Dunlop rubber factory at Montluçon in central France. The raid was unusual not only in the fact that it was against a single factory, but it was flown in moonlight conditions (bombers were generally stood down during full-moon periods) and involved control by an appointed master bomber (in this case Wing Commander E. Deane DFC). The raid was reported by returning crews to have been successful. Only three aircraft were lost from the force. Amongst them were two Halifaxes, one of which was a 427 RCAF Squadron Halifax V (DK253, ZL-M) piloted by Sergeant A. Chibanoff, RCAF. After taking off from Leeming at 8.30pm nothing more was heard, but it is clear that the aircraft reached the target. In the early hours of 16 September, the people of Harmondsworth heard an aircraft passing low overhead. It was ZL-M and reported by observers to be experiencing control difficulties. It appears that the Halifax may have had a hang up of some of its bombs as there were reports of bombs being jettisoned, but these remain unconfirmed. It is also possible that the stricken bomber was attempting to land at what was then London Airport (now Heathrow). At 2.50am the Halifax crashed at high speed near the River Colne, bouncing 25 feet back into the air, disintegrating as it went. The engines travelled for a quarter of a mile after the impact while the fuselage disintegrated and exploded on Middle Moor. All seven of the crew were killed instantly. The bomb aimer was Flying Officer Kendall Bell Begbie, RCAF. Aged 26, Begbie had come from Riverside, Ontario, to take part in the war effort. His parents were from Edinburgh and like many Scots had emigrated to Canada to secure a better future. Begbie was a married man and still had family in Edinburgh, as a notice in *The Scotsman,* placed by Begbie's uncle, showed. The Canadian's body was taken to Edinburgh (Warriston) Crematorium and over 300 people attended a service for the crew held at the crash site.[31]

The raid of October 8/9 was the last one in which Wellingtons took part. This remarkable and adaptable aircraft had taken part in the war from the very first and had made a massive contribution to the bomber offensive.

Bomber Command had been ordered by Sir Arthur Harris to prepare for its next major campaign, against the German capital, Berlin. In the build-up to this the pressure had to be maintained on other German city targets and there was a series of heavy raids throughout September, October and November. Three of these were on Berlin, with others on Munich, Hanover and Stuttgart amongst others. The crews of 8th Group (Pathfinders) led the way to these targets and their duties, aside from bombing, were to drop marker and illumination flares to guide the main force to the target area. Theirs was an incredibly dangerous job as they were often amongst the first over the target and they had to fly a longer operational tour than those of the main force (forty-five operations compared to thirty).

Flying the reliable Avro Lancaster, 97 Squadron, based at Bourn, had joined the Pathfinders in April. Amongst its most reliable crews over that summer was that of Flight Lieutenant Duncan McNaught Moodie DFM,

RCAF. Moodie was born in 1916 in Shanghai but his boyhood home had been Edinburgh and his parents still lived in the city. After education at Edinburgh Academy[32] he went on to a career at the Leith shipowners C. Salvesen & Co for five years, followed by a move to the firm of Hadden & Co, shipbrokers, Batavia. He joined the RCAF in 1941 and by 1942 was a pilot officer. Volunteering for Pathfinder duty, Moodie quickly established a reliable reputation on the squadron including one very 'dicey' operation to Hamburg on the night of 27/28 July (the firestorm raid) when his aircraft was coned by searchlights before being attacked by a night-fighter. Having evaded these attacks, the bombs were dropped on target and the navigator, Flight Sergeant J.T. Bundle DFM, plotted a new course back to base. On the night of 2/3 August the crew were again attacking Hamburg when heavy icing made control of the Lancaster difficult. Moodie, however, struggled on and successfully bombed the target before returning home.

Shortly after 5.30pm on 18 October, Moodie and his crew set out on a raid to Hanover. This was the fourth time they had been sent to this target (they had been forced to abort one operation due to an oxygen failure). On this night they were part of a force of 360 Lancasters. The sky over the target was cloudy and the Pathfinders were unable to mark the target resulting in the raid being scattered, with most bombs falling in open country to the north of the city. Eighteen Lancasters failed to return including Lancaster III (JB220, OF-O) of 97 Squadron. The pilot, Flight Lieutenant Donald M. Moodie, and his crew had crashed near Nienburg on the bank of the River Weser at Erichshagen. Six of the seven-man crew had been killed, with the only survivor being the bomb aimer Flight Sergeant H.W.N. Clausen DFM. A postscript to the loss of this crew was that, after the first operation to Hamburg, Moodie had been recommended for the DFC while his navigator and his bomb aimer had been recommended for the DFM. These awards were subsequently promulgated in November. Moodie's citation stated that he was the 'captain of a most reliable and capable crew'.[33] Flight Lieutenant Moodie and those who were killed were buried at Becklingen War Cemetery.[34]

Such was the cost of building a modern four-engined bomber that every care was taken to ensure that damaged aircraft which might be salvaged were repaired and sent back into action. Even quite heavily damaged bombers could be repaired and sent back to fight once again. With the public donating huge amounts of money to pay for the cost of new bombers and the expansion of Bomber Command, the press was co-opted to inform readers of the determination not to waste any of the precious aircraft. In October

The Sphere and other journals and newspapers ran stories describing the salvage efforts which went into repairing damaged bombers. The article in *The Sphere* recounted the story of Lancaster T for Tilly. The Lancaster had returned from a raid badly damaged and had crash-landed. The damage consisted of a smashed undercarriage, broken propellers and one engine burnt out. Readers were told how the bomber was taken to pieces, then moved to a specialised repair facility before being restored to airworthiness and sent back to a front-line squadron to carry on with the war.

At the end of October Mr and Mrs Richard Gray of 37 Third Row, Linton Colliery, Morpeth, Northumberland, received confirmation that their son William, who had been posted missing after an operation in May, was now listed as missing believed killed in action. William Dixon Gray had been a good pupil at Linton Council School and had earned himself a scholarship to attend Morpeth Grammar School where he spent five years. After leaving school he obtained work in the office at Linton Colliery but joined up shortly after the war began. Volunteering for aircrew duty, William was selected for navigational training and was sent to the USA and Canada to complete the majority of his aircrew navigator training syllabus. Aged 20 in 1943 Sergeant William Dixon Gray was posted to 35 (Madras Presidency) Squadron at RAF Gravely as navigator in the crew of Sergeant A.R. Sargent. This squadron was a member of 8th (Pathfinder) Group and was responsible for leading bombing raids and marking targets with flares; as such they were exposed to even greater danger at times.

On the night of 29 May Sergeant Sargent's crew had taken off from Gravely in their Halifax II (W7876, TL-K) tasked with a raid on Wuppertal. The raid was a part of the Battle of the Ruhr and W7876 was one of 719 aircraft from Bomber Command to take part in the operation. The raid has been called 'the outstanding success of the Battle of the Ruhr' with huge amounts of damage being caused and a small firestorm developing in the town. Approximately 1,000 acres of the old centre of the town were burnt out, over 80 per cent of the town's major industrial concerns were destroyed whilst 211 smaller industrial premises were also destroyed and an estimated 3,400 people killed. Losses for Bomber Command were thirty-three aircraft including ten Halifaxes of which W7876 was one. It later transpired that Sergeant Sargent's crew had been shot down in the early hours by a night-fighter. Fortunately, five of the crew managed to escape the bomber to be taken prisoner, but Sergeant Gray and the crew's rear gunner Flight Sergeant Colin Henry Garner were killed.[35]

With the technological battle swinging to and fro, November 3/4 saw yet another development when a raid on Düsseldorf by Lancasters of 3 and 6 (RCAF) Groups saw the use of G-H for the first time.

The first raid in the main phase of the Battle of Berlin was launched on the night of 18/19 November and consisted of a force of 440 Lancasters and 4 Mosquitoes whilst a diversionary raid by 248 Halifaxes, 114 Stirlings and 33 Lancasters was made on Mannheim/Ludwigshafen. Weather over the target was poor and although a large number of bombs fell on the German capital, the raid was scattered over the vast city and there was no concentration of bombing. Amongst the nine Lancasters to be lost on the operation was the 9 Squadron Lancaster III| (DV284, WS-G) piloted by Pilot Officer G.A. Graham, RCAF. The wireless operator/air gunner in this crew was 20-year-old Sergeant Arthur Fenwick Williamson from Northumberland Terrace, Tynemouth. The Lancaster was shot down by anti-aircraft fire and crashed shortly before 10pm at Burgwerben killing all eight crewmen who were subsequently buried at the Berlin 1939-1945 War Cemetery.[36]

With Wellingtons already having been withdrawn from the front-line strength of Bomber Command, the Stirling casualties continued to escalate and Harris took the decision to withdraw the type from Main Force operations over Germany and so the first of the RAF four-engined bombers was reduced to secondary status. The final raid over Germany involving Stirlings took place on the night of 22/23 November in an attack on Berlin.

On the night of 4/5 December Stirling III (LK387, IC-P) took off from RAF Downham Market on a 'gardening' operation to the Frisians. The crew was captained by Pilot Officer N.J. Keech, RAAF, but the aircraft failed to return to base and it was later assumed that it had been shot down by a night fighter over the Waddenzee. The crew were all reported as being missing believed killed. It was particularly tragic that the crew be lost on this night as it was the last operation by 623 Squadron. The squadron was disbanded the next day.[37]

In response to the growing ability of the German night-fighters to penetrate the bomber stream and amidst rising casualties, the Mosquitos and Beaufighters of 141 Squadron were used for the first time as intruders, with orders to intercept enemy night-fighters along the route of the bomber stream. In doing so they were able to use the Serrate device to home in on the radar emissions of the enemy night-fighters during the Berlin raid of 16/17 December.

CHAPTER 6

1944 – A Year of Changes

Summary of the Year

As the Battle of Berlin continued to take a heavy toll of Bomber Command, Harris continued determinedly with the offensive. Morale amongst the crews of Bomber Command was being maintained but, in some squadrons which had suffered particularly heavy losses morale was, undoubtedly, beginning to suffer. The year began badly with heavy losses on several Berlin operations and towards the end of January the greatest loss of the war on a single raid was inflicted upon the command when 62 aircraft failed to return from a raid on Magdeburg.

Harris was increasingly desperate to prove his theory regarding strategic bombing as he was aware that his command over his force was shortly to be curtailed as the demands of the forthcoming invasion of Normandy took priority and Bomber Command was increasingly asked to attack targets which were on the Transportation Plan designed to isolate the landing area so that German reinforcements could not reach the beachhead. This effort to prove the worth of strategic bombing and the increasingly heavy losses of raids in this period culminated in the disastrous Nuremburg Raid of 30/31 March which saw a force of 795 bombers savaged by night fighters under a full moon and 95 of the bombers shot down.

The command also increasingly focused on precision targets during this year. The commanding officer of 5 Group, Air Vice Marshal Cochrane, had for some time been agitating for permission for his Group to operate semi-independently, attacking more precision and hard to hit targets, using its own target marking force. To this end, 617 Squadron had been experimenting with a variety of low and high-level marking techniques. Wing Commander Leonard Cheshire was a particular exponent of the low-level marking technique and over the course of a series of raids this method was perfected, first using Lancasters, then Mosquitoes and, finally, Mustang fighter aircraft. Following the successful demonstration of these techniques, including in an attack on an aircraft factory at Toulouse on 5/6 April, Harris gave Cochrane the permission he sought.

This was probably, in retrospect, a wise decision but it did cause a great deal of resentment. The 8 (PFF) Group squadrons which had originated in 5 Group were transferred back and a great deal of rivalry and resentment built up between the two Groups. Other main force Group crews simply saw this as further proof that 5 Group and its crews were the favoured sons of Bomber Command HQ at High Wycombe.

Many of the precision targets attacked during this period fell into three categories. The first was those targets on the Transportation Plan list (most often railway and marshalling yards but also canals and other transport hubs). The second was a response to the flying-bomb campaign being mounted against London and southern England. The third type of operation was targeted against tactical targets that would impact upon the D-Day invasion. Many of these targets were in France and the crews, by and large, welcomed the shorter flights over targets which were generally less well defended than the German cities that they were used to flying over. Far less welcome was the attitude of Bomber Command in ordering that these operations would only count as one-third of an operation when it came to tallying the number of operations a crew had completed.

The crews were right to be dismayed for on several occasions the German night fighter force got in amongst the bombers on such operations and the resulting casualties were high. This culminated on the night of 3/4 May when the target was a German panzer base at Mailly-le-Camp. Difficulties in marking the target forced the main force to orbit the target and 42 Lancasters from 360 aircraft, from 1 and 5 Groups, despatched were lost, mainly to night fighters. This represented some 12 per cent of the number of Lancasters which were on the operation. The results of the raid appalled Bomber Command with a number of main force bomber captains abusing the master bombers over the R/T as they were forced to orbit the target and became prey to the prowling night fighters. The marking force was supplied by 5 Group (Leonard Cheshire was Master Bomber) and the resulting carnage caused even greater resentment amongst the surviving 1 Group crews towards their comrades in 5 Group. A more positive result of the disastrous raid was the revoking of the one-third rule for French targets.

With D-Day rapidly approaching the pace of Bomber Command operations heightened and on the night of 5/6 June the command flew 1,211 sorties, dropping 5,000 tons of bombs. The majority of these were aimed at various coastal batteries in Normandy and the crews could see the invasion fleet on their H2S radar screens as they made their way back to base.

In the weeks and months following the invasion Bomber Command aided the invasion forces by attacking a variety of tactical targets including German troop and defensive positions, French ports used by the E-boats which could have mauled the shipping on the Channel, fuel and ammunition dumps, as well as the continuing attack on transportation hubs.

Despite the focus on these targets, the growing strength of Bomber Command was brought into the battle against the German synthetic-oil industry upon which much of the Wehrmacht relied. These were small precision targets and it was hoped that the new techniques being developed by 3 and 5 Groups, along with the increasing accuracy of 8 (PFF) Group, would at last allow these targets to be hit. The US Eighth Air Force had already been successful with some of these targets but Bomber Command, flying by night, was asked to attack the plants in the Ruhr in order to save exposing the US daylight bombers to the concentrated flak over the Ruhr.

The tactics behind these raids was sound, despite Harris's continuing dislike and distrust of panacea targets, but the efforts of Bomber Command were distracted by the flying-bomb attacks on London and southern England. These necessitated the use of some of the bomber force to attack a variety of sites used to launch these weapons and other sites which stored the bombs. Once again, these were precision targets and the success of Bomber Command in hitting these sites demonstrated the growing capabilities of the force to be capable of hitting precision targets by day or night. These attacks continued until August when the advancing Allied armies overran the flying-bomb sites.

The focus on these targets meant that Bomber Command did not visit Germany in force throughout the entire month of June, but Harris did launch five raids in July. The summer also saw – thanks to the growing aerial dominance of the Allies – the re-introduction of daylight attacks. Harris was initially very reluctant to use his bombers in this way, remembering well the painful losses of earlier in the war, but was pleasantly surprised by the success of the daylight raids so long as they were strongly escorted. With many of the targets requiring precision bombing new tactics were developed with Oboe-equipped aircraft leading small formations of heavies. This method proved to be extremely accurate and, together, with new daylight marking techniques, boded well for the future. Experiments were also begun with G-H formation bombing techniques.

By mid-August the Allied armies had broken out of Normandy and were at the German frontier. Bomber Command once again stood at a crossroads. Recent months had shown that the command had the ability to hit precision targets both day and night but Harris still cherished hopes of proving his strategic bombing theories. While still operating within the tactical framework of the Allies, Harris was now largely released from the restrictions of spring and summer. By this stage in the war Bomber Command had vast assets and was capable of mounting huge and devastating operations. Harris, to his credit, never shirked when called upon to mount tactical operations. The command was split between two schools of thought; some believed that continued oil attacks would result in Germany being unable to continue the war, while others that attacks on the communications network would be the quickest way to victory. A smaller, third group, believed that the strategic campaign should be reinstated. The RAF, through Sir Charles Portal, generally supported the oil option while Allied commanders in Europe, led by Air Chief Marshal Sir Arthur Tedder, supported the transportation option that had worked so well in Normandy.

The debate over which targets to focus on was won by those who favoured attacking the German oil industry and both Bomber Command and the Eighth Air Force were ordered to focus on these targets over the next months. Harris reacted with typical contempt, scribbling a contemptuous comment in the margin of the order. He still maintained that limitations in the accuracy of his force meant that concentrating on such precision targets was a mistake and, furthermore, he doubted the opinions of the strategy makers who came up with panacea targets designed to quickly end the war. For Harris, the strategic bombing of German towns and cities and the resulting collapse in both industry and morale in Germany was still the surest way of winning the war.

He was boosted in this by the fact that lessening casualties and the growing capacity of the aircraft industry in Britain and the Empire (along with the huge numbers of aircrew coming through the training schemes) meant that Bomber Command expanded dramatically during 1944. The number of front-line aircraft available to Harris expanded by 50 per cent and these were all of the latest modern types. The growing force could now deliver bomb tonnages undreamt of in earlier years. The months from August 1944 to the end of the war saw the huge tonnages dropped which added up to 46 per cent of the total dropped by the command during the entire war. The availability of more Mosquitoes meant that the Light Night Striking Force (LNSF) could also be reinforced and this provided Harris with options to mount ever-increasing raids.

By now there were few remaining bomber aircrew who had been operational at the beginning of the war and who were still operating. Unfortunately, 1944 saw several of these veterans meet their ends. The heady, intoxicating, life experienced upon an operational squadron often infected these men and drove them onwards to continue flying on operations even when they could easily have been rested or gone on to other duties. Amongst those lost during the year were Squadron Leader Alec Cranswick DSO DFC, who was killed on his 107th operation and, perhaps the most famous member of Bomber Command, Wing Commander Guy Gibson VC DSO (and bar) DFC (and bar), who was killed in mysterious circumstances while returning from an operation to Rheydt in September.

We have previously seen how there had been high hopes for the new radar bombing tool named G-H and by October approximately one-third of 3 Group's Lancasters had been equipped with the device. As a result of this, Air Vice Marshal R. Harrison and his group had been given a new independent role, as had 5 Group. Not only was this a sign of just how powerful a force Bomber Command had become, but it also offered a new tactic. The group was to be used on days when a target was cloud covered but the cloud tops did not reach 18,000 feet. The aircrew of 3 Group had been practising for this new role and had developed a system whereby two non G-H equipped Lancasters would form up closely with one of the G-H equipped Lancasters (easily recognised by the prominent designs painted upon their tails) and would release their bombs at the same time as the G-H aircraft.

By the middle of the month 3 Group was ready to test out the new tactics in force. Harrison had asked that Bonn be used as the testing ground for the new tactic. Bonn was a relatively unimportant town but had not been bombed before and so post-raid photographic reconnaissance would not be confused by previous bomb damage. On 18 October 3 Group dispatched 128 Lancasters on this raid. Reconnaissance photographs revealed that it had been a complete success and the heart of Bonn had been almost completely destroyed. Local reports agreed with this, claiming that some 700 buildings had been totally destroyed, 1,000 more seriously damaged and 313 people had been killed. Only one Lancaster failed to return from the operation. The test having proven a success, 3 Group would continue in this role for the remainder of the war.

The raid on Bonn is a clear example of pure area bombing. The command acknowledged that Bonn was an unimportant target, hence its having never been bombed but at this stage of the war it was still seen as a viable target, if for no other reason than to test this new tactic. Amongst the destruction in old Bonn the town's university had been destroyed along with many other buildings of cultural significance. Local reports stated that a house which had been occupied by Beethoven was saved by the courageous efforts of its caretakers. Bomber Command's war was indeed merciless, but Harris would remain unapologetic for such raids and, indeed, the operation, however, horrific, did have a military purpose in testing the new tactic.

The year ended with an attack on Cologen/Kalk on 30/31 December when the Kalk-Nord railway yards were targeted. Demonstrating the increasing collapse of German defences and the growing abilities of Bomber Command, just two bombers (a Lancaster and a Halifax) were lost from a force of 470 aircraft, and despite the target being obscured by cloud the rail yards were hit successfully.

The Campaign

As the Bomber Command campaign against Berlin continued, the loss of life amongst aircrew continued to rise. No doubt the men of the command were exhausted when they were ordered to attack the German capital once more on the night of 1/2 January as, for many, this would be the second Berlin raid in four nights and the third in just over a week and they were most likely hoping for a quiet New Year's night. For this attack 421 Lancasters took off for the target (the Halifax bomber force had been temporarily rested as they had suffered such heavy casualties on recent raids). The raid proved to be a disappointment as heavy cloud once again obscured the city and the scattered nature of the bombing resulted in only twenty-one houses and a single industrial building being destroyed according to German reports. The Luftwaffe night-fighters infiltrated the bomber stream long before the target was reached, and several bombers were seen to be shot down although only two were lost over the target itself.

The experienced crew of Flight Lieutenant Douglas Allister MacDonald DFC, RCAF, of 630 Squadron, had taken off from RAF East Kirkby but failed to return. Subsequent enquiries revealed that their Lancaster III (JB532, LE-X) had been homebound after bombing the target when it was hit by flak which blew one engine completely out of the airframe. The bomber dived steeply and crashed at Grossbeuthen, killing all eight men aboard including the 20-year-old Canadian pilot from Saskatchewan. The bomb aimer was Flight Sergeant John Mowbray Turnbull (22). The young airman, a native of Sunderland, left behind his parents, George and Edith.[1]

Another Sunderland native who was killed in that night's operation was Sergeant Thomas Henry Mallett (20) who was the mid-upper gunner in Lancaster III (JB645, ZN-F) of 106 Squadron. The bomber had taken off shortly after midnight with Pilot Officer Edwin Cecil Holbourn, of Worthing in Sussex, at the controls but nothing more was heard, and the seven-man crew were later revealed to have all been buried in the Berlin 1939-1945 War Cemetery.

So far in January there had been three attacks on Berlin which had cost the command sixty-eight Lancasters and twenty-two Halifaxes. The casualties amongst the squadrons flying the latter type had been so severe recently that Harris had rested them from several recent Berlin raids, but on the last one the Halifax force had lost 8.3 per cent. For 102 Squadron at RAF Pocklington the Berlin raid of 20/21 January had been disastrous. The Halifax squadron had dispatched sixteen aircraft. Five had failed to return from the operation and two more crashed in England upon their return.

Interspersed amongst the Berlin raids in early to mid-January had been operations to other targets including Stettin and Brunswick. The Stettin raid had involved only 358 aircraft, including ten Halifaxes. This was the first large raid on this target since 1941 and cost the command sixteen aircraft. It was regarded as an acceptable number for such a raid, but the Halifax crews once again suffered badly with two failing to return. The Brunswick operation, which took place on 14/15 January, just one night before a Berlin raid, involved 496 Lancasters and just two Halifaxes but, worryingly for Harris, the new German night-fighter tactics had worked extremely well once again with the night-fighters being guided by an accurate running commentary on the progress of the bomber stream. Wireless interception showed that the Germans were aware of the bomber stream from a point where it was just 40 miles from the English coast. Little damage was done in Brunswick, but thirty-eight Lancasters (7.6 per cent) were lost, the majority of them to night-fighters. The serious losses were having a massive impact upon the Pathfinders and on this night 8 (PFF) Group lost eleven aircraft.

For the tired crews of Bomber Command who had returned from Berlin in the early hours of 21 January there was little rest and as they filed into the briefing rooms once more there must have been consternation at another long-range target. However, the target for that night was a virgin one, Magdeburg. It was a large raid, consisting of 648 aircraft, with the Halifax crews taking part. Once again the bomber stream was monitored while it was still over the sea and many night-fighters were able to get amongst the bombers. The German controller was very reluctant to name Magdeburg as the target, probably assuming this was another Berlin raid, but this hardly mattered due to the 'Wilde Sau' (Wild Boar) tactics being used by the majority of night-fighters. This tactic removed many of the fighters from having to depend upon ground control stations to vector them onto individual bombers, with them, instead, being set free to detect and enter the bomber stream at any point, the earlier the better, using a running commentary and their radar equipment to home in on and attack bombers, especially those using H2S. Fifty-seven aircraft were lost as a result – 8.8 per cent of the force – and, once again, night-fighters – many of them now equipped with *Schräge Musik* cannons (upward firing autocannon or machine guns) – were responsible for the vast majority of losses. Although the majority of aircraft on the raid were Lancasters (421) there were more Halifaxes lost. Thirty-five of the Halifaxes failed to return, this represented 15.6 per cent losses for the Halifax squadrons and it was becoming increasingly clear that the Halifax, especially the older types, were no longer viable for attacking long-range German targets. Demonstrating the increasing use of diversions, a small force of Lancasters and Mosquitoes of 5 and 8 Groups carried out a diversionary raid on Berlin using bombs and target indicators. However, due to the '*Wilde Sau*' ('Wild Boar', German night-fighter intercept tactics), it was largely ignored, although one Lancaster failed to return.

In addition to its main work, Bomber Command had two detached squadrons which worked as Special Duties units (138 and 161 Squadrons) dropping supplies and agents into occupied Europe. This was a very hazardous, but important, duty and many crews lost their lives. The squadrons also flew air-sea rescue operations attempting to find airmen who had been unlucky enough to have come down in the sea. On the night of 23 January 161 Squadron sent aircraft off on just such an operation. Two of its Halifax V aircraft failed to return and were presumed to have been unlucky enough to collide with one another over the North Sea with the loss of all fourteen airmen aboard. Halifax V (LL182, MA-V) was under the command of Flight Sergeant James William Robertson

(20) from Renfrewshire. Demonstrating the youth of many members of Bomber Command, his flight engineer, a Sunderland man, Sergeant Edward Robert Richardson was aged 19.[2] Halifax V (DG272, MA-U) was under the command of Flying Officer Kenneth Ferris Smith, a 23-year-old from Cheshire.[3]

Harris followed up this raid with another to Berlin on 27/28 January. The Halifax crews were rested for this operation and 515 Lancasters and 15 Mosquitoes were dispatched to the capital. Once more the force was detected early and on this night German night-fighters were even sent out to intercept the bomber stream while it was still 75 miles out from the Dutch coast. Once more, however, Bomber Command had mounted a series of feints and diversions, this time involving 140 aircraft. Eighty Stirlings and Wellingtons flew to lay mines off the Dutch coast (one Stirling was lost) while 21 Halifaxes did the same, but at Heligoland. It was hoped that these diversions would lure the night-fighters into taking off early so that they would be low on fuel when the bomber stream approached. In addition, nine aircraft flew radio countermeasure operations and twelve Mosquitoes flew Serrate patrols to attack enemy night-fighters. Finally, eighteen Mosquitoes were engaged in dropping dummy fighter flares away from the bomber stream. Many of the night-fighters were lured away by the Halifax force and casualties were lighter than recently with thirty-three Lancasters failing to return. Once again damage assessment was difficult, but it is known that fifty industrial premises were destroyed or damaged, 567 people were killed and 20,000 Berliners were bombed out.

The following night 677 crews were no doubt dismayed to be sent back to Berlin. Harris recalled the Halifax squadrons for this raid. Once again diversions played their part in drawing off some of the night-fighters while the northerly route which the bombers took, although lightening bomb loads, meant that some night-fighters had insufficient fuel to reach the stream. The Germans were, however, able to assemble a number of fighters over Berlin and forty-six bombers failed to return. Once again, the Halifaxes suffered disproportionately with 26 out of 241 lost (10.8 per cent).

For once the cloud over Berlin was broken and some ground marking was possible. Once again, however, accurate assessment is difficult although Bomber Command believed that this was one of the most concentrated attacks on the capital. Amongst the diversionary activities on this night were 'gardening' sorties, Serrate patrols, the bombing of German airfields by Mosquitoes, a diversionary raid by four Mosquitoes and, most interestingly of all, an attack on Berlin which was carried out four hours before the main attack by six Mosquitoes. Two Stirling minelayers were lost along with one Serrate Mosquito.

The crews had one night of rest before Harris once again sent them to Berlin. On this occasion 534 aircraft were dispatched but, interestingly, there were no early diversions. The German controllers failed to infiltrate the bomber stream early, but as the bombers approached the target the night-fighters became active and they remained active as the bombers made their way home. As a result, some thirty-three aircraft were lost.

The moon period now precluded Main Force operations for some time but on the night of 8/9 February twelve Lancasters of 617 (Dam Busters) Squadron attacked the Gnome-Rhone aero engine factory at Limoges, France. For some time the commanding officer of 617 Squadron, Wing Commander Leonard Cheshire DSO (and two bars), DFC (later adding the VC), had been pressing his beliefs in low-level marking as an aid to accuracy in attacking precision targets at night. Cheshire had been the youngest Group Captain in the RAF when the vacancy to command 617 had occurred and he had immediately volunteered to step down a rank in order to take over the squadron. A firm believer in precision bombing, he saw an opportunity to make a great difference at 617. Cheshire went on to become one of the most famous of Bomber Command pilots to survive the war, observed the atomic bomb on Nagasaki and became a post-war philanthropist, founding the Cheshire Homes. Wing Commander Leonard Cheshire marked the target at low level in a Lancaster, using this technique for the first time. This raid came about as a result of his determination to very accurately mark small targets so as to find a role for 617 Squadron, which had been struggling to find a suitable role since the Dams raid. The factory had been chosen because it was very lightly defended but surrounded by the houses of French civilians and Air Vice Marshal Cochrane felt that it would be a suitable test to see if Cheshire could indeed mark a precision target at low level while avoiding civilian casualties.

After making three runs over the target so as to alert the French workers, Cheshire guided the Lancaster down and dropped incendiaries from a very low level, between 50-100 feet. The main force of eleven Lancasters then dropped their 12,000lb bombs with remarkable accuracy. Ten of the bombs were direct hits on the factory, while the remaining bomb tumbled as it dropped, but fortunately dropped in the river. The factory, needless to say, was very heavily damaged and all production was halted. Even more encouraging for Cheshire and Cochrane was the fact that not a single French civilian had been killed or injured (indeed, the people of the town afterwards got a message through expressing their thanks for the warning before bombing commenced).

For Cheshire and Cochrane this was the proof needed to demonstrate to Harris that low-level marking of very small targets was possible and that 617 Squadron could bomb accurately enough following this method of marking. Cheshire, however, had doubts about the use of the Lancaster for this low-level work and believed that the Mosquito would be the ideal aircraft, especially when targets were more heavily defended.

After the moon period Harris immediately dispatched another heavy raid on Berlin. This was the heaviest attack of the war on the German capital. After a rest period of two weeks 891 aircraft were sent to Berlin with the Halifaxes once more recalled. There were a number of firsts, it was the largest non-1,000 force raid and saw the heaviest weight of bombs dropped at 2,642 tons. There were only minor diversionary sorties and the German controllers were able to direct their night-fighters to the bomber stream shortly after it left the English coast. Once again, however, the northerly route enabled the bomber stream to evade some of the fighters. Furthermore, the night-fighters were ordered to avoid Berlin in order to give free reign to the flak and searchlight defences. Many of the night-fighter crews, however, avoided this instruction and forty-three Bomber Command aircraft failed to return. The attack, made on skymarkers as Berlin was once again completely cloud covered, was successful and large areas of the city were damaged.

Harris then allowed his force three nights rest before sending 823 aircraft to Leipzig. This raid was disastrous. A significant number of Halifaxes (and others) turned back with mechanical difficulties, but the minelaying diversion at Kiel largely failed and the bomber stream fell under attack as soon as it crossed the Dutch coast. It remained under attack for the entire route to the target. In another disastrous turn the wind forecasts were wrong and many bombers arrived early over the target and were forced to circle waiting for the Pathfinder markers to go down. Seventy-eight bombers failed to return from Leipzig, 9.9 per cent of the total force dispatched. The rate of loss amongst the Halifax squadrons was 13.3 per cent of those dispatched and 14.9 per cent of those which had not turned back early. This was now incontrovertible proof that the older marks of the Halifax were no longer suitable for long range raids on Germany and Harris decided after this raid that the Halifax IIs and Vs were to be immediately withdrawn from operations over Germany.

After this several heavy raids were launched against a number of targets as Harris began to run out of time before his command was turned over to support the preparations for Operation Overlord. Targets in February and early March included Stuttgart (twice), Schweinfurt and Augsburg. The Stuttgart operations resulted in relatively light losses. The attack on Schweinfurt was an example of Harris following his orders despite his antagonism towards what he referred to as panacea targets. Schweinfurt was the home of the German ball-bearing industry and the night of 24/25 February would be Bomber Command's first to this target. It was a follow-up raid to an attack made by the USAAF Eighth Air Force the previous day and there was an innovative tactic used to attempt to lower losses on this distant target. The 734 aircraft which took part were divided into two waves which were separated by a two-hour gap. This appears to have worked as the first wave suffered twenty-two aircraft lost while the second lost only eleven. The bombing, however, on this difficult to find target was disappointing.

Amongst the aircraft which failed to return was Halifax III (LV778, C6-B) of 51 Squadron, based at RAF Snaith. Pilot Officer Douglas Jackson had taken off shortly before 6.30pm but nothing more was heard from the crew until there was notification that they had been killed and were buried at Durnach War Cemetery. The crew of eight men included airmen from four different countries with representatives of the RAF, RAAF, RCAF and RNZAF. The crew were: second pilot, Pilot Officer Frederick George Langford, RCAF (27); flight engineer, Sergeant Ronald Jack Colley, RAF (21); Flying Officer Francis Richard Rohrer, RAF; bomb-aimer, Flight Sergeant Leslie Noel Atkinson, RNZAF (29); wireless operator, Flight Sergeant John Francis Brown, RAF (24); mid-upper gunner, Flight Sergeant John Arthur Lloyd Carmichael, RAAF (25) and rear gunner, Sergeant John Cameron Harthill, RAF (24). For the Harthill family this must have come as a shattering blow as John's elder brother had also been killed aboard a bomber. On 24 November 1943 Pilot Officer James Cameron Harthill was serving as a bomb-aimer in the Mediterranean with 40 Squadron when his Wellington crashed into a mountain while on an operation to Turin.[4]

On the next night 594 aircraft were sent to attack Augsburg. This was the first large raid to Augsburg, which was relatively lightly defended, and the bombing was very successful. Indeed, the bombing was unusually concentrated, and the old centre of the historic town was almost completely destroyed while the bombing largely failed to spread to the more modern, industrialised areas. This prompted the Germans to allege that the Augsburg raid was a prime example of the RAF's terror tactics. Nevertheless, there were industries in Augsburg, making it a viable target, and some were destroyed or damaged on this night.

In preparation for the attacks on relatively small targets in France as part of the Transportation Plan in advance of Operation Overlord, and to find a use for the Halifax force which had recently been retired from German raids, Harris sent a force of 117 Halifaxes and six Mosquitoes from 4, 6 and 8 Groups to attack the S.N.C.A. aircraft factory at Meulan-les-Mureaux. The raid demonstrated the accuracy of Oboe marking and the factory was very seriously damaged with no losses to the bombing force.

Just three nights later came Bomber Command's first participation in the Transportation Plan when 261 Halifaxes and six Mosquitoes were sent to bomb railway marshalling yards at Trappes. The night was clear, the Oboe marking accurate and the Main Force responded well. Photo reconnaissance showed that massive damage had been done in the yards. The Trappes raid was the first in a series of attacks on French targets. The following night, for example, saw 304 aircraft attack a similar target at Le Mans. Although this time the target was cloud-covered, the use of Oboe once again saved the day and heavy damage was once again done. This was a bright start to the Bomber Command part of the Transportation Plan. Great damage had been done to the selected targets for no losses.

By this time Air Vice Marshal Cochrane was beginning to formulate his plans to potentially use 5 Group as a separate force capable of precision attacks. On 10/11 March 102 Lancasters from his group attacked four factories in France in conditions of moonlight. All of the attacks were judged to have been successful and only one aircraft was lost. Lancaster III (ND513, EM-R) of 206 Squadron had been tasked with attacking the Michelin tyre factory at Clermont-Ferrand but was shot down in the target area, killing all eight men aboard. The skipper of the crew was Squadron Leader Dudley George Hart Pike MiD, of Herne Hill, London.[5]

Another aircraft lost by Bomber Command on this night was engaged upon clandestine duties on behalf of SOE (Special Operations Executive). Stirling III (LJ509, WP-F) of 90 Squadron was, like many of the obsolescent Stirlings, being used for supply work. LJ509, with Squadron

Leader Terence Sydney Raymond King MiD, was carrying fifteen canisters of supplies for the French Resistance but crashed near Dijon, killing the entire crew.

On the night of 15/16 March Harris continued his campaign against Stuttgart by sending 863 aircraft to bomb the city. Once again there were fierce air-to-air combats and thirty-seven aircraft failed to return. Two of these losses, both Lancasters, made forced-landings in Switzerland. Another crew attempted to make for that neutral country but were overtaken by tragedy. This was Lancaster III (JB474, DX-F) of 57 Squadron. Piloted by Pilot Officer Samuel Cunningham Atcheson DFC, the Lancaster had been approaching the target when all four engines suddenly caught fire. Atcheson made for Switzerland and once he believed himself over the border ordered the crew to bale out. Sadly, only mid-upper gunner, Flight Sergeant K.A. Reece, was able to do so before control was lost and the bomber crashed at Saignelégier. Flight Sergeant Reece was interned by the Swiss authorities, but the rest of his crew were killed.[6]

After two attacks on Frankfurt and several smaller raids Harris made yet another attempt to successfully attack Berlin on 24/25 March. The Halifax force had by now been strengthened by the arrival of more of the newer and more effective Halifax IIIs and Harris sent 811 aircraft (including 216 Halifax IIIs) to the German capital. On this night, however, an unprecedentedly strong wind from the north (a jet-stream) developed and many of the bombers were carried far south of their track. To make matters worse the procedure put in place to warn crews of such a development failed and the bomber stream became badly fragmented. This allowed radar-controlled flak to pick off many of the bombers. The winds also caused problems over the target with skymarkers being blown rapidly across and away from the city. Because of the sheer weight of the attack, damage was still done in the capital but 126 towns and villages outside Berlin also reported suffering damage. Losses were very heavy with seventy-two aircraft failing to return. It is estimated that, unusually, the vast majority (fifty) were destroyed by flak.

Harris's time was now nearly up, and he was increasingly convinced that the Battle of Berlin was lost. With his force suffering unsustainable losses on deep penetration raids to the capital and the lighter nights approaching it was increasingly clear that a different approach was needed. Until a solution could be found to the new German night-fighter tactics, such raids would have to restricted. In fact, though no-one was aware of it and no announcement was ever made, this was the last occasion that a major RAF raid was launched on Berlin although the Mosquitoes of the Light Night Striking Force (LNSF) continued to harass the city.

Amongst the aircraft lost were three Lancaster IIs from 115 Squadron based at RAF Witchford. Lancaster II (DS678, KO-J) had taken off at 6.49pm with Pilot Officer Leonard Myles McCann, RCAF, at the controls. His wireless operator/air gunner was Sergeant William Bowey (21). The son of William and Elizabeth Crossley Bowey of Sunderland, he perished with four of his crew (two survived as PoWs) when their Lancaster was shot down from 20,000 feet by a night-fighter in the vicinity of Leipzig. The five men who died had, for many years, no known graves and are commemorated on the Runnymede Memorial, but evidence recently came to light that Sergeant Bowey and his crewmates had been buried at Ohrdruf Cemetery, but subsequently lost. The panel on the Runnymede Memorial will thus be removed as they are now commemorated on special memorials at the Niederzwehren Cemetery, Kassel, with the inscription 'WHO WAS BURIED AT THE TIME IN OHRDRUF CEMETERY, BUT WHOSE GRAVE CANNOT NOW BE FOUND. THEIR GLORY SHALL NOT BE BLOTTED OUT'.

With Bomber Command was now increasingly tasked with targets which were part of the Transportation Plan designed to severely disrupt the transport network in occupied Europe, especially France, in order to prepare for Operation Overlord. Following an unsuccessful Transportation Plan raid on Aulnoye on 25/26 March Harris launched a heavy attack by 705 aircraft on the Ruhr city of Essen. The Germans were taken by surprise by this sudden alteration of tactics to a shorter-range target and only nine aircraft were lost. Oboe once again marked accurately and Essen once more suffered heavy damage.

Just three nights later Harris ordered a raid on the railway yards at Vaires on the night of 29/30 March. With Harris still pre-occupied with the ongoing Battle of Berlin, many of these Transport Plan raids at this stage were carried out by the older Halifaxes which had been withdrawn from the Battle of Berlin. The raid on Vaires was typical of this. The operation involved 76 Halifaxes and eight Mosquitoes drawn from 4, 6 (RCAF) and 8 (PFF) Groups. The majority of the Halifaxes were provided by 8 (RCAF) Group which put up 49 aircraft from five squadrons (419, 427, 428, 431, and 434). The operation took place under very bright moonlight (thought necessary to identify these precision targets) and the bombing was very accurate with a highlight of the raid being the violent explosion in which two ammunition trains blew up. Post-raid intelligence gathered from secret sources reported that 1,270 German soldiers were killed in the attack. Only one of Bomber Command's aircraft failed to return, a Halifax from 419 Squadron. Halifax II (HR912, VR-F) took off from RAF Middleton St George at 6.19pm but nothing further was heard from the crew of Warrant Officer 2nd Class John Alexander Greenidge, RCAF. The 26-year-old hailed from Port of Spain, Trinidad. Greenidge was one of a number of Caribbean volunteers who had made their way to Canada to offer their services.[7]

On the night of 30/31 March most of the airmen of Bomber Command were looking forward to one of their regular stand-down periods due to the moon and were no doubt somewhat dismayed to be called for a briefing for what was obviously a maximum effort raid. This dismay deepened when the operation was revealed at briefing to be a deep penetration to Nuremberg. Many of the airmen, especially the more senior ones, had the feeling that such a raid was not on in the current conditions. Indeed, many of Harris's command staff at High Wycombe thought that perhaps there was some special, secret, reason for the raid while others, both at HQ and on the squadrons, thought it likely the raid would be scrubbed. Even more concerning was the fact that the route into the target did not feature any of the now traditional jinks and course alterations but a long straight leg to Nuremberg. Even worse, several of the Pathfinders realised that the route took them perilously close to a known fighter assembly beacon. Complaints were made to have the route altered but these were turned down and the operation went ahead as planned. A Met Flight Mosquito reported back that cloud, which it was hoped would offer protection to the bombers on the route to the target, would not be present. Despite all of these concerns the operation was approved.

On a night when many things went wrong for Bomber Command even the atmospheric conditions were against the bomber crews as they found themselves leaving long contrails at their operational heights and the 795 aircraft were silhouetted against a backdrop of cloud. The German controller ignored the diversions and assembled his night-fighters along the bomber stream route and at the previously mentioned beacon. A vicious fight developed along the route to the target and terrified crews repeatedly witnessed their comrades plummeting to the ground in flames. Many of the more senior crews realised that on this night it would be safer to be out of the bomber stream for once, while others dropped their height to try to evade notice. The city was covered by cloud and the raid failed to cause serious damage to Nuremberg with much of the bombing falling on Schweinfurt.

Upon return, officers debriefing the crews were stunned by the estimates of losses which were being reported. One Canadian pilot had been told before take-off that 796 aircraft were being sent to Nuremberg and, upon his return, he told his commanding officer, with remarkable accuracy, that Bomber Command could strike off the odd ninety-six. In fact, ninety-five bombers failed to return from Nuremberg and a Halifax flying an SOE mission was also shot down over Belgium. This was the biggest Bomber Command loss of the entire war – 545 Bomber Command aircrew lost their lives, more than had been lost by Fighter Command during the entire Battle of Britain.

Amongst them was Flying Officer Leslie Simpson (33) of 101 Squadron. The air gunner left behind his widow, Marguerite, at their Fulwell, Middlesex home. Squadron 101 was flying normal bomber operations but was a specialised squadron which had been issued with a device known as ABC which helped to jam enemy communications, and necessitated the addition of an extra, German-speaking, crewman as a special operator. Unfortunately, it would seem that it could also be tracked by some enemy radar systems and made the Lancasters of the squadron more vulnerable. On the night of the Nuremberg raid 101 Squadron suffered the loss of no fewer than seven of its aircraft. Amongst them was Lancaster I (LL832, SR-K2) which took off from RAF Ludford Magna shortly after 10pm under the command of 22-year-old Flight Sergeant Gerald Tivey. Pilot Officer Simpson was the mid-upper gunner in the crew. The Lancaster, unlike so many on this raid, did not fall victim to a night-fighter but was shot down by flak, crashing near the village of Rubenach with the loss of all eight crewmen.[8]

The Nuremberg operation would prove to be the last for 22-year-old Pilot Officer Cyril Joe Barton of 578 Squadron. Barton, who had left his reserved occupation in an aircraft factory to join the RAF, and his crew had flown on six previous operations aboard their favourite Halifax which they had named Excalibur. They crew had taken off from RAF Bourne at 10.14pm aboard Halifax III (LK979, LK-E) but on the way to the target they were attacked and very badly damaged by two night-fighters. An engine was knocked out, two fuel tanks were punctured, the radio and rear turret were rendered inoperable, as was the crew intercom. In the ensuing confusion three of the crew in the front of the aircraft (navigator, bomb-aimer and wireless operator) baled out. This left the young pilot without his navigational and bombing team in a badly damaged bomber and it would have been perfectly understandable for him to bale out at this point. Barton, however, decided to press on. He nursed the stricken Halifax to Nuremberg where he dropped his bombload and then, with little navigational help, set course for home. A strong wind blew the Halifax northwards up the North Sea and the battered bomber made landfall over North East England. As the Halifax crossed the coast it was down to just one operational engine and the huge aircraft was too low for the remaining crew to bale out safely. Barton ordered the remaining crew to their crash positions and stood by to make a crash landing. Seeing a row of colliery houses at the village of Ryton, Barton managed to avoid these and then the bomber hit the ground. The three crewmen in the crash position survived but Barton was found to be dead when he was pulled from the wreckage. In addition, a miner on his way to work was also killed when the bomber struck him. This incredibly courageous young airman, who was, unusually, very religious, had, like many other skippers, given his life for his crew and Pilot Officer Cyril Joe Barton was, very deservedly, awarded the VC. His flight engineer and mid-upper gunner were awarded the DFM.[9]

The Nuremberg Raid was an unprecedented disaster for Bomber Command and brought to an end Harris's Main Offensive period. On the following day Bomber Command's efforts were switched to supporting the preparations for Overlord. Nuremberg had been a raid in which many things had gone wrong. Yes, the weather conditions played a role, but the raid seems to have been incredibly poorly planned when compared to comparable raids of the period. Harris would appear to have wanted one last big area attack, but in undertaking such an attack in bright moonlight and with such a poorly conceived plan he had made a grave error of judgement. For some time there had been mounting proof that deep penetration raids were becoming untenable due to a number of factors. Foremost amongst these was the new *Wilde Sau* tactics being used by the Luftwaffe for which Bomber Command at this time had no answer. Secondly was the poor armament of British bombers. This was compounded by a failure to realise that German night-fighters were able to home in on emissions from H2S sets aboard bombers and the lack of acknowledgment by intelligence that many German night-fighters were now using upwards firing, *Schrage Musik* cannons against which the majority of British bombers had little or no defence.

Harris's own attitude towards the Nuremberg operation is instructive. In his memoirs he completely fails to make any comment or reference to the raid. To not mention the final raid of his Main Offensive and the raid in which Bomber Command suffered its highest ever losses is, quite frankly, stunning. His account of the bomber war is a fair one overall but in failing to mention this disastrous raid he renders much of his account dubious as he was obviously seeking to ignore, or at the very least not draw further attention to his errors in the conception and planning of this raid.

By now Harris was firmly entrenched in his command and had cemented his place with both the politicians and the British public and his removal would have been extremely difficult, almost unthinkable, at the time. The losses over the winter of 1943-1944, however, should probably have led to serious questions being asked about him. Certainly, other commanders of Bomber Command had been removed for less. This is in no way to criticise Harris's achievements to date. He had taken over a weak and demoralised force in 1942 and had turned it into an extremely powerful tool in the national armoury and much of his Main Offensive had been a relative success. The Ruhr, Hamburg, Peenemunde, all had been valuable contributions to the war effort. Raids on other towns and cities had varied in effectiveness but valuable damage had been done to German industry and the raids had provided a valuable propaganda tool at a time when opportunities for hitting back at Germany were extremely restricted. The general public enthusiasm for Bomber Command at the time is proof of this. It has to be argued, however, that during the winter of 1943-1944 Harris had overstretched his command and had allowed himself to be somewhat blinded to the restrictions of the force available to him. He should, perhaps, have assessed the results of the deep penetration raids earlier than he did and come to the judgement that it would have been better to restrict his raids to fewer deep penetration operations in order to further build up his strength.

Although it was the aircrew members of Bomber Command who received the most attention from the public, press and politicians, their work would have been utterly impossible had it not been for the efforts of countless groundcrew, administrative personnel, WAAFs and other staff who made up the human population of a Bomber Command airfield. Each raid required a massive expenditure of energy on the part of these hard-worked, but determined, men and women. Aircraft had to be readied and tested, loaded with fuel, ammunition and bombs, parachutes had to be re-packed, checked and issued, bomb cameras checked and loaded, flying meals prepared, food and hot drink readied for the aircrew to consume on their flights, intelligence materials readied, briefings prepared and a myriad of other tasks undertaken before one bomber could take off.

Now, Harris would find his selection of targets severely curtailed and much of the effort would be against the extensive list of pre-invasion targets. Raids on German cities would only be made on a few occasions when Bomber Command was not required for these invasion operations and even then, conditions would have to be favourable before the valuable bombers were sent.

Harris had feared that Bomber Command would be unsuitable for making such raids on small, hard to locate, targets at night but his fears were proven largely false. The pioneering use and development of the Master Bomber technique, combined with increasing accuracy and the dedication of Main Force crews faced with less stressful operations, allowed Bomber Command to enjoy great success in its pre-invasion operations. All too often though, the crews of the Master Bombers paid the price as they were required to repeatedly circle the target, remaining in the target area for considerable periods.

The switch to precision targets also allowed 5 Group under Air Vice Marshal Cochrane to hone its techniques in preparation for his hoped-for free-range precision bombing role. On 5/6 April 144 Lancasters from 5 Group mounted an attack on an aircraft factory in Toulouse. The marking for the raid, crucially, was carried out not by the Pathfinders, but by 617 Squadron. Wing Commander Cheshire, flying a Mosquito for the first time on a low-level marking flight, dropped his markers onto the factory roof. Despite heavy defences the speed and agility of the Mosquito allowed Cheshire to escape unscathed. These initial markers were followed by markers dropped by two hand-picked Lancaster crews. Both sets of markers were highly accurate and the bombing remained extremely concentrated. The crews responsible for the bulk of the bombing were from ordinary 5 Group squadrons and most had received nothing in the way of special training. The factory was very badly damaged and put out of action, while civilian casualties were limited to twenty-two fatalities and forty-five injuries. Only one of the attacking aircraft was lost. Lancaster I (ME685, EM-C) of 207 Squadron, piloted by Warrant Officer John Raymond Senior, was hit by flak over the target and the bomber exploded in mid-air as its bomb load detonated. The crew of five British airmen and two Australians were all killed.

This raid had been the final test for 5 Group and 617 Squadron's low-level marking technique. Shortly afterwards Harris contacted his old friend Cochrane to inform him that from henceforth 5 Group would operate as a largely independent force utilising the marking techniques it was developing. Furthermore, and to Cochrane's delight and Air Vice Marshal Bennett's anger, the two Pathfinder squadrons which had previously belonged to 5 Group, 83 and 97 Squadrons, were to returned to Cochrane to form the basis of his marking force. More Mosquitoes were to be made available for the use of 617 Squadron and, again to Bennett's fury, a Pathfinder Mosquito squadron, 627, was to be transferred to 5 Group.

Cochrane and his squadron commanders quickly came up with a specialised marking technique which would allow it to make full use of the new tools at its disposal. The 5 Group technique consisted of low-level target identification and marking by Mosquitoes, followed by backing-up of markers by 83 and 97 Squadrons (which would also provide an advanced flare force) which would be assessed and corrected if necessary by more Mosquitoes, while the twelve main squadrons of 5 Group bombed the target. The methods of the now independent 5 Group proved to be highly successful over France and on some German targets and 5 Group's average bombing error was reduced to just 380 yards, better even than that possible with Oboe. The new technique did have several drawbacks, however. The marker force depended upon decent weather conditions and delays in establishing accurate marking could lead to fatal delays in calling in the Main Force while giving the Luftwaffe time to alert fighters.

Despite the loss of two Lancaster squadrons and a Mosquito squadron, Bennett's 8 (PFF) Group continued to strengthen its Mosquito force over the period and the LNSF began making ever more daring nuisance raids into Germany. In the Main Force the recent Battle of Berlin had seen a reduction in the growth of Lancaster squadrons and this in turn resulted in 3 Group's remaining Stirling squadrons being slow to re-equip with the Lancaster. More positively, the replacement of the older Halifax marks in 4 and 6 Groups with the more able Halifax III was completed shortly before D-Day. Some much-needed reinforcement for 4 Group came with the formation of 346 and 347 Squadrons. These were the first Free French squadrons in Bomber Command. To ensure that the Free French airmen had a relatively comfortable base, the long-suffering 77 Squadron was moved from its longstanding base at RAF Elvington to the less salubrious and just completed RAF Full Sutton.

Although the majority of aircrew appreciated the less dangerous focus of raids over Occupied France, they were less enthused by the decision to count these operations as only one-third of an operation. This requirement was quickly dropped in the aftermath of a raid which proved that 5 Group's new methods could quickly go wrong and result in disaster. The target on the night of 3/4 May was Mailly-le-Camp. The site had been identified, with the aid of the Resistance, to be the base for a Panzer division and, so, 5 Group enlisted the aid of 1 Group along with two Mosquitoes from 8 Group. The total number of aircraft dispatched was 362. The Master Bomber for the operation was Wing Commander Cheshire of 617 Squadron. His early markers and those of the 'backer-up' Lancasters which were to ensure the marking remained on-target were accurate but communication problems resulted in a delay in calling in the Main Force (the V.H.F. radio set of the Main Force Controller was drowned out by an American forces broadcast) and enemy night-fighters arrived in strength as the bewildered crews from 1 and 5 Groups circled the target waiting to be called in to bomb. The bombing was accurate, eventually, and heavy damage was done, but as the Main Force circled and night-fighters began claiming victim after victim radio discipline broke down to a degree with angry bomber skippers demanding to be allowed to either bomb or abort. Forty-two Lancasters (11.6 per cent of the force) failed to return.

The Lancasters of 1 Group, making up the second wave, bore the brunt of the night-fighter attacks and the Group lost twenty-eight from 173 aircraft (16.2 per cent). The Australian 460 Squadron had dispatched seventeen bombers from RAF Binbrook but lost five (29.4 per cent). There was already a great deal of resentment in Bomber Command towards 5 Group which many believed was given preferential treatment and, following this disaster, the recriminations between 1 Group and 5 Group squadrons were bitter and lasting. Other squadrons also lost heavily over Mailly-le-Camp with several squadrons losing more than two aircraft on the night.

Squadrons Suffering more than Two Losses at Mailly-le-Camp.[10]

Squadron	Losses
12	4
50	4
101	5
103	3
166	3
460	5
625	3
626	3

Amongst the aircraft lost during the Mailly-le-Camp operation was Lancaster III (JB402, OL-R) of 83 Squadron. This was piloted by the Deputy Main Force Controller, Squadron Leader E.N.M. Sparks. It was Sparks who had saved the day by calling the Main Force in when his leader could not communicate. He had remained in the target area to help control the attack and was homebound when he was shot down by a night-fighter. Thankfully, all of the crew survived. Sparks, along with his flight engineer, bomb-aimer, wireless operator and both air gunners managed to evade capture with the help of the Resistance, however both of his navigators were captured.

The nights of 21/22 May and 22/23 May saw a return to German targets. On the first night 532 aircraft were sent to bomb Duisburg in the Ruhr. Cloud covered the aiming point but with Oboe marking the bombing was accurate and heavy damage was once again done to this important target. On the second night Harris split his force into four distinct raids. The main target for the night was Dortmund with 375 aircraft from 1, 3, 6 and 8 Groups attacking the city for the loss of eighteen Lancasters. Meanwhile 1 and 5 Groups sent 235 aircraft to attack Brunswick, but the raid was a failure due to an incorrect weather forecast. Total and heavy cloud over the target area meant that the 5 Group marking effort failed and bombing was widely scattered. Thirteen Lancasters were lost during this failed operation[11] but 6 and 8 Groups had sent 133 aircraft to attack the Le Mans railway yards and this was carried out successfully. Along with the railway yards, a Gnome & Rhone aero engine factory nearby was also hit for the loss of one Halifax. The final raid of the day saw 128 aircraft from 4 and 8 Groups attack railway facilities at Orléans. Once again the raid was successful and the passenger station and the repair workshops were both damaged for the loss of one Halifax.

On 24/25 May Bomber Command launched a large raid on the town of Aachen. This was an important hub in the rail system which linked Germany and France and was, as such, a vital target in the build-up to D-Day. The raid consisted of 442 aircraft from every Group except 5 Group. Damage to the railway yards was severe and 14,800 residents of Aachen were bombed out. The raid cost eighteen Halifaxes and seven Lancasters.

Such was Bomber Command's strength by this stage of the war that, despite launching the major raid on Aachen mentioned above, Harris was also able to mount a raid on batteries at several locations on the French coast using 106 Halifaxes, 102 Lancasters and 16 Mosquitoes. These attacks were carried out without loss. Meanwhile, 5 Group was dispatching two raids itself. These targeted the Philips factory at Eindhoven and a Ford engine factory at Antwerp. At Eindhoven the Master Bomber aborted the attack due to cloud, but at Antwerp the bombers were able to attack but missed the target. There were no losses during either raid. At the same time as these raids were taking place Bomber Command was also undertaking a range of minor operations including fifteen Mosquitos of the LNSF attacking Berlin, thirty-one Serrate sorties and eight Intruder patrols over enemy airfields, six radio countermeasures operations, twenty-three sorties by OTU aircraft and eighteen Halifaxes and seven Stirling minelaying operations in the Frisians and off the coast of Brest. One Halifax making a radio countermeasures flight was lost.

In the afternoon and evening of 5 June the aircrew of Bomber Command found themselves being briefed for a wide variety of operations on a large scale. Indeed, the command set a record of 1,211 sorties flown during the night. For many of the airmen it was clear that this was the invasion. For those using H2S on their way over the Channel it became clear as the sea was packed with ships. The main invasion duties of Bomber Command were to bomb German gun positions, troop concentrations, fuel and ammunition dumps, to continue the offensive against the rail and road network and to attack French ports where E-Boats were assembling. Following the invasion this work required only part of Bomber Command.

We have already seen how the command was increasingly able to divide its forces in order to make multiple attacks on the same night. This ability was to come in very useful as it was also put to work making vital attacks on synthetic oil industry targets concentrated around the Ruhr. It was felt that the USAAF Eighth Air Force would suffer heavy casualties attacking these heavily defended targets by day, but Bomber Command, having proven its ability to hit small targets at night, was thought ideal for the task.

On the night of 5/6 June 1,012 aircraft were dispatched to attack a number of coastal batteries. Of these, 946 successfully claimed to have bombed their targets for the loss of three aircraft. Almost all of the bombing was carried out on Oboe marking due to cloudy conditions. The night also set a new record for the tonnage of bombs dropped by Bomber Command with over 5,000 tons. Two 4 Group Halifaxes were lost in the attack on the battery at Mont Fleury and a 6 Group Lancaster went down during the attack on Longues. The first aircraft lost was Halifax III (LW638, MP-W) of 76 Squadron. Pilot Officer Stanley Arthur Douglas Walker and his crew were killed when the Halifax was shot down. The second bomber to go down at Mont Fleury was Halifax III (MZ513, LK-K) of 578 Squadron. Squadron Leader Walter Geoffrey Watson DFC and the members of his crew were killed when their aircraft was hit by flak over the target and set on fire. Squadron Leader Watson headed back out to sea and his crew baled out, but Watson was still at the controls when the Halifax crashed into the sea. The three survivors from his crew were picked up by US Navy tank landing craft.

The Lancaster shot down on the Longues attack was Lancaster I (NE166, 60-D) of 582 Squadron. The very experienced and highly decorated crew of Squadron Leader Arthur William Raybould DSO DFM, vanished without trace.[12] Raybould was born at Dumfries but had spent much of his life in Cheshire and had been a student when he had enlisted in the RAF in 1940. He was a hugely experienced bomber pilot with seventy-eight sorties to his name despite being just 23 when he was killed. This courageous and skilled pilot had been awarded the DFM in August 1942 while serving with 101 Squadron and the DSO in November 1943 for his service with 105 Squadron.

From 426 Squadron another Halifax from the Houlgate force was lost when it exploded in the air outbound over Norfolk, while another Halifax, from 77 Squadron, crashed on take-off at Full Sutton.

In addition to these bombing attacks a number of other, more complicated operations were carried out by Bomber Command in support of the landings. For example, 110 aircraft of 1 and 100 Groups mounted bomber support operations designed to protect the aircraft targeting the coastal batteries. The 1 Group effort consisted of twenty-four Lancasters equipped with the ABC jamming equipment which patrolled likely night-fighter routes and their special operators (who were German speakers) used the equipment to jam the German radio guidance broadcasts. In addition, 100 Group undertook a variety of operations including radio countermeasures, Serrate and Intruder patrols. Two of the Intruder Mosquitoes and an ABC Lancaster were lost.

Meanwhile fifty-eight aircraft drawn from 3 and 5 Groups flew on a variety of operations whose purpose was to disguise the true location of the invasion fleets. Sixteen Lancasters from 617 Squadron, along with six G-H equipped Stirlings from 218 Squadron, flew extremely accurate courses dropping screens of Window in order to simulate the approach of a large convoy of vessels approaching the coast between Boulogne and Le Havre. So demanding was the navigation and flying of these courses, that the aircraft flew with extra navigators and pilots aboard and the crews had trained for their tasks for over a month. In addition, a mixed force of thirty-six Halifaxes and Stirlings drawn from four different squadrons dropped dummy paratroopers along with explosive devices to draw German forces away from the real invasion sites. Finally, thirty-one Mosquitoes attacked Osnabruck. Two Stirlings from the diversion force, both from 149 Squadron, were lost.

On 8/9 June Bomber Command made several attacks on a variety of railway targets in France but the night also marked the first dropping of the 12,000lb Tallboy bomb. Developed by Barnes Wallis, the first Tallboys were dropped during a raid by twenty-five Lancasters of 617 Squadron on a railway tunnel at Saumur. The target was first illuminated by flares dropped by four Lancasters from 83 Squadron and then marked at low-level by Mosquitoes, before the huge and precious 'earthquake' bombs were dropped with great accuracy. One of the Tallboys actually penetrated the roof of the tunnel and the result was that the tunnel was blocked for some time and Panzer reinforcements seriously delayed from reaching the battlefront.

On the following night Bomber Command launched an unusual attack with 410 aircraft which targeted four airfields in France. No clue was given as to why this operation was undertaken, but it is likely that it was in response to concerns that the Germans might attempt to fly reinforcements into the battle area (something which would have been almost suicidal given allied air superiority). All of the targets were successfully hit, but two Halifaxes were lost from a force attacking the airfield at Laval.

With Bomber Command tasked with attacking a number of well-defended synthetic oil plants as part of the new oil campaign, Harris ordered 303 aircraft from 1, 3 and 8 Groups to attack the Nordstern plant at Gelsenkirchen on the night of 12/13 June. The attack began very well with extremely accurate Oboe marking and bombing but deteriorated in its latter stages as cloud moved into the target area. Nevertheless, all production at the plant was halted, a loss to the Germans of 1,000 tons of aviation fuel per day. This loss of production lasted for several weeks and in addition other fuels were also lost. However, the target was indeed well-defended and seventeen Lancasters were lost in the attack.

On the day following the opening of the oil campaign Bomber Command launched its first daylight raid since May 1943 (when 2 Group left) when 221 Lancaster and 13 Mosquitoes of 1, 3, 5 and 8 Groups attacked E-boats and other light naval forces grouped in the harbour at Le Havre. The raid was split into two waves with the first attacking in the evening and the follow-up at dusk. The marking and bombing were accurate and very few E-boats escaped unscathed. The first wave was preceded by twenty-two Tallboy-armed Lancasters of 617 Squadron and three Mosquitoes. This force attacked the nearby U-boat pens and it is known that at least one Tallboy penetrated the pens successfully. The attack removed, once and for all, the threat to the invasion vessels from the E-boats. Arthur Harris still had doubts about risking his force in daylight and both waves of the attack were escorted by Spitfires. Only one Lancaster was lost.

Mid-June found Bomber Command very actively engaged in the oil campaign and the continuing support of the Allied invasion forces, but on 16/17 came a distraction. On this night 405 aircraft were sent to attack four newly identified V1 flying bomb sites in the Pas-de-Calais. All of the targets were marked by Oboe Mosquitoes and the attacks were judged to have been successful. On the same night 321 aircraft continued the oil campaign by attacking a synthetic-oil plant at Sterkrade/Holten. The weather, however, was poor and the target indicators quickly became obscured by cloud with the result that the Main Force could only use the glow as a marker for its bombing. The raid was scattered but some bombs did fall onto the plant although there was little overall effect on fuel production. To make matters worse the bomber stream was routed to pass over a night-fighter beacon at Bocholt and twenty-one bombers were lost to fighter attack to join the ten which had fallen to flak.

The Halifax component of the force suffered worst with twenty-two (13.6 per cent) of the 162 Halifaxes failing to return. As was known to happen, one squadron in particular was badly mauled. On this occasion the blow fell upon 77 Squadron which had despatched twenty-three aircraft on the raid and lost seven. Twenty-six airmen from 77 Squadron were killed, fifteen were captured and two evaded capture. The crew of one of the Halifaxes from 77 Squadron (MZ705, KN-Q) were all rescued after they ditched off Lowestoft.

Losses from 77 Squadron on 16/17 June.

Number	Code	Captain
MZ698	KN-J	F/Lt S.E. Wodehouse
MZ705	KN-Q	P/O S.E. Judd
MZ711	KN-T	F/Lt F.V.S. Goodman
MZ715	KN-Z	P/O A.I. Crain, RAAF
NA508	KN-A	Flt-Sgt R.A.W. Blair, RAAF
NA524	KN-F	F/O J.M. Shaw, USAAF
NA545	KN-R	P/O H.W. Bird, RAAF

Bomber Command continued to split its time between the flying-bomb threat and the Transportation Plan on the night of 4/5 July when 231 Lancasters and 15 Mosquitoes from 5 and 8 (PFF) Groups were sent to continue the bombing of the underground flying-bomb site at St-Leu-d'Esserent (617 Squadron had attacked the site earlier that day). The bombing was good but night fighters got in amongst the bomber stream and thirteen Lancasters were lost. The losses on this raid were spread between eight squadrons with 57, 106, 207, and 463 Squadrons each losing two bombers.

One of the 106 Squadron Lancasters to be lost on this night was that of Flying Officer Frank Crosier and crew aboard Lancaster III (WD339, ZN-U). The pilot was a native of Walthamstow and was aged just 20. It was the duty of this young man, like all pilots, to hold his aircraft steady if the crew had to bale out. Pilots knew that their chances of escape in such an event – especially in the Lancaster which had worse escape hatches than the Halifax – were extremely small and many lost their lives while struggling with the controls to give their comrades time to escape a falling, burning, bomber. Flying Officer Crosier lifted his Lancaster off from RAF Metheringham at 11.15pm but the crew failed to return and nothing further was heard. This brave young pilot, like so many others, had joined the ranks of those who had paid the ultimate price while allowing their crew to escape.[13]

The other raid on this night was made by 282 Lancasters and five Mosquitoes from 1, 6 (RCAF) and 8 (PFF) Groups, with the target being the railway yards at Orleans and Villeneuve. Both targets were bombed accurately but twenty Lancasters were lost (sixteen from the Villeneuve raid and four from Orleans). Accurate marking on these small precision targets in Occupied France was absolutely vital and on that night 35 (Madras Presidency) Squadron was sending fourteen of its Lancasters to mark Villeneuve. The squadron was providing the master bomber and his deputy, along with crews tasked as illuminators and backers-up.

Amongst the latter was the aircraft and crew of Squadron Leader Alec Panton Cranswick DSO DFC. The 24-year-old married man from Oxford was at the time, probably, the most experienced bomber pilot in Bomber Command. Over the course of the war he had flown 106 bomber operations over Europe and North Africa. Cranswick had talked his way back onto operations, despite the fact that he had already completed three operational tours, and was determined to complete his fourth tour which would bring him to 120 operations; this was his 107th operational flight and he was unaware that the authorities had decided that he would only be permitted to fly a further three operations before he was to be withdrawn. Cranswick eased Lancaster III (ND846, TL-J) off the runway at RAF Graveley at 11.16pm. This pathfinder squadron was used to losses but was stunned when TL-J and Cranswick failed to return from the operation. Cranswick's Lancaster had dropped its indicators at 8,000 feet over the target but was hit moments afterwards in the bomb-bay, which instantly caused a fierce fire. Cranswick assessed the situation within seconds and ordered his crew to bale out, but just moments later the stricken bomber either exploded or broke up in mid-air. The wireless operator, Flight Sergeant W.R. Horner DFC, was thrown clear and managed to deploy his parachute. He was picked up, very seriously injured, as a PoW but the remaining seven men, including Cranswick, were all killed.[14]

Cranswick's aircraft was one of two which failed to return to Graveley following this operation. The other was that of Squadron Leader George Frank Lambert DFC, a 24-year-old married man with two young sons. Lancaster III (ND731, TL-A) and its crew were also acting as backers-up on the operation and the Lancaster was shot down by a night fighter at approximately the same time, 1.33am, as the Cranswick crew. Four of the eight-man crew were able to bale out, with three being taken prisoner and one managing to evade capture. The remaining crew, including Squadron Leader Lambert, were killed aboard the crashing bomber.[15]

As was now usual, 100 Group put up a number of aircraft flying a variety of diversionary, countermeasure and intruder operations. These operations in themselves could often be highly dangerous as the heavy bomber aircraft flying RCM operations sometimes did not have the protection of the bomber stream and were themselves vulnerable to night fighter attack. On this night 35 RCM flights were made, and one Halifax failed to return to its base at RAF Foulsham. Flight Sergeant David McNab Thompson, RAAF, and his 192 Squadron crew were lost aboard Halifax III (LW621, DT-Q) which was believed to have crashed into the sea due to unknown reasons. The eight-man crew were all lost. Flight Sergeant Thompson was a 22-year-old from Yarraville, Victoria, and had married an English woman, Meriel Joyce Thompson, from Oxford.[16]

On 7 July Bomber Command had carried out an attack in support of the Army in the area of Caen, but this had been largely ineffective through poor target selection. On 18 July the British Second Army was about to launch an armoured attack on Caen, codenamed Operation Goodwood. Bomber Command was again called to support the attack by bombarding fortified villages to the east of the town. Four of the targets were marked by Oboe, but the fifth Oboe failed although the situation was redeemed by the Master Bomber and Pathfinder backers-up who marked the village using visual techniques. In total, 6,800 tons of bombs were dropped on the positions. USAAF bombers also attacked but, demonstrating the far greater carrying capacity of the British bombers, more than 5,000 tons of this total was dropped by Bomber Command. As a result of the accurate bombing, defending units from the 21st Panzer Division and the 16th Luftwaffe Field Division were severely disrupted, and the raid was said to be the most effective operation in support of the Allied armies to be carried out by Bomber Command. For the crews of Bomber Command, the attack gave them something different as most bombing runs were made between 5,000-9,000 feet, the flak being subdued by Allied artillery and naval bombardment; only six aircraft were lost.

On the night of 14/15 July Bomber Command made two attacks. The targets were the railway yards at Revigny and Villeneuve and flying-bomb sites at Anderbelck and Les Landes. By this stage of the war the command was capable of mounting large-scale support operations and on this night these operations consisted of a diversionary sweep over the North Sea by 132 aircraft, 42 Mosquitoes flying radar counter-measure (RCM) flights, 56 Mosquitoes flew intruder patrols, and eight Stirlings flew 'gardening' operations off the Biscay ports. A total of eight aircraft were lost on the night, seven Lancasters from the Revigny raid and a Mosquito intruder from 515 Squadron. Mosquito VI (PZ293) had taken off from RAF Little Snoring shortly before midnight, tasked with patrolling over enemy airfields. At 2.15am the pilot, Flight Lieutenant Hugh Arthur Lightbody (28) was blinded by searchlights in the vicinity of the airfield at Florennes. As a result, the Mosquito crashed and both the crew were killed. Flight Lieutenant Lightbody became one of at least 44 Jamiacan airmen to be killed during the war. He hailed from Malvern, Jamaica, and was an experienced pilot who had enlisted in the RAF Volunteer Reserve as a Sergeant Pilot in 1937 and had been called up for service at the very beginning of the war.[17]

On 27 August came yet another momentous sign that Bomber Command's war had changed dramatically when 243 aircraft, mainly Halifaxes of 4 Group, made the first major daylight raid on Germany in three years. The target was the Rheinpreussen synthetic oil refinery at Homberg (Meerbeck). The bomber armada, escorted by nine squadrons of Spitfires, ploughed through the enemy sky with air gunners no doubt anxiously scanning the skies. Showing the increasing aerial dominance that was enjoyed by the Allies, only one enemy aircraft was seen. Oboe Mosquitoes were somewhat thwarted by cloud, but accurate bombing was possible through gaps in the cloud cover and damage to the refinery was done. On the same day Bomber Command continued its offensive against flying-bomb sites, 226 aircraft accurately hit the site at Mimoyecques. The campaign against the flying-bomb (and V2 and other special weapons sites) continued throughout much of the rest of the war. No aircraft were lost from any of the Bomber Command sorties on this day.

Just days after the above daylight attack another, far larger, raid was made on 31 August against eight V2 rocket store sites with 601 bombers making what were claimed to be accurate attacks on these sites for the loss of six Lancasters. Amongst the losses was the aircraft of the commanding officer of 550 Squadron. Wing Commander Alan Francis Moir Sisley and his crew had taken off from RAF North Killingholme shortly after 1pm in Lancaster I (NF962, BQ-V) but the bomber crashed at L'Étoile on the northern side of the River Somme, killing all eight men aboard.[18] The flight engineer in the crew was 19-year-old Glaswegian, Sergeant Ronald MacLeod. Despite his youth Sergeant MacLeod was a married man with children and his widow had a very touching inscription, much of it in Gaelic, placed upon his headstone. The inscription read: ' GUS AM BRIS AN LA AGUS AN TEICH NA SGAILEAN. DADDY, MAMMY, MARGARET AND PEGGY'.[19]

Meanwhile, 165 Halifaxes of 6 (RCAF) Group, along with five Pathfinder Mosquitoes bombed a coastal battery at Ile de Céezembre, close to St Malo. The bombers flew into the target at a maximum height of just 3,000 feet and the site was very accurately bombed for the loss of just one Halifax, MZ879, BM-O, of 433 Squadron. Pilot Officer James Ralph Beveridge, RCAF, and his crew (consisting of five Canadians and an RAF flight engineer) was lost without trace.[20]

For the rest of the year Bomber Command continued its campaigns against multiple targets including oil facilities, transport hubs, V1 and V2 sites, and aiding Allied forces in a tactical bombing role. In addition to this Harris continued to send raids to Germany whenever this was feasible. A daylight raid on 8 September saw the last use of the Stirling on a bombing raid when four aircraft from 149 Squadron operated as part of a force of 333 aircraft sent to bomb German positions around Le Havre, which the British were preparing to assault. The final Stirling to drop bombs on enemy territory was believed to be that of Flying Officer J.J. McKee, RAAF, aboard LK396. The bombing around Le Havre continued for several days but was often frustrated by cloud or by smoke and dust curtailing raids. The heaviest raid in the short campaign occurred on 10 September when 992 aircraft bombed eight German positions for no loss. On the following day another attempt was made but the Master Bomber called a halt after 171 aircraft had bombed. Under attack from two British divisions, the garrison surrendered hours later.

On 19/20 September Bomber Command suffered a heavy blow to morale when Wing Commander Guy Penrose Gibson, VC DSO and Bar DFC and Bar, failed to return from an operation to bomb oil facilities at Mönchengladbach/Rheydt. For Wing Commander Gibson, his personal role in the war had become a cause of great irritation and his lack of operational activity a source of growing annoyance. Gibson was increasingly convinced that he was being kept out of action because of his fame, a suspicion which was undoubtedly correct, and this rankled with him. A complex and intelligent man, Gibson had fallen prey to the peculiar compulsion which affected some Bomber Command airmen and compelled them to return to operations time and time again even though they were tour-expired. Gibson was serving as Base Operations Officer at RAF Coningsby but was missing operations and was doing everything he could to get back to the squadrons he loved, officially or unofficially. On this occasion he appears to have secured permission to act as Master Bomber on the raid despite the fact that he was very inexperienced with the Mosquito.

After attending a staff officer training course from March until May, Gibson had been sent on leave. After he heard of the D-Day landings on 6 June he became increasingly anxious that the war would be ended before he had the chance to return to operations. As soon as his leave was over he sought an audience with Harris and asked for an operational posting. Harris, eager not to lose Gibson but recognising his agitation, arranged for a position as a staff officer at RAF East Kirby where he would shadow the Base Air Staff Officer to get a grasp of the planning and liaison activities necessary in such a role. On 5 July Gibson flew a Lancaster for the first time since leaving 617 Squadron, on a test flight, and a fortnight later he accompanied a crew on an operation to bomb a V1 site in France.

At the start of August Gibson had been posted to RAF Coningsby (54 Base). Coningsby was renowned for being a centre of innovative tactical planning in 5 Group and this was a high-profile posting. Gibson's new duties, however, gave him access to intelligence reports which led him to believe that the war might indeed be concluded before he became operational once more and his sense of agitation increased. It seems likely that, in response to this, Air Vice Marshal Cochrane, who enjoyed a good relationship with Gibson, agreed to him flying on limited operations with strict conditions meaning that such flying was to be in a non-participatory role (i.e. as a passenger/observer), involved only a short time over the target and was on a mission where there was fair chance of baling out over friendly territory if anything went wrong. Clearly, Bomber Command was still unwilling to risk losing such a valuable member in terms of propaganda value. In mid-August Gibson apparently once again flew as an observer on a daylight raid over Holland and on 2 September he had his first flight in a Mosquito when he flew to one of the Shetland Islands.

On 19 September a change in weather resulted in Bomber Command having to hurriedly prepare an operation on Mönchengladbach and Rheydt rather than the originally proposed target of Bremen. Responsibility for planning the operation was 5 Group's and the Group would also be responsible for marking and controlling the operation. The plan which was proposed for the raid, which involved 227 Lancasters and ten Mosquitoes from 1 and 5 Groups, was a very complicated one with three different areas being marked using an unfamiliar technique known as dispersed marking. Because of this complexity many of the crews were left perplexed and very surprised when it was announced that the untried (in this technique) Gibson would be Master Bomber. Many crews expected the choice to be an experienced Master Bomber from Coningsby or from 627 Squadron at RAF Woodhall Spa. Some even voiced the opinion that it might have been Gibson's inexperience in the planning of such operations that had resulted in such a complex plan.

Further problems arose with no serviceable Mosquito available at Coningsby meaning that Gibson had to journey to Woodhall Spa to borrow a Mosquito from 627 Squadron. In addition to this minor problem Gibson's first choice of navigator was ill and so he chose to be accompanied by the Station Navigation Officer at Coningsby, Squadron Leader Jim Warwick. Upon arrival at Woodhall Spa, Gibson refused to use the reserve aircraft and instead demanded the use of Mosquito XX (KB267, AZ-E). This caused some antagonism with the original crew of AZ-E and the groundcrew as it meant swapping bombloads over between aircraft.

Together with navigator Squadron Leader J.B. Warwick, DFC, Gibson took off from RAF Woodhall Spa in Mosquito XX (KB267, AZ-E). Main Force crews heard Gibson clearly giving directions over the target and returning crews told intelligence officers that he had given no indication of being in any difficulties during the course of the raid. The raid, however, was a disappointment due to the complicated marking plan. The plan called for the three aiming points (Green, Red and Yellow) to be moved mid-raid, a difficult proposition at the best of time, but with an inexperienced Master Bomber who had not flown operationally for some time, most improbable. The marking of the Red aiming point went wrong with the markers failing to identify the target. Gibson himself attempted to mark but his target indicators hung up. He then ordered the Main Force assigned to Red to hold causing them to turn away, something which exposed the force to greater risk of interception by night-fighters, as had happened at Mailly-le-Camp. Some crew, frustrated, took matters into their own hands and bombed the Green aiming point and, with little choice, Gibson gave permission for the rest of the force to bomb on Green.

It would appear that Gibson then remained in the target area for a couple of minutes to assess the scene and one crew from 61 Squadron reported at debriefing that they believed they had heard Gibson report that he had a damaged engine. As the crews returned from the operation and were debriefed it became clear that Gibson had not returned to RAF Woodhall Spa. At first this did not cause concern as many believed that he had made for RAF Coningsby where he was, after all, stationed. Meanwhile, at a foggy Coningsby it was believed he may have landed elsewhere due to weather. As time passed, however, it became clear that Gibson had not returned and the rumour that he was missing quickly spread throughout 5 Group. There appears to have been a marked reluctance to admit that Gibson was indeed missing and, although Churchill, who had grown quite close to Gibson, was notified one week later it was not until the end of November that Gibson was officially listed as being missing.

However, while over Holland on the return leg the Mosquito was seen in trouble at low-level, with the cockpit lights on and, according to some eyewitnesses, in flames. The aircraft crashed near Steenbergen-en-Kruisland killing both men. The initial investigation at Steenbergen concluded that there had only been one man in the cockpit when the Mosquito crashed, and Jim Warwick was identified by his identity tags. A third human hand was then discovered revealing that the recovered remains were those of two airmen. A sock with a laundry tag revealed the name of the second airman, W/CdrWing Commander Guy Penrose Gibson. The two men were given a decent funeral by the local Dutch community.

The cause of Gibson and Warwick's death will most likely never be known, but there have been many who have attempted to advance various theories. These have ranged from pilot (or crew) error, technical problems, damage caused by enemy action, to friendly fire. The most recent of these, unconfirmed, theories was advanced in 2011 following the death of a man who had flown on the operation as a rear gunner. The man, Sergeant Bernard McCormack, had left a taped confession before his death in 1992 stating how he had fired upon what he believed to be an enemy night-fighter over Steenbergen and that he had seen it go down. After questioning upon his return, he had become convinced that he had in fact shot down Gibson. There is absolutely no proof of this, but crews would not have expected to have seen Gibson's Mosquito over Steenbergen as he had been advised to return over France. Gibson had refused this option and favoured returning directly at a low altitude. The truth, despite Sergeant McCormack's heartfelt guilt, is that we shall probably never know how Guy Gibson came to lose his life. His death was a blow, but he had paid the price which tens of thousands of Bomber Command aircrew paid during the war.

By late 1944 the Allied air superiority was such that Bomber Command had begun to once more undertake massed daylight raids. Although many of these attacks continued to be part of the strategic offensive, some were tactical in nature. With the failure of Operation Market Garden, however, the Allied right flank near Nijmegen was left vulnerable. On 7 October Bomber Command thus launched raids on the towns of Kleve and Emmerich which stood on the approach roads to Nijmegen (other attacks took place on the sea walls at Walcheren while 617 Squadron launched an attack on the Kembs Dam which it was believed the Germans could use to flood the Rhine Valley should the Allies advance). The attack on Emmerich consisted of 340 Lancasters and 110 Mosquitoes and was very accurate with almost 2,500 buildings in the town being destroyed and 680,000 cubic feet of rubble having to be later removed from the town for the loss of only three of the attacking aircraft (all Lancasters). Amongst the aircraft which failed to return was Lancaster I (PD239, AS-Z) of 166 Squadron. The bomber had taken off from RAF Kirmington shortly before noon with 22-year-old Flight Lieutenant Geoffrey Underhill Fulford at the controls, but nothing more was heard, and the crew were declared missing. The mid-upper gunner in the crew was Sergeant William Skea, a 19-year-old Orcadian from Northill, Shapinsay. His parents, William and Mary Ann Skea, were informed that their son had failed to return from operations and nothing more was heard of him. As late as a year later his parents placed a notice in the *Orkney Herald* stating that their son had now been officially presumed to have lost his life on 7 October 1944. At some point afterwards the young air gunner's body must have been recovered as he and his entire crew are buried in the Reichswald War Cemetery.[21]

The attack on the Kembs Dam by 617 Squadron was made by thirteen Lancasters. Seven of these aircraft were to fly at 8,000 feet to draw the flak while the others were briefed to attack from below 1,000 feet in order to place their Tallboys, equipped with delayed fuses, alongside the lock gates of the dam. American Mustang fighters were to attempt to suppress the flak positions before the bombers attacked. The attack succeeded and the gates were destroyed but two of the Lancasters from the low force were lost. Lancaster III (LM482, KC-Q) had taken off from RAF Woodhill Spa at 1pm with Flight Lieutenant Christopher John Geoffrey Howard at the controls. Howard's aircraft failed to release its Tallboy on the first bomb run and was seen to turn away from the target before beginning a second bomb run. On this run the Lancaster was hit by light flak and it crashed inside the German border near the village of Efringen-Kirchen, killing the entire crew.[22]

The second Lancaster from 617 to be lost was that of 24-year-old Squadron Leader Drew Rothwell Cullen Wyness DFC. Lancaster III (NG180, KC-S) had taken off at 1.10pm and was nearing the aiming point when it was hit by light flak which caused both port engines to catch fire. Squadron Leader Wyness dropped his Tallboy, feathered the useless engines, and steered the stricken bomber north before putting it down in the Rhine close to Rheinweller. The crew survived the ditching and clambered aboard their dinghy. Seeing activity on the German bank of the Rhine, two of the crew, flight engineer Flight Sergeant James Hurdiss (23) and mid-upper gunner Flight Sergeant Thomas Horrocks, jumped overboard and swam to the French bank in Alsace. Shortly afterwards a German patrol boat was spotted and the rear gunner, Flying Officer George Edward Cansell (21), also jumped overboard and swam to the French bank. The soldiers aboard the patrol boat then fired warning shots and ordered the remaining crew to paddle to the German bank, from where they were taken to Rheinweller. The mayor of the town refused to be responsible for their custody and two local Gestapo agents were summoned. The Gestapo men, one of whom was Hugo Gruenner, and several gendarmes took the airmen to the riverbank where they were shot and their bodies thrown into the Rhine. Nothing more was heard of the three airmen who swam to France and it was later surmised that they too were captured and executed by the Gestapo. Their bodies were never discovered and some sources claim it is possible that they were cremated at Natzweiler Struthof SS Concentration Camp, near Strasbourg.[23] The other aircrew to be murdered were: Flight Lieutenant Ronald Henry Williams, DFC (22) (navigator); Flying Officer Herbert Walter Honig (22) (bomb aimer); and Flying Officer Bruce James Hosie (21), RNZAF (wireless operator).[24]

On 14/15 October Bomber Command launched Operation Hurricane. This was an operation which was intended to demonstrate to the German people that the Allied Air Forces enjoyed complete superiority even over Germany itself. Thus, Bomber Command and the US Eighth Air Force were to mount huge raids over the Ruhr. On 14 October a huge daylight raid consisting of 1,013 aircraft attacked Duisburg, dropping 3,574 tons of high-explosive and 820 tons of incendiaries (the lack of incendiaries was because of the simple fact that there was now little left to burn in the city). The attacking force lost fourteen aircraft of which thirteen were Lancasters. This was because the first waves were made up of this type and by the time the Halifaxes bombed the anti-aircraft defences of Duisburg had been overwhelmed. The Eighth Air Force's contribution was a raid by 1,251 bombers on the Cologne area. They were accompanied by 749 fighters and not a single enemy fighter was seen.

That night, Bomber Command continued the onslaught on Duisburg by sending 1,005 aircraft to attack in two waves separated by two hours. A further 4,040 tons of high-explosive and 500 tons of incendiaries fell on the battered city. Five Lancasters and two Halifaxes were lost on the operation. Duisburg had received almost 9,000 tons of bombs in just forty-eight hours during the course of this almost continuous raiding. Its defences had been completely overwhelmed and the Luftwaffe had utterly failed to protect the city. Detailed accounts from Duisburg are not available, but the damage and casualties were known to be very heavy, one report conceding that all of the local mines and coke ovens had been either destroyed or damaged so badly that they were inactive.

Demonstrating the now immense strength of Bomber Command, a force of 233 Lancasters and seven Mosquitoes from 5 Group was spared from revisiting Duisburg and instead were sent to Brunswick on the night of 14/15 October. A number of complex diversions along with support offered by RAF night-fighters resulted in only one Lancaster being lost from this force. This fifth attempt to knock Brunswick out of the war succeeded. The centre of the city was completely destroyed, and many outlying districts were also heavily damaged and so bad was the damage that officials in Brunswick estimated that this was a 1,000-bomber attack. At least 80,000 people were bombed out.

Despite these heavy attacks, Bomber Command continued with its extensive campaign of minelaying. This duty proved to be of great value to the war effort and provided many inexperienced Bomber Command airmen with their first taste of operational experience. These operations, however, were not without risk and many aircrew lost their lives on so-called 'gardening' operations. On the night of 15 October four aircraft (two Halifaxes and two Lancasters) were lost on such operations. Squadron Leader S.W. Hart and his crew took off from RAF Melbourne at 9.17pm to lay mines in Danish waters but failed to return. It was later revealed that Halifax III (MZ826, ZA-M) had gone down, but that the navigator, Flight Lieutenant S.A.F. McHardy had managed to evade capture. The remaining five men had been killed. The dead included wireless operator Pilot Officer Albert Lawrence Slatter, known to friends and family as Larry, who was a 28-year-old from Cheltenham. He was a married man and left behind his widow, Isobel, and 3-year-old son, Ian, in Aberdeen. Pilot Officer Slatter is buried at Vadum Cemetery in Denmark.

An experimental daylight cloud-cover raid on Bonn mounted by 128 Lancasters of the now G-H equipped 3 Group took place on 18 October. The raid, as described previously, was a complete success and a vindication of the G-H device and severe damage was done by highly accurate bombing for the loss of only one aircraft. Lancaster (HK544, KO-U) of 115 Squadron had taken off from RAF Witchford just after 8.:30am and had set course for the target. Nothing further was heard from the crew and they were posted missing. Flying Officer Kenneth Victor Smith, RAAF, a 21-year-old from New South Wales, and his crew were all killed.[25]

For the family members and friends of those who failed to return from Bomber Command operations the nature of the campaign meant that the majority of men who failed to return were declared missing and little was known of their fate. This state of affairs could last for many months or even years. The news which arrived by official telegram was usually dreaded but it did not always bring bad news. Sometimes a family received word that a loved one had survived the loss of his aircraft and that he had been captured by the enemy and was a PoW. Mr and Mrs Alfred Sheen of 2 Orchard View, Saughall, received just such a telegram at the end of October. This notified them that their son, Pilot Officer Thomas Alfred Sheen was a prisoner. Pilot Officer Sheen was an experienced airman who had flown approximately fifty operations, many of them with 83 Squadron in the Pathfinders.

On the night of 23/24 October Bomber Command revisited its old bête-noir, Essen. This was the largest raid of the war on this city with 1,055 aircraft dropping 4,538 tons of bombs on Essen. Due to earlier bombing there was so little left to burn in Essen that more than 90 per cent of the bombs were high explosive (including more than 500 of the 4,000lb high capacity bombs (cookies); 607 buildings were destroyed and over 800 seriously damaged. At least 662 people were killed for the loss of eight aircraft.

Just thirty-six hours later, on 25 October, Bomber Command revisited Essen by daylight when 771 aircraft found the target obscured by cloud and bombed on skymarkers. The attack was scattered, but serious damage was still done to Essen with 1,163 buildings destroyed and 820 people killed. Severe damage was caused to the remaining industrial concerns in the city, especially to the Krupps steelworks where the destruction of the power supply network caused a complete shutdown, and the Borbeck pig-iron works was shut down completely for the rest of the war. Four aircraft were lost. While Essen was being bombed a force of 243 aircraft attacked the oil plant at Homberg. Bombing was somewhat scattered, and the results are not known, but no aircraft were lost.

Three days later 733 aircraft of Bomber Command visited Cologne and caused catastrophic damage for the loss of seven aircraft. Entire areas of the city were almost completely devastated with 2,239 blocks of flats being destroyed along with fifteen industrial premises, dock facilities and other premises. More than 600 were killed and double that number injured. This raid was followed by another on 30/31 October by 905 aircraft. Aided by Oboe marking, but hindered by cloud cover, Bomber Command assessed that the bombing was scattered and that little damage had been done, but they were wrong. Massive damage had been caused by the raid in several suburbs by the 4,041 tons of bombs which fell on them. Property damage was colossal and almost 500 were killed. The St Gereon Church, which was some 1,000 years old, was hit by a cookie which caused damage which would not be repaired for over three decades. All of this damage was caused without loss to Bomber Command.

The next night 493 aircraft revisited Cologne on yet another Oboe attack which took place through almost complete cloud cover. Damage, while not as severe as in the recent raids, was still serious but assessment is almost impossible to evaluate as the system of recording damage in the city had now almost completely broken down in the face of the devastation. Two Lancasters were lost. The incredibly heavy pummelling continued through the early part of November with heavy raids causing massive damage to a number of towns and cities including Dusseldorf and Bochum. The latter city was visited by 749 aircraft on the night of 4/5 November and severe damage was done with over 4,000 buildings being destroyed in the city. The industrial areas were hit very hard indeed and nearly 1,000 people lost their lives. Unusually, however, the German night-fighters managed to strike back and twenty-eight bombers failed to return. For 346 (Free French) Squadron, based at RAF Elvington the operation was calamitous with five Halifaxes lost from the sixteen which it had sent.

On the same night 174 Lancasters and two Mosquitoes from 5 Group re-visited the partially repaired Dortmund-Ems Canal to the north of Munster and once again breached the canal, causing it to drain. The effects of such attacks on these targets can be seen by a report which was captured at the end of the war in which Speer informed Hitler that the damage to the canal prevented coke from the Ruhr reaching three vital steelworks at Brunswick and Osnabruck. When he was interrogated after the war Albert Speer admitted that the attacks on the Dortmund-Ems Canal caused more serious setbacks to industry in Germany than any other attacks at that period of the war. Three Lancasters were lost on the raid.

On 12 November a special operation was mounted by thirty Lancasters from 9 and 617 Squadron. The Lancasters, armed with Tallboys and accompanied by a Lancaster from 463 Squadron carrying a cameraman, took off from Lossiemouth bound for yet another attack on the *Tirpitz*. A raid on 29 October had damaged the mighty battleship but Bomber Command was determined to finally sink it. Upon reaching Tromso the bombers found clear weather conditions and the *Tirpitz* was struck by at least two of the massive bombs. The bombs caused immense damage and the *Tirpitz* suffered a magazine explosion and capsized. The Admiralty grumpily refused to acknowledge the *Tirpitz* as sunk because its upturned keel was still above water. Bomber Command had finally sunk the *Tirpitz* and only one Lancaster, from 9 Squadron, was damaged by flak before making a safe landing in Sweden where the crew were briefly interned. The raid could have been disastrous. The *Tirpitz*, at bay at Tromso, was protected by fighters stationed nearby but they did not take off due to communication problems.

On 21/22 November Bomber Command carried out five attacks on different targets. They included attacks on both the Dortmund-Ems Canal and the Mittelland Canal. Breaches were made in both canals and reconnaissance photographs showed that the Mittelland Canal had been drained over a length of 30 miles leaving a large number of barges stranded and industries without supplies. The attack on the Mittelland Canal cost Bomber Command two Lancasters from 5 Group.

December opened with the command launching its first attack on oil facilities in eastern Germany. Severe damage was done to the facilities at Leuna by 475 Lancasters, guided by twelve Mosquitoes. Five of the Lancasters were lost, but this was regarded as acceptable considering that Leuna lay west of Leiiepzig and was 250 miles from the western borders of Germany.

When the crews at briefing on the afternoon of 12 December saw that they were once again heading for Essen many must have wondered what was left to destroy in the city and whether or not they were just turning over the rubble. The command sent 540 aircraft to Essen that night in what was a very accurate attack on the battered Krupps works. The raid caused substantial further damage and was the final one mounted against Essen. Six Lancasters were lost.

With the surprise German Ardennes offensive gaining ground, Bomber Command was ordered to give assistance and on the nights between 19 and 26 December launched a number of assaults on communications hubs in order to restrict the flow of reinforcements, ammunition and fuel to the attacking forces. This demonstrated the many roles which Bomber Command could now fulfil. Even in 1943 many, including Harris, would have considered it impossible that Bomber Command was capable of being able to hit small, tactical, targets with sufficient accuracy. Oboe and the marking developments pioneered by 5 and 8 Groups had ended that debate while the growing aerial superiority meant that daylight bombing by huge forces was also now possible and the development of G-H bombing by 3 Group aided in increasing accurate daylight bombing by the Command.

On the last day of 1944 Bomber Command dispatched a dozen Mosquitoes from 627 Squadron to attack a Gestapo Headquarters headquarters at Oslo. Eight of the Mosquitoes bombed the target and recorded seeing hits on the building. On the same day two attacks were made on railway yards at Vohwinkel and Osterfeld. The G-H attack by 3 Group at the first target went wrong due to high winds which carried some of the bombing off-target, but serious damage was done by 1 and 8 Groups at the second target.

CHAPTER 7

1945 – Crushing Blows

Summary of the Year

The year opened with further attacks on the Dortmund-Ems and Mittelland Canals canals but, alongside such operations and the continued oil campaign, Harris remained determined to continue his bludgeoning attacks upon the towns and cities of Germany. Targets in Germany were, however, becoming harder to find and because of this a number of raids were mounted against more obscure towns which had hitherto escaped damage. Some old favourites which had proven hard to destroy also found themselves revisited.

Other operations in the early months of the year included raids of a more tactical nature to support Allied ground operations. A plan to isolate the Ruhr communities before their invasion saw Bomber Command used to attack series of canals and other communications targets which linked the area.

Many familiar targets from previous years were visited for the final time during the period, amongst them Munich, Stuttgart and Cologne. The strength of Bomber Command during this period was phenomenal and it was often possible to send out two large raids on separate targets at the same time which meant it was capable of delivering terrible, devastating blows. With the Luftwaffe and German ground defences increasingly in disarray, casualties fell dramatically although aircrew continued to lose their lives right up until the final days of the war in Europe.

This part of the war also saw some of the most controversial raids of the war. The most infamous of these was the attack on Dresden which took place on 13/14 February and which resulted in the deaths of at least 50,000 people in a firestorm. Shortly afterwards, when news of the attack surfaced, attitudes amongst some officials underwent a radical change. A number of politicians who had previously been eminently supportive of Bomber Command suddenly began to row back upon their previous support and sought to disassociate themselves from the campaign.

Foremost amongst them was Churchill who cynically sought to wash his hands of any involvement in the planning of the Dresden raid. His actions so infuriated Bomber Harris that a vicious memo was sent to the Prime Minister, after which Churchill moderated his tone, but remained critical in an effort to appear innocent of involvement.

Regardless of the controversies the war for the airmen of Bomber Command went on as usual amidst the sorrow and loss of comrades and the stress of front-line bomber operations. This period also saw the final Bomber Command VC of the war awarded to Captain Edwin Swales of the South African Air Force (SAAF).

Despite its weaknesses the Luftwaffe also proved that it could sometimes marshal its strength to deliver a sobering blow against its old adversary and there were several occasions where losses exceeded the now low normal. The most daring of these blows came in early March when 200 Luftwaffe fighters (as part of Operation Gisela) followed the bombers back home to their bases in England and succeeded in shooting down 20 aircraft.

Demonstrating how well the war was progressing for the Allies, the target list increasingly featured targets in the far east of Germany. The command continued to bolster its strength and this period also saw a number of very large raids which took place in daylight. These were planned not only as part of the strategic offensive, but also in an effort to show the German people that the war was lost and that continued resistance would only result in greater loss of life and damage to German cities. These operations included two raids by forces of over 1,000 bombers on consecutive days with the targets being Essen and Dortmund.

Meanwhile the command was increasingly capable of mounting more precise strikes. The most precision raids were often made by 617 Squadron (increasingly joined by 9 Squadron) and the unit now had even more tools at its disposal. In mid-March the squadron once again attacked the Bielefeld Viaduct (something of a bete noir for the unit) but this time the squadron dropped the first 22,000lb Grand Slam bomb of the war, causing the viaduct to collapse. The Grand Slams also proved their use in finally allowing Bomber Command to successfully attack the massive U-boat pens. Other precision targets were hit by 3 and 5 Groups, operating independently of the Main Force on many occasions. Meanwhile the Light Night Striking Force (LNSF) continued its campaign of visiting German cities when the heavies were busy elsewhere.

The beginning of April saw a momentous development when, partly in reaction to criticism over Dresden and partly due to the fact that there was an increasingly small number of targets of worth left for it to attack, area bombing was officially ended. The final major Bomber Command raid of the war came just days later when 440 bombers attacked Hamburg. Despite this, a number of targets continued to receive attention, although aiming points increasingly became focused on tactical objectives. Enemy naval assets were targeted and sunk and 617 Squadron finally managed to sink the *Tirpitz*.

The final heavy bomber raid of the war came on the night of 26 April when Bomber Command visited the Tonsberg oil refinery in southern Norway. Some of the final operations, however, were missions of mercy. From late April until VE-Day the command mounted Operation Exodus which saw 469 flights bring 75,000 PoWs back to Britain and Operation Manna which saw the bombers dropping vital food supplies to the starving population of Holland. During this period the command continued to mount some attacks and an attack on Kiel on the night of 2/3 May saw the final Bomber Command losses of the war.

The Campaign

On 2/3 January, for example, Bomber Command revisited Nuremberg, sending 514 aircraft in the hope that this elusive target, scene of the command's worst disaster, could finally be destroyed. The Pathfinders arrived in clear weather and received aid from a rising full moon (something which would have earlier in the war spelt disaster). They clearly marked the target and the Main Force thundered in. Much of the centre of the city was destroyed, more than 4,000 modern houses being destroyed alongside important industrial concerns such as the M.A.N. and Siemens factories in what has been referred to as 'a near-perfect example of area bombing'. In addition to the modern properties destroyed were 2,000 preserved medieval houses along with the castle, Rathaus and almost all of the historic churches in the city centre. Nuremberg had finally been vanquished, at the cost this night of just four Lancasters (although two more crashed in France).

The destruction being done to German towns and cities was now reaching catastrophic proportions but for Harris this was simply vindication of the claims he had made since taking over command. Support for the activities of Bomber Command remained high amongst the public and the press although there was some disquiet beginning to be voiced in certain political circles. The Nuremberg raid was followed up by heavy attacks on Hannover, Hanau and Munich on the nights of 5-8 January. This was followed up on 14/15 by an extremely successful attack on the oil facilities at Leuna and Dülmen, as well as an attack on the railway yards at Grevenbroich. Losses on these raids were generally light but the Hannover raid cost the command thirty-one aircraft. At the end of the month the final large raid on Stuttgart was mounted when 602 aircraft bombed the city on the night of 28/29 January. The force was drawn from 1, 4, 6, and 8 Groups and was split into two waves divided by three hours. Although an area attack, this operation did have specific targets. The first wave flew to the town of Kornwestheim, just to the north of the city, to attack the large rail yards there, while the second wave's aiming point was the suburb of Zuffenhausen, in which there was the Hirth engine factory. Cloud cover resulted in the force having to resort to skymarkers and bombing was, as a result, scattered.   Despite this, heavy damage was done, especially at Kornwestheim, and the Bosch factory in Stuttgart was also badly hit. A substantial number of bombers, however, bombed a large decoy site which was even firing rockets into the air to simulate target indicators exploding. A total of eleven aircraft were lost on the raid, including one Mosquito.

As the Allied armies advanced Bomber Command found itself called once more into the role of tactical bombing. On 7 February, for example, British armies were poised to advance across the German border and requested preparatory support from Bomber Command. As a result, the fortified towns of Goch and Kleve were attacked overnight. The main target was Goch and a force of 464 aircraft attacked here. As was now usual a Master Bomber controlled the operation. On this occasion, with accuracy key, he called the Main Force to come below the cloud-base to attack. Most of the bombers therefore attacked from approximately 5,000 feet. Because of this the attack developed with great accuracy but the Master Bomber called a halt to the attack after 155 aircraft had bombed as dust and smoke caused by the raid had made effective control of the raid all but impossible. Despite this there was massive damage in the town and the defences were reduced significantly.

At Kleve 285 aircraft bombed and the damage was even more severe. After the war Kleve claimed that it was the most destroyed town of any of comparable size within Germany. There was, however, some rancour over the operation as the commanding officer of the infantry attack claimed later that he had asked for a purely incendiary attack, but Bomber Command had dropped 1,384 tons of high-explosives instead. This seems to have been a case of an officer, after the casualties caused by Allied bombing had become clear, trying to divorce himself from responsibility. There is no reason to expect that an attack on prepared defensive positions would be made with incendiaries, high-explosive bombs were clearly more suited to this task.

The Bombing of Dresden

Having seen the adaptability of Bomber Command shown by the attacks in support of the British Army, the 13/14 February saw the most controversial raid of the entire war when 805 aircraft were sent to bomb Dresden. The city was one of several on a list which had been passed to Bomber Command at the behest of Stalin and through Churchill and the Air Ministry. The list of targets and accompanying memo urged (ordered) Bomber Command to mount attacks on several towns and cities which were being used as transport hubs for the transferral of troops between the Eastern and Western Fronts. The list included Berlin, Chemnitz and Dresden amongst others, but Chemnitz and Dresden were given particular importance as targets. The attack on these targets was given the codename Operation Thunderclap and Churchill played a clear role in the final planning.

The attack consisted of two separate raids and, in total, 1,478 tons of high-explosives and 1,182 tons of incendiaries fell on the town. It was the second attack which did most damage and a huge firestorm developed which quickly enveloped the city. To this day no-one knows exactly how many died in Dresden, with estimates varying, but it seems highly likely that the figure may well have exceeded 50,000. Six Lancasters were lost along with two more in France and one which crashed upon its return to England. The attack was followed up the next day by the US Eighth Air Force.[1]

Much was subsequently made of this attack. Critics have decried the Dresden raid as a terror attack, ignoring the fact that, as a transport hub, it was a legitimate military target and the fact that for the last three years Bomber Command had been carrying out area attacks with the same intent of what happened at Dresden – the total destruction of an urban target. The reasons for the criticism seem to be mainly that the attack came towards the end of the war with Germany and that such high casualties resulted. Neither of these factors are really valid. No-one knew how long Germany might continue resisting and while it was clear that she would lose the war, the British people would certainly not have expected Bomber Command to show mercy to the enemy or to call off attacks if such a choice might mean the war going on one day more and cost more Allied lives.

The actions of Winston Churchill in this matter were nothing short of disgraceful. Churchill had been one of the most vociferous and active advocates of Bomber Command and of Harris's area bombing campaign. Churchill had been heavily involved in the demand for a raid on Dresden but backpedalled immediately when the results of the raid began to become known. He sent a memo out querying whether the time had come for calling off such attacks if they were achieving nothing but inflicting terror on the population of Germany and causing damage that the Allies would have to cope with after Germany's surrender. Portal and Harris were, unsurprisingly appalled and disgusted by this betrayal and, following an exchange of messages, Churchill modified his original memo but still distanced himself from Dresden and the command came in for sole blame over Dresden despite the US Eighth Air Force raids. The Americans were more politically savvy and had, since the opening of their bombing campaign, made the claim, false as it was, that they were engaged solely in attacking military objectives. Indeed, by this stage of the war it could certainly be argued that Bomber Command was capable of greater accuracy than their American counterparts. Dresden was a human catastrophe, yes, but it was not a war crime and the men who flew on the operation, and indeed, those who planned it, should certainly not be vilified for their part in it.

On the following night Bomber Command sent 499 Lancasters and 218 Halifaxes to attack Chemnitz. Once again, the raid was split and divided by three hours. One of the main features of this raid was an elaborate series of diversions which deceived German defences and meant that only thirteen aircraft were lost. Chemnitz, however, escaped major damage as extensive cloud meant that much of the bombing fell in open countryside.

Harris was unwilling to send his Main Force back to Berlin but beginning on the night of 20/21 February the Mosquitoes of the LNSF launched raids on the German capital on 36 thirty-six consecutive nights. The LNSF was now at its fullest strength and a force which had started as little more than an afterthought was playing a substantial role in the bomber war. The nuisance raids of the LNSF to targets across Germany ensured that the German defences could not rest or be concentrated on specific areas. The damage caused by the Mosquitoes, which were often carrying cookies, was also a factor. The remarkable aircraft was so effective that it was not uncommon for a Mosquito of the LNSF to bomb Berlin, return, be refuelled and checked and, with a new crew, return to the target in one night.

Once again reverting to the tactical role, Bomber Command launched a series of attacks on a number of targets on the night of 21/22 February with the intention of isolating the Ruhr area from the rest of Germany. These attacks were successful. On the following night Pforzheim was the target for 367 Lancasters and thirteen Mosquitoes of 1, 6 and 8 Groups. This was the first and last attack by Bomber Command on this target and was made from just 8,000 feet. The marking and bombing were very accurate and in only twenty-two minutes 1,825 tons of bombs fell upon the town. There was a miniature firestorm on the town and more than 17,000 people were killed. Post-war assessment of the damage to Pforzheim claimed that 83 per cent of the town had been completely destroyed.

The raid also saw an action which led to the award of the final Bomber Command VC of the war. Captain Edwin Swales, DFC, of the South African Air Force (SAAF), of 582 Squadron was Master Bomber on the operation. His Lancaster was attacked twice over the target area and two engines and his rear turret were knocked out. Captain Swales could not take evasive action because he was continuing to broadcast instructions to the Main Force. He managed to nurse his Lancaster out of the target area, but upon encountering turbulence in cloud he ordered his crew to bale out. They did so, but Swales, like so many bomber pilots, paid the ultimate price and could not escape after holding the Lancaster steady for his comrades and was killed when his bomber crashed in Belgium.

On the night of 3/4 March the Luftwaffe demonstrated that it might have taken a beating but that it could still show considerable initiative and act against Bomber Command. Typically, the Luftwaffe of Goering mounted the operation, codenamed Gisela, on the 2,000th night of the war. Using 200 fighters they followed the raiding RAF bombers back to Britain before attacking as they approached their bases. On this night 446 aircraft had been sent to attack both the oil refinery at Kamen and the Dortmund-Ems Canal. Eight aircraft were lost over Germany, but twenty British bombers were shot down over England by aircraft involved in operation Operation Gisela. The Halifaxes of 4 Group were particularly hard-hit, losing eight aircraft over England, but losses came from a variety of units including aircraft from Heavy Conversion Units (HCUs) which were involved in training flights. Even with this blow, however, such was the strength of Bomber Command that the losses on the night amounted to what was regarded as an affordable 3.6 per cent.

Bomber Command continued pounding targets both new and old and on 11 March Essen was visited for the last time. This was the largest attack of the war so far with 1,079 aircraft taking part. With accurate Oboe marking the city suffered a blow which finally and completely paralysed it when 4,661 tons of bombs fell in just minutes, killing almost 900 people. Such was the state of Essen that when American troops later entered the city they were left astounded by the devastation of this one-time industrial powerhouse. The majority of the city was in complete ruin and the bombing of Essen had resulted in 7,000 deaths in the city while the population of the city had fallen by 338,000, as people left to find safer places away from the bombing. The defences, by this stage of the war, were so overwhelmed that only three Lancasters were lost on the raid.

The record set over Essen did not last long. The next day 1,108 aircraft were sent to attack Dortmund. Here 4,851 tons of bombs fell on the city and, even though the raid was carried out through cloud, immense damage was done. By this stage the systems for recording damage had largely broken down, but post-war assessment stated that this final raid on Dortmund had completely halted industrial production and that the recovery of the city would take many months.

Two days later Bomber Command dropped its heaviest bomb of the war for the first time. Thirty-two Lancasters and five Mosquitoes of 5 and 8 Groups were sent to attack the Bielefeld and Arnsberg viaducts. The viaducts had proven difficult to destroy as they were so difficult to hit but with 12,000lb Tallboys and the first operational use of the 22,000lb Grand Slam, it was hoped that the destruction of the targets would be assured. The attack, by 9 Squadron, at Arnsberg failed but at Bielefeld the viaduct collapsed. The aircraft of Squadron Leader C.C. Calder of 617 Squadron dropped the first Grand Slam of the war. The Grand Slams could only be produced in very small numbers and were used sparingly on specialised targets. At the end of March 617 Squadron used the new bomb to penetrate and destroy the massive U-boat pens close to Bremen. The majority of the damage was done by just two Grand Slams.

By this stage Germany was on its knees and it was clear that the dogs of Bomber Command would shortly be called off and old targets were raided for the last time. Hamburg was attacked by 440 aircraft on the night of 8/9 April for the loss of six aircraft. Kiel was attacked by 599 bombers the next night. It was during this raid that the *Admiral Scheer* was at last sunk and the *Admiral Hipper* was badly damaged. On 16 April 617 Squadron launched an attack on the pocket battleship *Lützow* at Swinemünde. Flak was intense and the squadron suffered its last loss of the war when Lancaster I (NG228, KC-V) had its port wing blown off by flak. 29-year-old Squadron Leader John Leonard Powell, DFC, (29) of Glamorgan, and his crew became the final wartime losses from 617 Squadron.

On 25/26 April the crews of 107 Lancasters and twelve Mosquitoes of 5 Group were briefed for what would turn out to be the final heavy bomber raid carried out by Bomber Command. The target was the oil refinery at Tonsberg in Norway. Given the state of the war and the fact that this target lay in an occupied country, this seems a peculiar target to have selected, nevertheless, the crews set off and an accurate attack seriously damaged the refinery. There was only one casualty. Lancaster I (RA542, JO-Z) of 463 Squadron was badly damaged by a night-fighter (which may itself have been shot down) and, with three of the crew wounded, the pilot, Flying Officer A. Cox set course for neutral Sweden. Cox made an emergency landing at Satenas airfield and the most seriously injured of the crew, bomb-aimer Flight Sergeant R. Smurthwaite was taken to hospital for treatment. The crew were interned until the end of the war days later. Flying Officer Cox and his navigator, Flying Officer J.A. Wainwright were both awarded the DSO, while the flight engineer, Sergeant G.W. Simpson, was awarded the Conspicuous Gallantry Medal (CGM).[2]

Bomber Command's war ended with a raid on Kiel by 179 Mosquitoes of 8 and 100 Groups on 2/3 May. It was believed that the Germans were gathering ships at Kiel to take troops to Norway in order to continue the war. One Mosquito was lost but considerable damage was done. Bomber Command's offensive ended, however, on a tragic note when two Halifaxes from 100 Group which were engaged on radio countermeasure work to support the Kiel raid collided and crashed with the loss of thirteen men.

Thus, twelve British airmen and one from the Irish Republic became the final Bomber Command casualties of the offensive.[3]

The men and aircraft of Bomber Command were given a particularly useful duty at the end of the war. From 26 April to 7 May the Lancasters of 1, 5, 6, and 8 Groups were put to work on Operation Exodus. The Lancasters flew to Brussels and other airfields where they picked up British PoWs who had been liberated and flew them back to Britain without delay. Many of these men had been captives since 1940 and so, getting them back home speedily, was a great end to the war for the men of Bomber Command. Over the course of Exodus some 75,000 men were flown back to Britain.

For others, the war ended with a different mercy mission. The population of western Holland was starving and there were fears of famine, already a large number of the old and sick had succumbed. After a truce was arranged with the local German commander the Lancasters of 1, 3 and 8 Groups were loaded with food and flew over the area to drop these much-needed supplies. The drop zones were marked by Pathfinder Mosquitoes. During Operation Manna Bomber Command successfully dropped 6,672 tons of food in the course of 2,835 Lancaster and 124 Mosquito sorties; a fitting end for the men of Bomber Command.

During Bomber Command's war 55,573 aircrew
had paid the ultimate price.

Conclusion

The dedication of the ground crews, administrative and intelligence staff, WAAFs and all those involved with Bomber Command – and without whom the operations of the command would not have been viable – are immensely praiseworthy and these often forgotten men and women deserve equal praise to any who served during the war. The aircrew who flew on bomber operations displayed incredible courage, great skill and remarkable fortitude in the face of formidable odds and the knowledge, for many who served during the majority of the war, that casualties were very high and the chances of making it through one operational tour, far less the mandatory two, were very slim indeed.

None of the operations of Bomber Command would have been possible had it not been for the monumental efforts and sacrifices of the ground-crews. The erks (as they were known) worked tirelessly throughout the war. Often, they faced incredibly harsh conditions in wintery weather on the barren and exposed airfields and they received little reward for their toils other than the gratitude of the crews that they looked after. For many of these men the loss of 'their' aircraft and its crew was a devastating blow which was repeated time and again throughout the war. Likewise, the WAAFs who provided so many services to Bomber Command throughout the war. Acting as drivers, mechanics, intelligence officers, flying control staff, parachute packers, cooks, batwomen and many other duties they saw young men (and many of them had become sweethearts) go to their deaths night after night and many of them paid a terrible emotional price. For reasons of length the stories of these men and women could not be adequately covered here but they surely deserve books of their own.

The actions of the aircrew were quickly and cynically overlooked by politicians and many others at the end of the war because the policy of area bombing had become far less popular in peacetime. The decision to deny a campaign medal to the men and women of Bomber Command remains a hugely dishonourable stain upon the political leaders of this country.

For the aircrew who were fortunate enough to have survived their time with Bomber Command there could be no such forgetting. The mental and physical scars of their service remained with many of these men for the remainder of their lives and many were tortured by the memories which they carried with them. The majority had lost friends while others suffered nightmares and other difficulties which would now be termed as symptoms of Post-traumatic Stress Disorder.

Likewise, the sacrifices of the aircrew were not so easily forgotten or brushed aside by those who had suffered the agonies of having lost a loved one who was serving with Bomber Command. Each loss sent ripples of grief through families and communities and for many families the fact that a loved one had simply been posted as missing, with no other information forthcoming, led to indescribably sad and long-lasting agonies of suffering and grief.[1]

In the aftermath of the war the RAF and the authorities did their best to ascertain the fate of those many airmen declared missing believed killed but it was often impossible. The Missing Research and Enquiry Bureau was seen as a beacon of hope by many of the bereaved. Others, unwilling to accept the loss of their loved one did not accept any facts put forward by the bureau and undertook their own research. Let two such stories suffice for the thousands of bereaved families of the missing.

As was mentioned in a previous chapter, Stirling III (LK837, IC-P) of 623 Squadron was lost on the night of 4/5 December 1943 while on a 'gardening' operation off the Frisian Isles. The bomb-aimer in IC-P was Flight Sergeant Wilfred Kastner Sutherland, RCAF. As we have already seen, the families of those who were posted missing could sometimes wait for months or even years before anything new might be received as to the fate of a loved one while others would never hear anything further.

For some families, this agony was all-consuming. Flight Sergeant Sutherland's family were left devastated by his loss and his father relentlessly pursued leads as to what had happened to his son. Mr John L. Sutherland, a building contractor from Vancouver, like so many, refused to believe that his son was dead, and clung to the hope that he had somehow survived but had not been able to contact his family. In March 1948 he visited Britain in order to better pursue leads as to his son's fate. He became a frequent visitor to the bureau but one day in November he claimed to have seen his son. He had been standing underneath the clock at King's Cross station when he saw a man whom he claimed was his son. He described how the man had stood approximately 12 feet from him, that he had been wearing dark, rough, European clothes and a round worker's hat, and that the man had looked at him strangely. Mr Sutherland described how he was convinced that it was indeed his son and that he had wanted to rush to him and embrace him but shock had rooted him to the spot and when he recovered his composure the man had moved off through the crowd towards platform six. Mr Sutherland had rushed after him shouting his son's name but had been unable to find him. Determined to find the man he believed to be his son, he had identified the train at the platform as having been bound for Durham and had called at all of the stations on the route begging for information on the man.

Mr Sutherland refused to admit defeat and even travelled to Holland where he questioned officials and fishermen, but none were able to shed any light on the fate of his son or his crew. He also took to returning to King's Cross in the hope that the man would re-appear and he became well known to the staff at the station where he was often to be seen standing under the clock. The stationmaster and porters would tell people that he would stand for ten hours at a time, barely taking breaks to grab a cup of tea, and inform people that he was searching for his son. Nothing could convince Mr Sutherland that Wilfred was dead. He returned to Canada at the end of November but vowed to return to King's Cross.

Sergeant Thomas Frederick Stott was a 21-year-old air gunner serving with 103 Squadron at RAF Elsham Wolds when he was posted missing on the night of 18 October. The young air gunner was the son of Herbert Reginald and Laura Stott of Leeds and, like so many fathers, Mr Stott refused to believe that his son had been killed, instead preferring to cling to the theory that he was still in Germany somewhere but unaware of his own identity. Mr Stott had been informed by the bureau that the evidence pointed to his son having lost his life on 18 October, but he visited the offices of the bureau to tell them that he was not convinced and insisted that his son was alive and that he would find him himself. To this end he took evening classes to learn German and then visited the country, but no matter how many people he questioned he could turn up no new evidence. Despite the further attempts of the bureau to convince hm that his son was indeed dead, Mr Stott refused to believe it. He even went against this own son's wishes for, heartbreakingly, the young airman had written a last letter home to his parents in which he said 'Don't worry, Dad, if I don't come back. Just try hard to forget me.'

Both Flight Sergeant Wilfred Kustner Sutherland, RCAF,
and Sergeant Thomas Frederick Stott, RAF,
remain missing to this day.

Endnotes

Chapter 1

1. Callaway was replaced on 11 September 1939 by Air Vice Marshal Arthur Harris.
2. F/O O'Neill appears to have survived the war.
3. Those recovered were: F/Sgt Turner; Sgt Donald Edward Jarvis (24) (2nd Pilot); and Aircraftman 2nd Class (AC2) Kenneth George Day (20) (Wireless Operator/Air Gunner). F/Sgt Turner and his second pilot are both buried at Sage War Cemetery while AC2 Day is buried at Becklingen War Cemetery.
4. *Halifax Courier*, 9th September 1939, p. 6.
5. This was the first complete crew to be taken as PoWs.
6. The other crewmen were Sergeant William McKenzie Gunn (27) (observer) and AC1 John Bateson (24) (wireless operator/air gunner). All are commemorated on the Runnymede Memorial.
7. F/O Baughan and P/O Coste survived to be taken PoW with both surviving the war and ending the war as Flight Lieutenants, P/O Coste being held at Stalag Luft 7.
8. Helmut Lent went on to rise to the rank of Oberleutnant and had 110 victories when he was killed on 7 October 1944. AC1 Geddes is buried at Sage War Cemetery.
9. The crew were: 22-year-old Flying Officer Michael Franklin Briden (Pilot); 21-year-old Pilot Officer William Stanley Francis Brown (2nd Pilot); Sergeant Valentine Henry Garner Richardson (Observer); 19-year-old AC2 Isaac Davidson Leighton (Air Gunner); AC1 Peter John Warren (Wireless Op/Air Gunner) and AC1 Alan Gordon Foster (Wireless Op/Air Gunner). The body of AC1 Foster was later washed ashore whilst the others are commemorated on the Runnymede Memorial.
10. Aircraftman Leighton had been in the RAF for two years and was approaching his 20th birthday when he lost his life. His father, Robert, and stepmother Florence lived in Dudley, Northumberland.

Chapter 2

1. The crew were: F/Lt J.E. Baskerville (pilot); P/O Emery Orville Fennell (2nd pilot); Sgt Bertram David Shepperson (observer); LAC Leslie Close (wireless operator/air gunner) and LAC William George Newton (wireless operator/air gunner).
2. F/O Saddington had the unusual honour of holding the award of the Czechoslovak War Cross. This had been awarded after his participation in Nickel operations over that country.
3. John Hannah contracted tuberculosis in 1941, due to his injuries, and was discharged with a full pension. He attempted to earn a living driving a taxi but found supporting his wife and three young children more and more problematic and his health continue to deteriorate. After a period of four months in the Markfield Sanatorium Hannah died on 7 June 1947.

Chapter 3

1. The Beaufort was shot down and the crew killed. The pilot, F/O Kenneth Campbell was awarded the VC.

Chapter 4

1. Sir Arthur's nickname was one which was largely coined by the press. Within his command, to the airmen of Bomber Command, he was largely known, half-bitterly, half affectionately, as 'Butcher'.
2. The two decorated men were P/O Donald Arthur Howard, DFM (pilot), and Flt-Sgt Kenneth McKenzie (20), DFM, of Leith.
3. Sgt Cadman is buried at Sage War Cemetery.
4. The crew were: Flt-Sgt Basil Courtney Wescombe (pilot); Flt-Sgt Frederick Edward Thomas (2nd pilot); Sgt Eeric Ronald Harper (observer); Flt-Sgt Leonard Sieve (wireless operator/air gunner); Sgt Claude Raymond Westbury (wireless operator/air gunner); Sgt John Thomas Howe (air gunner); and Sgt Maurice Robert Walker (air gunner).
5. This was the last Wellington to be lost by 99 Squadron as part of Bomber Command. Shortly afterwards the squadron was posted to India.

6. The crew was: F/Lt Basil John Adam, RAAF, of Victoria; Sgt Joseph Arthur Willis of Gillingham; and F/O Frederick Walter Ollis Street-Porter. All are commemorated at Runnymede.

7. The dead men were P/O Parsons, Sgt William Thomas Holmes (observer), Sgt Thomas Arthur Butterworth (air gunner), and Sgt Kenneth William McCaskill (wireless operator/air gunner).

8. S/Ldr Cross did not survive the war. In March 1944 he was part of the large group of officers who escaped from their PoW camp at Sagan. After his recapture he was handed over to the Gestapo and was murdered on 30 March. He now lies in Poznan Old Garrison Cemetery. The two crew who lost their lives were Sgt Melville James and Flt-Sgt Donald Richard George Holmes.

9. *Lincolnshire Echo*, 13 February 1942, p.4.

10. *Ibid.*

11. The dead men were wireless operator/air gunner Sgt Kenneth Bertram Harvey (20) of Great Dunmow and air gunner Sgt William Ronald Gregory (18) from Liverpool.

12. Lubeck was never raided again by the RAF. An agreement was reached that the port would not be targeted again so long as it was used for the shipment of Red Cross supplies.

13. Flying with a different crew Sgt Wheeler, DFM, was killed on 5 May 1942 while on an operation to Pilsen.

14. For the Maygothling family this was a particularly tragic loss as P/O Maygothling's father, S/Ldr George John Maygothling died while on active service in 1940, aged 52.

15. Sherwood retired from the RAF as an Acting Wing Commander in 1958 on his 60th birthday. He died in 1973.

16. *Gloucestershire Echo*, 28 April 1942, p.3.

17. The dead crew were: P.O David Malcolm Johnson (21) (pilot); W/O Oldrich Jambor (Czechoslovakian) (29) (2nd pilot); F/Lt Hector Austin Charles Batten (observer); Flt-Sgt Josiah Robert Connor (22) (wireless operator/air gunner); and Flt-Sgt John McKenzie McLean (22) (air gunner).

18. P/O Foers recovered from his severe injuries, was promoted to F/Lt, but was killed on 2 October 1942 flying with a new crew, still with 78 Squadron, on an operation to Krefeld. There were two survivors from his eight-man crew (they were carrying a second-dickie pilot for

experience). Foers and those who died are buried in Rheinburg War Cemetery.

19. Sgt Waddicar survived the war and by 1944 he was a Flight Lieutenant. Sgt Sewell is buried Eastbourne (Ocklynge) Cemetery. The remaining crew all appear to have survived the war.

20. Little is known of Sgt Leo, but it is known that he had enlisted in Rhodesia.

21. *The Sphere*, 17 October 1942, p.67.

22. *Ibid.*

Chapter 5

1. Interestingly the 1953 film *Appointment in London* features, in a minor role, a black, RAF bomber pilot. The film remains probably the best depiction of a Bomber Command squadron at war. It was based on a story written by former bomber pilot John Wooldridge. Wooldridge had flown 108 sorties during the war including some as a flight commander in 106 Squadron under Guy Gibson and the main character, W/Cdr Tim Mason (played by Dirk Bogarde), is loosely based on Gibson. The film is a remarkably accurate depiction of the bomber war of 1943, albeit from a very officer-centred viewpoint. John Wooldridge became a noted composer for film scores but was killed in a car accident in 1958.

2. This was an experienced and courageous crew with three of the officers having been decorated. They were F/L E.F.G. Healey DFC DFM (pilot), Sgt Dunbar (flight engineer), F/O J.R. Pennington DFC (navigator), P/O D.M. Crozier DFM RCAF (bomb aimer), P/O M.H. Lumley (wireless operator), Sgt C.H. Jurgensen (mid upper gunner), and Sgt F.J. Edwards (rear gunner).

3. The remaining crew were: P/O Michael Hope Lumley (wireless operator); Sgt Caspar Harold Jurgensen (mid-upper gunner); and Sgt Frank John Edwards (rear gunner).

4. The remaining crew were: Flt-Sgt Leslie William Cronk (2nd pilot); P/O Duncan Hugh Alexander Dewar, RCAF (navigator); Flt-Sgt Joseph Aleo, RCAF (bomb-aimer); Sgt George Ernest Patrick O'Connor (wireless operator); and Flt-Sgt James Edward Quinn (rear gunner). All are buried at the Reichswald Forest War Cemetery.

5. In addition to S/Ldr Smith, DFC, MiD, the crew of R9264 was: Flt-Sgt Robin Neville Benedict Brooker, DFM (flight engineer); F/Lt Barry Martin, DFC, RNZAF (navigator); Flt-Sgt William Joseph Dempster, DFM, RCAF (bomb-aimer); Flt-Sgt Francis Quigley (wireless operator); Flt-Sgt J.P. Bragg (id-upper gunner); and Sgt R.G. Newman (rear gunner).

6. All of the eight-man crew are commemorated on the Runnymede Memorial.

7. Sergeant Carr left behind his parents in Newcastle. There is some confusion over Carr's rank as the CWGC lists him clearly as a Pilot Officer whilst W.R. Chorley, *Bomber Command Losses of the Second World War, 1943*, names him as a Sergeant. The eight men of the crew are all commemorated on the Runnymede Memorial.

8. *The Journal*, 23 February 1943, p.4.

9. *Orkney Herald*, 14 April 1943, p.3.

10. Sgt Bell was buried far from home at Sutton-in-the-Forest Church Cemetery. Unusually for an evader, Conroy, now commissioned as a F/O returned to action with 429 Squadron but shortly after his return his Halifax was shot down over Berlin on 24/25 March 1944. The courageous young Nova-Scotian remained at the controls long enough for his crew to successfully escape their stricken bomber, but he was killed when the Halifax crashed. F/O Controy is buried in the Berlin 1939-1945 War Cemetery.

11. The crew consisted of: Sergeant Alexander Greig (22), RAF (pilot); Flight Sergeant James Mead (24), RAF (2nd pilot); Sgt Douglas William Perch, RAF (flight engineer), Sgt Peter Bailey (21), RAF (navigator), F/Sgt John Campbell Paton (29), RAF (from Glasgow) (bomb aimer), Sgt Charles Victor Ellen (23), RAF (wireless operator), Sgt Norman Frederick Trigg, RAF (air gunner), and WO David Wesley Lowther (28), RCAF (air gunner).

12. S/Ldr Sage had joined the RAF in 1936 and remained until 1964. From 1984 until his death in 1994 he was Life President of the Yorkshire Air Museum at Elvington.

13. The crew consisted of: F/L H.G. Shockley, RCAF (pilot); P/O B.H. Labarge, RCAF (2nd pilot); Sgt C.O. Henderson, RCAF (flight engineer); P/O W.W. Kirkpatrick, RAFVR (navigator); P/O F. Holland, RAFVR (bomb aimer); F/O W.M. Palmer, RCAF (wireless operator);

Sgt M.W. MacKenzie, RAFVR (mid-upper gunner); and P/O J. Henderson, RAFVR (rear gunner).

14. S/Ldr Grimston's younger brother, F/Lt The Hon. Bruce David Grimston was killed on 13th July 1944 while flying a Wellington of 524 Squadron with Coastal Command on an anti-shipping mission off the French coast. Both brothers are commemorated on the Runnymede Memorial.

15. The other 103 Squadron crew which failed to return on this night ditched in the sea off Falmouth and the crew were picked up safely.

16. Middlebrook, M & Everitt, C, *The Bomber Command War Diaries. An operational reference book 1939-1945* (Midland, 1996), pp. 384-5.

17. Holland, James, *Dam Busters* (Corgi, 2013), p.376.

18. Sergeant Charles McAllister Jarvie, aged just 21, has no known grave and is commemorated on the Runnymede Memorial along with five of his crew (the only body recovered was that of the rear gunner). The crew of AJ-K were: Pilot Officer Vernon William Byers, RCAF (pilot); Flying Officer James Herbert Warner (navigator); Pilot Officer Arthur Neville Whittaker (bomb aimer); Sergeant Alistair James Taylor (flight engineer); Sergeant John Wilkinson (radio operator); Sergeant Charles McAllister Jarvie (front gunner); and Flight Sergeant James McDowell, RCAF (rear gunner).

19. Pilot Officer Gray's pilot was 21-year-old Flight Sergeant Frederick Joseph Alexander Steel from Carlisle. He was married to Undine Frances Gwilliam Steel and is buried at Gateshead. Tragically, 515 Squadron exchanged their Defiants for the far more effective Beaufighter later that month.

20. Stirlings were always at risk from flak as they could not fly as high as the other bombers which accompanied them. The seven men who died lie in Schoonselhof Cemetery, Antwerp, Belgium. In April 1992 the *Evening Chronicle* had a request for any information on F/Sgt McQuillan or P/O Curtis from a Mr Cynrik De Decker who was writing a book on local air crashes for the local history society and the crash was the subject of a display in the local library.

21. It is likely that the Lancaster exploded in mid-air and that the pilot was blown from the aircraft but was wearing a seat-type parachute harness enabling him to descend safely. Aside from Pilot Officer Armstrong the deceased were: Sgt Mervyn Jones (Flight Engineer); Flying Officer Frederick Leonard Yates (Air Bomber); Sgt Peter Williams

(Wireless Operator/Air Gunner); Sgt Derek Murphy (Mid Upper Air Gunner); and Sgt John Albert Thomas Newton (Rear Air Gunner).

22. The crew were: Pilot Officer A.O. Smuck (Pilot), RCAF; Sgt Foggon; Flying Officer J.J. Kelly (Navigator); Sgt B. Domigan (Air Bomber); Sgt R. Barneveld (Wireless operator/Air Gunner); Sgt D.G. McKay, RCAF (Mid Upper Air Gunner); and Sgt D.L.G. Brown, RCAF (Rear Air Gunner).

23. F/Lt Ferguson later escaped from captivity during the chaos following the Italian surrender.

24. *Evening Chronicle*, 23rd August 1943, p. 4.

25. The body of Squadron Leader Todd-White was also recovered and he lies in Kviberg cemetery in Sweden. The remaining crew were never found and are commemorated on the Runnymede Memorial.

26. By 1943 Thomas was flying Spitfire photo-reconnaissance aircraft with 541 Squadron from RAF Benson. During a period of leave he found the time to marry his Tynemouth-born sweetheart, Lance Corporal Thelma Robson, Auxiliary Territorial Service (ATS), at Holy Saviour's Church in Tynemouth on 17th March. However, like many wartime marriages this one ended in tragedy when Mr and Mrs Goulden received notification at their home at Cricket Field Cottage, Preston Avenue, that their eldest son had been posted missing. On 28th May Thomas, then a Flight Sergeant, had been flying a photo-reconnaissance mission to Lubeck in a Spitfire PRXI (EN411) but failed to return and there was no news of him.

27. The eight-man all-RAF crew consisted of: F/Sgt. A.J.E. Long (pilot); F/O C.L. Barbezat (second-pilot); Sgt D.A. Galloway (flight engineer); Sgt J.J.V. Heal (navigator); Sgt J. Cooper (bomb aimer); Sgt L.H. Sefton (wireless operator); Sgt D. Goulden (mid-upper gunner); Sgt F. Willetts (rear gunner). Although the average age of the crew was just 23 the second pilot that they took along with them that night was aged 34. All are commemorated on the Runnymede Memorial.

28. Sergeant Bell is buried at Stoneykirk Cemetery in Wigtownshire. The senior navigator aboard the Anson was Sergeant John Robson of High Spen (he had attended school in Blaydon). The pilot and both navigators were killed instantly whilst the staff/instructor wireless operator, Flight Sergeant G.H Scully died whilst being taken to hospital and the pupil wireless operator, Sergeant W. Shapcott, RAAF, died of his injuries on 6 September.

29. Sergeant Ridley is buried at Durnbach War Cemetery along with his flight engineer (Sgt B.H. Cockcroft) and rear gunner (P/O W.G. Brown).

30. Amongst the other crews lost on this night were that of the new commanding officer S/L G.W. Holden, DSO, DFC & bar, and the crew which had flown with Guy Gibson on the dams raid, and another of the dams raid survivors, F/L L.G. Knight DSO, RAAF. This raid demonstrated that low-level attacks on German targets were not viable in large heavy bombers and were discontinued as a result.

31. The rest of the crew were: Sgt A. Chibanoff, RCAF (pilot); Sgt D.R. Coe (flight engineer); F/O F.V. Webb, RCAF (navigator); F/O K.B. Begbie, RCAF (bomb aimer); Sgt A.R.J. Gaiger (wireless operator); Sgt E.T. Potts (mid-upper gunner); and Sgt H.W. Frost, RCAF (rear gunner).

32. Edinburgh Academy produced a roll of honour which detailed the loss of 177 academicals who had lost their lives during the war and of 1,817 academicals and eight masters who had served in the armed forces during the war.

33. *The Scotsman*, 16 November 1943, p.6.

34. The crew consisted of F/L D.M. Moodie DFC, RCAF (pilot); Sgt E.L. Melbourne (flight engineer); F/S J.T. Bundle DFM (navigator); F/S H.W.N. Clausen DFM (bomb aimer); F/S T.E. Stamp (wireless operator); F/S L.A. Drummond (mid-upper gunner); F/S F.A. Hughes (rear gunner).

35. Sergeant Gray's body lies in Rheinburg War Cemetery, as does that of his crewmate Flight Sergeant Garner (from Staplehurst, Kent). Sergeant Gray's headstone has the following inscription upon it: 'Deep in our hearts A memory is kept of one we loved And will never forget'. W7876 was one of four losses suffered from 35 Squadron on this night; 40% of the total Halifax losses for the night.

36. The other crewmen were: Pilot Officer G.A. Graham, RCAF (pilot); Flight Sergeant J.G. McComb, RAF (second pilot); Sergeant W.G. Statham, RAF (flight engineer); Flying Officer D. MacDonald, RAF (navigator); Sergeant R.M. Inness, RAF (bomb aimer); Flight Sergeant H.F. Altus, RAAF (mid upper gunner); and Sergeant K. Mellor, RAF (rear gunner). It is likely that the crew of P/O Graham were well advanced in their tour of operations as they were trusted to have an inexperienced second pilot with them.

37. 623 Squadron had been formed on 10 August 1943 but was only operational for three months. During this time the squadron suffered a very high loss rate, losing ten aircraft. LK387 had itself flown on only four previous operations (two of them 'gardening' operations, a raid on Mannheim and a raid on Leverkusen) when it was lost.

Chapter 6

1. All of the crew are buried at Berlin 1939-1945 War Cemetery.
2. The rest of the crew were: F/O John Morrice Keay (navigator); Sgt Henry Charles Walton (bomb-aimer) (22); Sgt Edward Heaton (wireless operator) (21); Sgt William Meikle (mid-upper gunner) (20); Sgt Lyal Harvey (rear gunner) (29).
3. F/O Smith's crew consisted of: Sgt Keith Cushing (flight engineer); Flt-Sgt Kenneth James Roberts (navigator) (21); Flt-Sgt John Richard Bradshaw (bomb-aimer); F/O Wilfred Preston, DFC (wireless operator) (22); Flt-Sgt John Anderson Whyte (mid-upper gunner) (23); and Flt-Sgt Mathew Livingstone, DFM (rear gunner) (28). F/O Preston had been awarded his DFC in May 1943 for service with 10 Squadron. Flt-Sgt Livingstone had been awarded his DFM in November 1943 for service with 138 Squadron.
4. The Harthill family lived at Lossiemouth.
5. Other than S/Ldr Pike the crew consisted of: Sgt Norman Charles New (flight engineer); F/O Albert Alan Boad (navigator); P/O Eric Henry Moulden (bomb-aimer); P/O Reginald Augustus Wheeler (wireless operator); Sgt John Hesketh (air gunner); Sgt James Arthur Little (mid-upper gunner); F/Lt James Gilhulme Moor, DFM (rear gunner). It is not known why the crew included an additional air gunner.
6. Those killed were: P/O Samuel Cunningham Atcheson, DFC (pilot); Sgt Brian Henry Maude Thomas (flight engineer); P/O Antony Patrick McCall (navigator); Flt-Sgt Jack Greenhalgh (bomb-aimer); Sgt Frank Slater Weaver (wireless operator); and Sgt James Willie Naylor (rear gunner). All are buried at Vevey (St Martin's) Cemetery.
7. The crew were: W/O2 J.A. Greenidge, RCAF (pilot); Sgt W.A. Sinclair, RAF (flight engineer); F/Sgt T.B. Lowe, RCAF (navigator); Sgt V.N. Lunney, RCAF (bomb aimer); W/O1 E.O.E. Humphreys, RCAF (wireless operator); Sgt M.,W. Wheeler, RCAF (air gunner); and Sgt E.G. Surridge, RCAF (air gunner). All are commemorated on

the Runnymede Memorial. Just five months after the crew had failed to return the parents of John Greenidge received the news that another son had been killed. John's younger brother, James Douglas Greenidge was serving with the Canadian Grenadier Guards, 22nd Armoured Regiment, when he was killed in France on 15 August 1944.

8. All of the crew rest in the Rheinberg War Cemetery.

9. The rear gunner was not decorated. P/O Barton was the only Halifax pilot to be awarded the VC. The miner who was killed was George Dodds Heads (58) of 8 South View, Ryhope.

10. One of the 101 Squadron crews was flying a bomber borrowed from 460 Squadron meaning that 460 lost five crews on the night but six aircraft.

11. Reconnaissance flight just an hour after the attack found no cloud.

12. The other crew lost with S/Ldr Raybould DSO, DFM, were: F/O Gerald Longfield Ramsay (flight engineer); F/Lt Arthur Feeley, DFC (navigator); F/O Arthur Hugh Grange, RCAF (bomb-aimer); W/O Henry Kitto, DFM (wireless operator); P/O John Norris Papworth, DFC (mid-upper gunner); and F/Lt Dennis Johnson, DFC (rear gunner). F/Lt Feeley had been awarded his DFC in October 1943 for service with 83 Squadron. W/O Kitto had joined the RAF in 1938 and received his DFM in November 1942 for work with 83 Squadron. F/Lt Johnson was a pre-war regular officer who had trained as an air gunner. He had been awarded his DFC in May 1943 for service with 83 Squadron.

13. The crew were: F/O F. Crozier, RAF (pilot); Sgt R.R. Mosley, RAF (flight engineer); F/Sgt A.G. Ross, RCAF (navigator); P/O G.A. Price, RNZAF (bomb aimer); Sgt T.H. Perera, RAF (wireless operator); Sgt W.J. Hardisty, RAF (air gunner); and Sgt C.K. Churchyard, RAF (air gunner). The pilot was killed and Sgt Perera and Sgt Churchyard were both taken prisoner but the remaining four men evaded capture.

14. The all-RAF crew were: S/Ldr A.P. Cranswick, DSO, DFC (pilot); Sgt C. Erikson (flight engineer); F/O R.H. Kille (navigator); F/Lt P.R. Burt, DFC (bomb aimer); F/Lt A.C.M.G. Taylor (2nd bomb aimer); F/Sgt W.R. Horner (wireless operator); F/Sgt A.H. Wood (air gunner); and F/Sgt E. McH. Davies (air gunner). All the dead are buried at Clichy New Communal Cemetery. For many years it was assumed that Cranswick and his crew fell victim to flak but more recent research has established that the crew fell victim to a night fighter.

15. The crew were: S/Ldr G.F. Lambert, DFC, RAF (pilot); W/O R.J. Goode, RAF (flight engineer); F/O F. Salt, RAF (navigator); F/Lt D.R. Hall, RAF (bomb aimer); F/O P. Moorhead, RAF (2nd bomb aimer); F/Lt F.D. Round, DFM, RAF (wireless operator); F/Lt J.G. Coke, RAF (air gunner); and F/O F.E. O'Connell, RAAF (air gunner). The pilot, wireless operator and both air gunners are buried at Emance Communal Cemetery. F/O Moorhead evaded capture.

16. The crew were: F/Sgt D.MCN. Thompson, RAAF (pilot); Sgt E.A. Padley, RAF (flight engineer); P/O W. Birkin, RAF (navigator); P/O A. Aiston, RAF (bomb aimer); F/Sgt T. Charlesworth, RAF (wireless operator); F/O R.L. Smith, RAF (specialist operator); Sgt G. Richards, RAF (air gunner); and Sgt W.F. Schofield, RAF (air gunner). F/Sgt Thompson's body lies at Calais Canadian War Cemetery, Sgt Padley in Dieppe Canadian War Cemetery, and P/O Aiston at Mahon-Plage Communal Cemetery. The remaining crew are commemorated on the Runnymede Memorial.

17. Both F/Lt Lightbody and his navigator/radar operator, F/Sgt E.J.A Broomfield, rest in Hotton War Cemetery in Belgium.

18. W/Cdr Sisley's crew consisted of: P/O Peter Charles Siddall, RNZAF (2nd pilot); Sgt Ronald MacLeod (flight engineer); Sgt Hugh Henry Mills Connolly (navigator); Flt-Sgt Harold George Thomas (bomb-aimer); Flt-Sgt Arthur Stuart Parsons (wireless operator); Sgt Derek Picken Gates (mid-upper gunner); and Sgt Thomas Hamilton (rear gunner).

19. Roughly translated this Biblical quote reads: until day breaks and the shadows shall flee.

20. The engineer, Sgt Charles William Garrett was a married man from West Dulwich, London, and, at 36 years old, he was older than most aircrew.

21. The crew were: F/Lt G.U. Pulford (pilot); Sgt D.M. Hughes (flight engineer); Sgt J.W. Barnden (navigator); Sgt W.F.W. Jones (bomb-aimer); Sgt R.E.T. Burns (wireless op/air gunner); Sgt W. Skea (mid-upper air gunner); Sgt J.P. Van Der Linde (rear air gunner).

22. This all-RAF crew were: F/Lt C.J.G. Howard (pilot); P/O F.C. Hawkins (flight engineer); F/Lt T.J. Tate (navigator); P/O E.A. Hartley (bomb aimer); P/O R.D Lucan, DFM (wireless operator); W/O P.E. Woods (air gunner); F/Sgt H.G. Clarke, MiD (air gunner); and F/O D.T. Watkins, DFC (air gunner).

23. After the war Hugo Gruenner was awaiting trial after being captured by British forces but he escaped and with help from unknown sources fled under a false name to Argentina where he died in 1971.

24. Several days later the bodies of S/Ldr Wyness and F/O Hosie, RNZAF, were recovered from the Rhine and are now buried at Choloy War Cemetery. A fortnight later the bodies of F/Lt Williams and F/O Honig were also recovered and both now lie in the Durnbach War Cemetery. The remaining crew are commemorated on the Runnymede Memorial.

25. The crew were: F/O Kenneth Victor Smith (21), RAAF (pilot); Sgt George Jack Rutson (31), RAF (flight engineer); Sgt Thomas Greener, RAF (navigator); F/O Ivan George Skelton (23), RAF (bomb aimer); F/Sgt Robert Russell Denholm (22), RAAF (wireless operator/air gunner); Sgt Eric Thomas Mason, RAF (mid-upper air gunner); and Sgt John Charles Constable (20), RAF (rear air gunner). All are commemorated on the Runnymede Memorial.

Chapter 7

1. The Americans returned to Dresden on 15 February and 2 March but the main damage was done during the RAF raid. The US raid on 15 February was also controversial as the Mustang fighter escort was ordered to strafe roads in the vicinity of Dresden.

2. It is known that JO-Z was restored by the Swedish Air Force but it is not known whether the Lancaster ever flew again. It is known that it was scrapped in 1946.

3. Most of the victims were men who had already completed at least one operational tour.

Conclusion

1. This was despite the massive efforts of the Missing Research Section and the Missing Research and Enquiry Service which did its very best to track and identify missing airmen in the months and years following the end of the war.

Index